Citizen Quinn

D0814836

Citizen Quinn

GAVIN DALY AND
IAN KEHOE

PENGUIN

IRELAND

PENGUIN IRELAND

Published by the Penguin Group
Penguin Ireland, 25 St Stephen's Green, Dublin 2, Ireland
(a division of Penguin Books Ltd)
Penguin Books Ltd, 80 Strand, London WC2R ORL, England
Penguin Group (USA) Inc., 375 Hudson Street, New York, New York 10014, USA
Penguin Group (Australia), 707 Collins Street, Melbourne, Victoria 3008, Australia
(a division of Pearson Australia Group Pty Ltd)
Penguin Group (Canada), 90 Eglinton Avenue East, Suite 700, Toronto, Ontario, Canada M4P 2Y3
(a division of Pearson Penguin Canada Inc.)
Penguin Books India Pvt Ltd, 11 Community Centre,
Panchsheel Park, New Delhi – 110 017, India
Penguin Group (NZ), 67 Apollo Drive, Rosedale, Auckland 0632, New Zealand
(a division of Pearson New Zealand Ltd)
Penguin Books (South Africa) (Pty) Ltd, Block D, Rosebank Office Park,
181 Jan Smuts Avenue, Parktown North, Gauteng 2193, South Africa

Penguin Books Ltd, Registered Offices: 80 Strand, London WC2R ORL, England

www.penguin.com

First published 2013
003

Copyright © Gavin Daly and Ian Kehoe, 2013

The moral right of the authors has been asserted

Typeset in 12/14.75 pt Bembo Book MT Std
by Palimpsest Book Production Ltd, Falkirk, Stirlingshire
Printed in Great Britain by Clays Ltd, St Ives plc

A CIP catalogue record for this book is available from the British Library

ISBN: 978-1-844-88314-1

www.greenpenguin.co.uk

For our families

Contents

Prologue

Around the border towns of Derrylin and Ballyconnell, the locals like to tell a story. They say it shows what sort of a man Sean Quinn really is, and why they support him. It is the story of how he hired his pilot.

In 2005, with more than three decades in business behind him, Sean Quinn decided to buy a private jet. The reticent tycoon already had a helicopter, an eight-seater 2000 Agusta A109E, liveried in a distinctive blue. He used the chopper to get to meetings, GAA matches and the occasional social event around Ireland and Britain. During the 2002 General Election campaign, Quinn had even loaned the helicopter to the Taoiseach, Bertie Ahern, on his canvass of the country.

By 2005, the geographical scope of Quinn's investment interests was expanding. A jet would allow him to go further, faster. He settled on a ten-seater Dassault Falcon 2000EX, a €16.5 million aircraft with a range of 6,000 kilometres. It had soft beige leather seats, maple wood-panelled walls and customized gold-plated fittings in the bathroom and galley kitchen.

The Falcon was a statement of intent as well as a handy way to travel. Richard Branson, the Virgin tycoon, had a Falcon; so too did Dermot Desmond, the billionaire financier. Quinn's Falcon would be registered G-KWIN, a personal touch, and emblazoned with the blue and gold Quinn Group logo. All Quinn needed was someone to fly it.

The story goes that, one afternoon, as he sat in his home, Sean Quinn looked out the window and surveyed the championship golf course at his Slieve Russell Hotel. It was early, the course was quiet, and the only figure to be seen was a young greenkeeper tending to the grass. Quinn recognized him immediately; he was a local lad who had recently lost a parent. The businessman went out and summoned the greenkeeper into the house. He offered the young man sympathy for his loss, and got him chatting about his career plans. The green-keeper squirmed awkwardly in the face of questioning from the boss, a man not known for his small talk.

Would he fancy becoming a pilot? Quinn asked.

The squirm turned to a smile.

Training was quickly organized, and the young greenkeeper eventually qualified as a pilot and took control of the Falcon. From St Angelo Airport, a modest airfield outside Enniskillen, the Falcon took flight to Dublin and London, Zurich, Prague and Moscow.

Once, at a dinner in Eastern Europe, a celebration of his latest overseas property purchase, Quinn regaled his assembled guests with the tale. He had flown there on the Falcon, one of 337 times the jet would be used by Quinn, his family and employees over a six-year period. At the end of his story, he pointed to the pilot and quipped: 'Now, Captain, I hope you have the greens just the way I like them?'

Everyone laughed, including the pilot.

By 2012, however, Sean Quinn's wings were well and truly clipped. His jet and helicopter were on the block, deemed 'non-core assets' in the financial restructuring of the Quinn Group. In a rapid unravelling of his decades of work, Quinn – once ranked in the top 200 richest people in the world by *Forbes* magazine – had lost control of his manufacturing group, his insurance company and most of his property empire.

His aircraft and other assets would be sold and the proceeds used to chip away at the Quinn Group's €1.3 billion debt mountain, owed to banks and bondholders. The helicopter, with 2,145 hours of flying time on the clock, was the first to go. Castle Air, a British helicopter operator, snapped up the Agusta in early 2012 for the knockdown price of about €1 million.

In late autumn 2012, the Falcon, which had been on the market for €12 million through a Florida aircraft dealership, also flew the coop. Its destination remained a mystery until November, when the Irish edition of the *Sunday Times* reported on its new home – in Iran, where it had been acquired by the Islamic Republic's civil aviation organization.

Aviation websites showed pictures of the luxury jet at a dusty

Tehran Mehrabad Airport. The Quinn Group's logo was still on its body and tail fin, but the plane had been stripped of its G-KWIN lettering; the new code was M-ABFF, an off-the-shelf registration from the Isle of Man.

How did the plane end up in Iran?

No comment, said a spokesman for Quinn Group, now in the grip of its lenders.

How much did it sell for?

No comment.

By the time the jet's destination had been traced, Sean Quinn was in a cell in the training unit of Mountjoy Prison in Dublin, jailed for nine weeks for contempt of court. Literally and figuratively, Sean Quinn's once mighty empire was grounded. It was one of the most dramatic reversals of fortune in the boom and bust of the first decade of the twenty-first century.

But just what happened? Where did it all go wrong?

This is the story of a man who built an empire from a sandpit and lost it all on a fabulous financial folly; a gifted industrialist who sullied his name and his legacy by sanctioning a scheme to cheat a nationalized bank of hundreds of millions of euro. It is the story of how a 'chieftain' to an impoverished region ended up a bankrupt prisoner, a forlorn figure undone by unfettered ambition.

This is the story of how a billionaire became a bankrupt.

This is the story of Sean Quinn.

I

'I was always very greedy'

The 'Jesus Christ' Hotel, they called it in the early days. When people came around the bend in the road, where scrubby fields made way for landscaped grounds, an impressive fountain and a vast white edifice, that was the usual reaction: 'Jesus Christ.'

Just a few miles south of the border between Co. Cavan and Co. Fermanagh, the Slieve Russell Hotel sharply divided opinion when it opened in 1991. The locals loved it. Sceptics said it was a white elephant in the middle of nowhere. But the Russell endured and expanded, ultimately sprawling to 222 bedrooms, a helicopter hangar, a spa and a function room that could hold 1,200 people. An 18-hole championship golf course emerged from the soggy land; a megalithic wedge tomb was relocated to the 300-acre grounds from nearby Slieve Rushen, from which the hotel adapted its name. The 4,000-year-old tomb, known in local folklore as the Giant's Grave, had stood in the way of a quarry being developed by Sean Quinn. With government permission and the supervision of an archaeologist, he simply moved it.

In the Kells Bar, with its stained-glass skylight and enormous circular bar, Quinn placed a reproduction Book of Kells. In the lobby, he put a bronze sculpture depicting Emer, wife of Cúchulainn, the warrior champion of Ulster, double-crossed and killed by an accomplice of Queen Maeve of Connacht. Legend has it that Cúchulainn, knowing he was mortally wounded, tied himself to a pillar to face down his enemies. It was only when a raven landed undisturbed on his shoulder that his enemies were sure he was dead and dared to approach him.

★

On 7 March 2007, there was standing room only in the Slieve Russell function room. The mood was expectant, excited. People had come in their hundreds to hear what Sean Quinn had to say. On paper, it was just another conference, organized by Cavan County Enterprise Board with some funds from Europe, the kind of event with a few run-of-the-mill speakers and a decent dinner. But with Quinn on the bill, this one was different.

They had crowded around Quinn when he arrived, straining to see him, speak to him, maybe even get an autograph. Everybody knew the story: the farmer's son from down the road in Derrylin, Co. Fermanagh, had left school at fourteen and built a billion-euro business on gravel, cement, building products, glass, insurance and property investment. Yet he remained an enigma, a man who kept his own counsel and treasured his privacy. He rarely gave interviews, and he was not in the habit of making speeches.

Quinn, sixty years old, took a deep breath and got to his feet. He would have recognized plenty of faces as he moved to the podium – local business people, friends, members of the Russell golf club. He was on his home turf, but he seemed nervous.

From their home, 500 metres down the road, Quinn and his wife, Patricia, had watched the Russell grow. He'd walked the land, overseen the construction, supervised the layout of the rooms. His children had picked stones from the fields that would become fairways and greens. Now, at every opportunity, Quinn got a crowd into the Russell, whether it was a local GAA gala or professional advisers to his Quinn Group. He often ate his lunch or dinner in the Kells Bar and walked the golf course greeting guests.

Quinn's daughter, Brenda, the youngest of five children, owned the Russell; the eldest, Colette, was its ultimate boss. Colette had earned her stripes in hotel management in Switzerland, then completed a commerce degree. Ciara, the second-eldest of the Quinn children, a claims handler in the family-owned Quinn Insurance, was preparing for her wedding. The venue for the event, naturally, was to be the Slieve Russell.

So if Sean Quinn was ever going to share his thoughts, the Slieve

Russell was the place to do it. And in March 2007, there was no shortage of things to talk about.

Quinn Group was thriving. The Irish building boom was in full swing and there was strong demand for the products Quinn's workers were churning out just down the road. Quinn's wind turbines spun on the skyline, helping to power the string of plants along the road between Ballyconnell and Derrylin where cement, concrete products, roof tiles, insulation, glass bottles, radiators and plastics were manufactured. In all, there were twenty separate Quinn facilities spanning the border.

The scale of the manufacturing businesses was astonishing, and it was not limited to the Cavan–Fermanagh borderlands. In addition to a glass factory in Derrylin capable of making a billion bottles a year, there was a bottling plant in England with capacity for nearly 1.5 billion bottles. The plastics business had factories in Ireland, the UK and continental Europe. Quinn Group operated the biggest radiator factory in Europe, based in Newport in South Wales, with capacity to produce four million radiators a year.

Six months earlier, Quinn Direct, the insurance operation, had announced 1,000 new jobs at its offices in Cavan, Fermanagh and Dublin. Two months earlier, Quinn had moved into health insurance with the acquisition of Bupa Ireland. Now Quinn was going further afield to find new investments. He had been to Poland, Bulgaria, the Czech Republic, to Russia, India and Ukraine. He had 40 people working on overseas property projects. The biggest to date, the Kutuzoff Tower, a twenty-storey high-spec office block in Moscow, was just about complete.

The Quinn Group accounts for 2006 would show profits of €430 million. Quinn's five children, the eldest just thirty-one years old in March 2007, owned the lot. How had he done it? That's all anyone wanted to know.

Quinn stumbled over the first few sentences of his speech. He had, he said, been 'cajogled' into speaking by Vincent Reynolds, the chief executive of the enterprise board. It was ten years since he had spoken in public and it would be ten years before he did so again, if he had anything to do with it, Quinn said to laughter from the audience. 'I'm not a very good speaker, so I'll just run through some of the bits of stuff that we have found handy,' he said.

He shared anecdotes from his thirty-four years in business, starting in 1973 with IR£100 and a farm of gravelly land. He lost track of himself more than once. 'I had stuff wrote down to say, and I'm not sure where I am in all of that now,' he said. No one was complaining. They were hanging on every word.

'We came from a very simple background and we tried to make business always simple,' Quinn said. 'We don't believe in too much fuss, we never got a feasibility study done in our lives in thirty-three, thirty-four years. I don't use a mobile phone. I play cards in a house at night where you have to go out into the front street to go to the toilet.

'I enjoy that, I live a very simple life and that's the way I want to continue living that life. It doesn't mean that I can't go and meet people in Russia or India or Dublin or whatever the case might be. I'm not overly shy, but I much prefer to just sit back and enjoy what I'm doing, my two dogs, the wellingtons on, dodge about the mountain, and that's the way I like doing it.'

By the time Quinn finished speaking, forty-five minutes later, holding forth on the inequity in the health insurance market, dominated by the state-owned VHI, he seemed to be enjoying himself. 'I was never more enthusiastic than I am at the moment, so we look forward to the next few years with pride and with interest,' he said. 'We feel that we have been a great success story, we feel we have done very well. We are not getting hung up on it. We think we can do a lot more. I think that, in the next five years, the growth in the Quinn Group will not be less than it has been in the last five years.'

Five years would bring Quinn to 2012 and the age of sixty-five, though there was no sign that he had any intention of retiring.

No one who heard the Slieve Russell speech, with its extraordinary mix of naked capitalism and homespun wisdom, could be in any doubt about Sean Quinn's motivations. 'I was always very greedy,' he had said at the outset. 'I was never happy with whatever we had, and I was always looking for new opportunities.' Later, as he wrapped up his talk, he returned to the theme. His plan, he said, was to share future profits with his management and staff. 'I don't think it's good if it all goes to the Quinn family. We were too greedy for too long and we are still too greedy. But the intention would be over the next few years to leverage a lot of profits towards our management and staff. That's my final ambition in the business world.'

The day after Quinn gave his Slieve Russell address, *Forbes*, the US business magazine, published its annual ranking of the world's billionaires. It estimated that Quinn's wealth had nearly doubled over the previous year, rising by $2 billion to $4.5 billion. The farmer's son and school dropout was the 177th richest person in the world.

Sean Quinn was born on 3 September 1946 in his family's small farmhouse in the townland of Teemore, Co. Fermanagh, close to Derrylin. He was part of the fifth generation of his family to live in the farmhouse, just a mile from the border with the Republic. They were difficult, uncertain times. In the aftermath of the Second World War, nothing was plentiful in Derrylin, a one-street town surrounded by dark hedgerows and small farms of bad land.

Quinn was never academically minded. On the day he was to sit the eleven-plus examination – which would decide whether he would make it into a grammar school, or go to a technical school and learn a trade – he told the crowd at the Slieve Russell, 'I lay in the whins halfway between my home and the school. Once I seen the bus leaving the school [for the exam centre], I hopped up and out with me little blue suit and short trousers and arrived over to the school. The teacher wasn't best pleased.'

Nor was Quinn's mother. 'I think the whip was on its way when me father walked in,' Quinn recalled. 'He says: "Ah, he'll be fine. He'll help me with the farm and it'll be alright."'

Quinn left school at fourteen to work on the farm. He lined out for Teemore Shamrocks, the local Gaelic football team, and played a drum with the local Mountain Road Pipe Band. Quinn's brother, Peter, three years his senior, would go on to university and become an accountant. His two sisters, Miriam and Bernie, trained as teachers.

In 1967, when Quinn was 21, his father died and he became the man of the house. The farm had 23 acres of land, mostly stony and prone to flooding. Quinn started working as an agricultural contractor, rotavating soil and mowing hay for local farmers. He disliked it as much as he had disliked school. He would later say he was the worst farmer in Europe.

The Cavan–Fermanagh border in the early 1970s was a bleak and mistrusting place. On 21 September 1972, IRA gunmen entered a farmhouse at Aghalane, just down the road from the Quinn farm. Thomas Bullock, a 53-year-old farmer and part-time member of the Ulster Defence Regiment (UDR), a reserve regiment of the British Army, was watching television with his wife, Emily. The gunmen shot Emily Bullock after she answered the door, then shot Thomas Bullock in his armchair. The gunmen escaped across the fields.

Two months later, the local bridge over the Woodford River at Aghalane was blown up, physically severing the main route between the Republic and Northern Ireland. The link between the communities in Derrylin and Teemore in the north and Belturbet in the south was broken. Loyalist paramilitaries were blamed for the bridge bombing.

A temporary bridge was put in place before Christmas 1972, reopening the route. It would not be open for long. On 28 December 1972, a car bomb went off in the Diamond in the centre of Belturbet, an old Ulster Plantation town. Two teenagers, Geraldine Reilly, a fifteen-year-old local girl, and Patrick Stanley, a sixteen-year-old from Clara in Co. Offaly, were killed. Dozens of others were injured.

In the aftermath of the bombing, the temporary bridge at Aghalane, thought to be the route the terrorists had taken into Belturbet, was blown up too. What had been a short hop from the north into Belturbet became a twelve-mile journey via an intimidating British Army border checkpoint and Ballyconnell town. Few people bothered going the extra distance.

It was in that environment that Sean Quinn, tired of farming and with limited options, considered his future. The following year, 1973, would change his life. At a dance, he met his future wife, Patricia, a Galway woman six years his junior who shared his surname. And he made what he would later describe as a 'very fortunate' discovery.

When the glaciers ground their way through Fermanagh and Cavan during the Ice Age, they left a pattern of drumlins – distinctive small rounded hills – in their wake. The land in the area was often difficult to farm, but drumlin geology had its advantages, too: beneath a thin coating of clay on the Quinn farm lay what Quinn described as 'very substantial deposits of sand and gravel'. In 1973, Quinn, aged 27 and by now captain of the Fermanagh Gaelic football team, started to dig it out. The family farm would be his first quarry.

He sold the sand and gravel, first in wheelbarrow loads, then from a Bedford truck with his name plastered on the front. 'When we started off with the sand and gravel, that time I only had two hundred quid, so I had to be very careful with what I did with it,' he told the audience at the Slieve Russell. 'I wasn't able to do very much with it and the banks weren't overly keen to give me too much money. So we just had to flooter about with bits of lorries and securing the deeds of the farm to get a few pound from the bank.'

There were other people doing the same thing locally and it was difficult to make a living at first. Quinn needed to add some value, so he borrowed £100 sterling, sank a well and started to wash the gravel on site before selling it on. He undercut other suppliers and made use of his GAA contacts. People liked him and trusted him. They wanted him to succeed.

Quinn was ambitious from the start, setting a target of 20 per cent annual growth in profits. That meant expansion. He looked at his basic products – sand and gravel – and decided to go to the next step. Nobody made concrete blocks locally, so Quinn started making concrete products. If you needed stone, sand, gravel or cement blocks, Sean Quinn was your man.

'We worked very local, we worked very tight, and we started to get a bit of cash,' he said in an interview decades later.

They were busy times on the family front, too. The Quinns' first daughter, Colette, was born in July 1975. Ciara arrived just over a year later, in August 1976, followed by Sean, their only son, in February 1979. Aoife was born in October 1981 and their youngest daughter, Brenda, in 1987.

In 1982, Quinn started manufacturing roof tiles in a purpose-built factory in Derrylin. The following year, he bought two quarries – one close to home in Fermanagh and one at Williamstown in Co. Galway. Quarrying was a business Quinn knew and liked, and the Williamstown acquisition was the first step in making his local business into a national concern.

In 1984, he started making pre-stressed concrete products, including precast stairs, floors and roof units. 'If we were in sand and gravel, we wanted to go into blocks and readymix; if we were in blocks and readymix, we wanted to go into roof tiles and we wanted to go into floors,' Quinn said. 'So we always wanted to expand.'

The writer Colm Tóibín met Quinn at his business near Derrylin in 1986. Tóibín was walking the length of the border, gathering material for a book with Tony O'Shea, a photographer. It was a grim time politically. In February 1985, the IRA had killed Jimmy Graham, a bus driver and part-time member of the UDR, on the street in Derrylin. Graham was sitting in his bus, waiting to bring children to a swimming pool, when IRA gunmen fired two shots at him. Then they got into the bus and fired twenty-four more. They escaped in a van.

The IRA had tried to kill Jimmy Graham before, in 1980, but he had fought them off and been awarded the British Empire Medal as a result. The following year, in June 1981, the IRA killed Graham's brother, Ronnie, while he was delivering coal near his home in Lisnaskea, about nine miles from Derrylin. Five months after Ronnie Graham's murder, in November 1981, the IRA killed Cecil Graham, a brother of Ronnie and Jimmy. He was shot sixteen times outside his wife's parents' house. In 1985, the IRA finally killed Jimmy, the third brother.

The killing of Jimmy Graham was still a fresh memory in Derrylin when Tóibín arrived. Michael Harding, then the local priest and later an author and *Irish Times* columnist, had been across the road from where the shooting took place. He described to Tóibín how the killers had fired in the air and roared 'Ya-hoo, ya-hoo, ya-hoo' as they drove away, delighted with their handiwork.

Tóibín found Derrylin and Ballyconnell depressed and depressing.

Young people were emigrating and the weather was so bad that farmers in the south were sending truckloads of hay north for farmers whose crops had been destroyed by the rain. The area was lucky in one respect, however: it had Sean Quinn. There were hundreds of local people working in Quinn's quarries and factories. There were no trade unions in the business and everyone was paid according to productivity. Quinn trucks crammed the narrow roads, dashing back to base each evening to get another load away before the end of the business day. It was said the drivers kept to the middle of the road because if a truck were scratched on the ditches, the driver had to pay for the damage.

Tóibín found Quinn 'a dark, good-looking, gruff man in his late thirties, wearing an old grey pullover', completely at ease with his workers. 'He didn't act like the boss. And he certainly didn't look like a millionaire.'

The border was a nuisance for Quinn, but not an obstacle. Certain things, such as tyres and road tax, were cheaper in the Republic, but he could take advantage of elements of the tax regime in Northern Ireland, where there was a 100 per cent tax-free allowance on profits that were reinvested. Quinn, a nationalist, told Tóibín that a friend had been shot dead by the IRA for doing business with the British security forces. Quinn didn't have any dealings himself with the British – 'I didn't think it was prudent,' he said – though he employed a few local Protestants.

There was rarely any trouble, apart from Quinn's frustration that his trucks were delayed for a couple of minutes at the British Army checkpoint each time they crossed the border. All that wasted time added up – and time meant money. Quinn had calculated the cost: it was about the same as keeping one lorry on the road full-time, he said.

Quinn confirmed one extraordinary incident that Tóibín had heard about. He was crossing the border one day to go to a funeral, already late and anxious. The British soldiers stopped him, made him drive into the side of the checkpoint and held him there. They wouldn't let him go, even though he passed through several times a day and his name was written on all the green-liveried trucks that went through the checkpoint. After half an hour, Quinn told the British soldier he was going anyway, whether the soldier agreed or not. He knocked the soldier over, got in his car and drove off. There was no retaliation. Sean Quinn was too important, the locals told Tóibín. In the aftermath of the incident, Quinn's already sizeable status grew larger.

When Tóibín told Quinn he heard the soldiers carried truncheons after the episode, the businessman 'chuckled to himself' and said nothing. 'He was interested in making money and having a good time,' Tóibín wrote. If that was the case, Quinn was doing well on both counts.

In 1984 he had bought the Cat & Cage pub in Drumcondra, in Dublin, for IR£640,000. It was a huge sum, but Quinn's motivation was simple: when he went to football matches in Croke Park, the pubs were always full and he found it difficult to get a drink. 'I said to myself: This has to be a simple business, because they're charging a ransom for the beer and they get paid for the beer before they pay Guinness, so this seems to be a good business,' he told the Slieve Russell crowd twenty-three years later.

He wasn't just investing in physical businesses. During Tóibín's visit to his office, Quinn took a phone call from a man with a 'strong British accent', and started writing down figures in a notebook, issuing instructions about buying and selling. Tóibín asked him what the call had been about.

> Stocks and shares, he said. He had started, six months before, to play the stock market. He showed me the list of items he dealt in – gold, oil, the Swiss franc against the dollar, aluminium. His broker, he said, phoned twice or three times a day and he told him what to do. A salesman brought him out the *Financial Times* from Enniskillen, so that he could read about his investments. It was interesting, he said, suggesting that playing the stock market was a form of amusement, implying somehow that it was a common pastime around Derrylin and Teemore.

If investing in stocks and shares was a form of amusement for Quinn, he had another plan that was deadly serious.

Sean Quinn had decided to build a cement plant at Derrylin, a move that would put him in direct competition with Irish Cement, part of Cement Roadstone Holdings (CRH). In business since the late 1930s, Irish Cement had a virtual monopoly on cement supply in the Republic. It also supplied the market leader in Northern Ireland, Blue Circle, which resold Irish Cement's product to northern customers.

Quinn's intention was to build his factory just beside the border and supply the whole island. It was an ambitious plan. He had no experience of cement manufacturing and would be competing head-to-head with both Irish Cement and Blue Circle. Undaunted, Quinn gave one of his former salesmen the job of making sure the highly complex factory, with its crushers and kilns and packaging machines, was built on time and within budget.

Quinn's friends and associates said he was mad. He was spending about £30 million sterling on the plant, which would have the capacity to produce 500,000 tonnes of cement a year. That was equivalent to 22 per cent of the cement market on the island of Ireland. That would mean 22 per cent less business for Irish Cement and Blue Circle. 'They are not overjoyed,' he told Tóibín, with some understatement.

A special 45-minute programme on the cement industry on RTÉ's *Today Tonight* in November 1987 highlighted the scale of the challenge facing Quinn. A number of cement industry operators described how CRH, which had just reported annual profits of IR£46 million, went to extraordinary lengths to scupper competition. The company was accused of spying on competitors, following their trucks, putting pressure on their customers and attempting to fix prices. The only allegation the cement company denied was the one of price fixing. Imported cement was rendered almost unusable by certification requirements imposed by the Irish government. Quinn would be the first new manufacturer to challenge the status quo.

Interviewed by *Today Tonight*, Quinn said his cement would be significantly cheaper than Irish Cement's product. Using Quinn cement would cut the cost of an average house by £500. 'That'll be of great benefit not only to the consumer but to the nation,' he said. Asked why people in the Republic should buy cement made in Northern Ireland, Quinn laid out his credentials. 'Our cement is coming from a Southern quarry. All the limestone, which is 70 per cent of the manufacture, is coming from a Southern quarry. We have 200 Southern employees. I live in the South. Why would they not buy our cement, at a price cheaper than [cement] presently is? We would expect that we would get the support of people that are interested in making money.'

But a gain for the consumer would be a loss for Irish Cement and CRH. Quinn's new plant would be a double whammy: it would eat into Irish Cement's market share while also forcing prices down. CRH wasn't going to sit back and let him build his factory unhindered.

'They used to fly an airplane over here about every six weeks or so to see how we were getting on and take aerial photographs,' Quinn told *Today Tonight*. 'They felt they might be able to find something in the aerial photographs that might be contrary to what planners would require. As well as that, I'm sure they wanted to see how we were getting on, or when we might go bankrupt, or if we were overspending.'

CRH also went directly to Quinn's bankers, Security Pacific in London and Northern Bank, to try to influence their decision to back the businessman. 'I'd say it was a bit below the belt,' said Quinn matter-of-factly, adding mischievously, 'but maybe if I was as uncompetitive as CRH is, then I might have to do something similar.'

Quinn had hoped the Industrial Development Board in Northern Ireland would give grant aid to cover around half the cost of the Derrylin factory. But Irish Cement brought an action before the European Commission challenging the grant aid. Irish Cement argued it had received just 10 per cent grant aid from the Irish government when it was expanding its factory in Limerick. A much higher level of state aid to Quinn would distort competition and damage the cement market as a whole, it said. Irish Cement also claimed Quinn's factory would not create net new employment because it would lead to lay-offs at Irish Cement's existing plants. That would not be compatible with the EC's policies governing grant aid.

'I suppose they felt that, with a small company like ourselves, if we weren't able to get grants to the tune of 40–50 per cent, we wouldn't be able to raise the money to build the factory,' Quinn said. After CRH's intervention, he was offered a 20 per cent grant, and accepted it. 'We were very disappointed when the grant was reduced in October from 20 per cent to 12.5 per cent and the grant is now off altogether,' he told *Today Tonight*. 'So we have to finish the factory without grants. We think that we have been fairly harshly treated.'

On the *Today Tonight* programme, Declan Doyle, then managing director of Irish Cement, admitted it viewed the challenge from Quinn very seriously. 'Sean Quinn's advent was a major event in the market. We have to react,' he said. 'It's necessary in business to know the strength and weaknesses of your competitors ... We have to defend our volumes.'

Quinn's cement plant opened in 1989, drawing limestone and sand from the Quinn quarries, processing it into cement, bagging it, and selling each bag for a couple of pounds less than Irish Cement and Blue Circle. The strategy worked. He won steady business, particularly in the border region and the north-west of the country.

At the same time, Quinn was expanding his hospitality interests, buying pubs and hotels, including the Kilmore Hotel, close to Cavan town, fifteen miles from Ballyconnell. Then he decided to build his own: the Slieve Russell. It was an intensely personal project for Quinn, built in the fields directly beside his home. In the 2007 speech, he described it as 'a baby of our own conception that we looked at twenty years ago when I used to be walking into Ballyconnell for a couple of pints'.

Quinn was convinced the Slieve Russell would be a success, despite its rural, border location more than two hours' drive from both Dublin and Belfast. It would have luxury bedrooms and restaurants, a leisure centre and golf course capable of hosting a major international tournament. He micro-managed the project, at one point insisting an expensive wooden bar be ripped out and dumped simply because it didn't look right to him. By the time it opened its doors in 1991, the hotel had cost IR£14 million, a vast sum at the time. Millions more would be invested in the golf course and later expansions, including road upgrades and building accommodation for staff. His vision paid off – visitors flocked to the Slieve Russell, liked what they saw, and came back for more.

The hotel would become the flagship of Quinn's burgeoning hospitality business, which by the mid 1990s had grown to comprise twelve pubs and seven hotels, including Buswells Hotel across the road from the Dáil in Dublin. He also owned the Iveagh Fitness Centre, a modern gym in a hundred-year-old former public baths in Dublin city centre. The pubs were mostly in busy city locations, reflecting what was said to be Quinn's rule of not buying pubs with car parks. There would surely be a crackdown on drink-driving, he believed, and any pub that relied on customers who came by car would suffer.

There were hiccups. Hoping to capitalize on growth in Europe after the fall of the Berlin Wall, Quinn invested about £5 million sterling in a bar in Berlin, Sean Og's. Despite a location in Berlin's trendy eastern district of Prenzlauer Berg and favourable international reviews, it was a disaster. Berliners didn't drink the way Irish people did.

'There was as many people there as there was in Tallaght, but they weren't working,' Quinn said in 2007. 'Three or four of them would go into a pub, they'd buy one bottle of mineral water and they'd drink it between them and sit there for three hours. And that's a fact.' He pulled the plug on Sean Og's after two years.

Quinn could afford the odd mistake. The building-products businesses were throwing off cash and the banks were happy to lend to them. As the group expanded, Quinn moved to build a management team. He had worked largely alone in the early years, but in 1989 he hired David Mackey, a soft-spoken former manager of Cavan County Council, as general manager of the group. Born in Letterkenny, Co. Donegal, in January 1949, Mackey was of Quinn's vintage. He shared Quinn's vision and way of doing things; he described him as 'such a bloody genius of a man'. Quinn respected Mackey's calm professionalism. The men became friends and confidants.

Liam McCaffrey, a young accountant, was another key appointee.

He was working at Coopers & Lybrand as an external auditor to the Quinn Group before Quinn hired him as company accountant in 1990, aged twenty-seven. Peter Quinn, Sean's brother, an experienced business adviser and accountant, helped the business, too. In 1991, Peter was elected president of the Gaelic Athletic Association, as the association faced a decade of transformation. He would be regarded as one of the strongest presidents the association ever had, credited as the brains behind transforming Croke Park, the GAA's Dublin headquarters, into a world-class stadium.

The 1990s brought a flurry of activity for Quinn. In 1994, the group erected its first wind turbines on the slopes of Slieve Rushen, behind the Derrylin headquarters. The Quinn Energy installation, one of the first wind energy projects in the country, helped power the factories, and would later be extended significantly.

Quinn launched Quinn Environmental, which developed a waste disposal facility in Co. Armagh. It burned the gas produced from the decomposing waste to generate electricity, which Quinn could sell into the electricity grid in Northern Ireland.

Quinn Tarmac was introduced to capitalize on road-building projects on both sides of the border. The group acquired Lite Pac, a thermal insulation business with a factory in Granard, Co. Longford; then it combined its knowledge of block-making with insulation, adding lightweight thermal blocks to its line-up. More factories, more jobs, more profits.

David Mackey, the general manager, was appointed chief executive, and Liam McCaffrey, the young accountant, became financial controller. Quinn, however, was the man in charge and his biggest move was yet to come.

As his business grew, Quinn faced increasing bills for insuring his assets – the fleets of trucks, the expensive machinery, the factories, hotels and pubs. He looked into setting up an insurance operation to self-insure his own interests, and then decided to go a step further. 'We realized that if we can do this for ourselves, we can do it for other people,' Quinn said. The Irish insurance market was dominated by international insurance companies such as Guardian

PMPA, CGU and Norwich Union but Quinn believed there was room in the market for a local operator with better customer service. Direct Line Insurance was taking off in Britain, promising hassle-free insurance over the phone, but there was no Irish equivalent.

Mackey worked up licensing applications for the Department of Enterprise and Employment, which had responsibility for regulating insurance companies. In January 1996, the department gave the green light, granting Quinn a licence to write general insurance. Swiss Re was signed up to provide reinsurance to the company. Quinn Direct Insurance opened with fifteen staff, specializing in commercial and motor insurance. It would sell policies directly to the public over the phone and not use brokers or agents.

'We are doing it in a quiet, controlled way and letting it develop slowly,' Mackey told the *Irish Times*. The insurance company would be a separate entity from the Quinn Group, said Mackey, who declined to discuss the licence details or capital requirements of the company. Quinn Direct later opened an office on O'Connell Street, Dublin's main thoroughfare, supported by a call centre in an impressive new insurance headquarters building in Cavan, beside Quinn's Kilmore Hotel.

Quinn Direct arrived into a crowded insurance market. There were already more than thirty companies in the general insurance market, and several new arrivals starting to offer direct phone services. Almost 80 per cent of the insurance market was controlled by five players. The common wisdom in the industry was that an insurer needed at least 5 per cent market share to generate a proper return. Why should Sean Quinn succeed where so many others were struggling?

Helped by public goodwill towards Quinn, particularly in the border region where he had a large workforce, Quinn Direct had a steady start. It had revenues of IR£12 million in 1996, its first year in business, and IR£19 million in 1997. By the end of 1997, Quinn was claiming 30,000 policyholders, amounting to 2 per cent of the market.

Selling insurance was radically different from quarrying gravel, but Quinn used broadly the same strategy for both sectors, undercutting rivals to gain market share. About 70 per cent of the Quinn

Direct business was private motor insurance, and Quinn was top-heavy with younger drivers who found it difficult to get cover elsewhere or were priced out of the market. To build market share, Quinn offered deliberately low introductory premiums and bet that he could hold on to the business through customer loyalty, even if prices went up in subsequent years. Quinn Direct was virtually the only insurer that would take on seventeen-year-old drivers and one of the few that would insure male drivers under twenty-five. It was the riskiest end of the insurance market, one that competitors deliberately avoided.

The bet on young drivers, and on customer loyalty, did not completely pay off. Official figures from the Department of the Environment showed Quinn Direct had by far the highest number of motor insurance cancellations in the industry: almost 3,800 customers cancelled their policies in 1997, more than 10 per cent of the 30,000 customers claimed by Quinn. The following year, more than 5,600 Quinn customers cancelled. Motor insurance policies are cancelled for two main reasons. Either the insurer discovers that the customer did not disclose all the relevant facts on their application, or the customer fails to pay their premium. Either way, it was bad news for Quinn.

In an article in *Business & Finance* magazine, rival insurers anonymously suggested Quinn Direct was getting cold feet about some of the risks it was taking on. Quinn Direct denied that was the case. 'Given that we in Quinn Direct are one of the very few insurers offering cover to younger drivers and we provide direct debit facilities to all ages, it is to be expected that there will be higher than average default on policies,' it said.

Rivals also queried whether Quinn was putting aside sufficiently large capital reserves to cover future claims. With its large cohort of more accident-prone younger drivers, Quinn would need particularly large reserves. Though Quinn's rivals routinely questioned how sustainable his business could be, he shrugged off his detractors. By dealing with customers over the phone, having staff in lower-cost regional locations, and settling legitimate claims quickly, Quinn Direct had lower costs than most insurers, he argued.

Quinn loved the insurance business. Compared to quarrying and manufacturing cement, it was a tidy way to make money. The insurer got the cash up front when customers paid their premiums. One former senior Quinn executive recalled another reason why Sean Quinn was fond of insurance: 'He had four hundred truck drivers on the road and no way of knowing what they were doing at any point in the day. With insurance, he could walk into the office and see 80 per cent of his people under one roof. They were accountable. It was as easy as pie. And he was making millions doing it.'

It was a highly simplistic view that overlooked the risks inherent in writing insurance and the cyclical nature of the business. Even the world's biggest insurers weren't always profitable. Big claims and poor investment decisions could quickly plunge an insurer into the red. Yet Sean Quinn, with virtually no formal education and no background in financial services, genuinely believed he had created a new insurance model.

Quinn Direct was still in its infancy when Quinn decided to embark on another new venture. The hospitality business had opened Quinn's eyes to the glass industry, which, like cement back in the 1980s, was in the hands of a near-monopoly: the Irish Glass Bottle Company, owned by Dublin-based Ardagh.

In his quarries, Quinn had an abundance of sand, the key raw material for making glass. He decided to build a glass plant at Derrylin. He would adopt the same approach as he had with cement, building a modern factory and undercutting his rivals slightly on price. 'He loved the challenge of taking on a dominant player,' said a former director of Quinn Group. 'His view was that if he used the highest-quality machines to make the lowest-cost product, he would win against his competitors. It was just a matter of time, but he would win.'

Speaking at the time, Quinn said, 'We are going to have the most modern factory in Britain and Ireland. I think we can produce the cheapest glass, and we will try to get the best price for it.'

Quinn's rivals knew his modus operandi by now and took the threat seriously. The British Glass Confederation, a Sheffield-based industry group whose members had business in Ireland, strongly opposed the project, claiming there was already over-capacity in Irish glass-making. Quinn's entry into the market would lead to job losses, they said, mirroring Irish Cement's campaign against Quinn a decade earlier. They objected to grant aid for the factory and searched for grounds on which it could be stalled or halted.

'They hired a group of consultants from Belfast and went through it inch by inch for more than a year and tried to find a way of stopping the project,' Quinn said in an interview several years later. They failed. After a £60 million sterling investment, the bottling plant opened on a greenfield site in Derrylin at the end of 1998. The Northern Ireland Industrial Development Board again backed the project with a hefty grant. The scale of the operation was staggering – the highly automated factory could produce enough glass containers to supply the whole glass market in the Republic. The sand came from a Quinn quarry just a few hundred metres from the factory. Almost all of the 340 staff were drawn from the local area.

A little over a year later, Quinn opened a second cement manufacturing plant outside Ballyconnell, south of the border. It was a IR£70 million investment. The new factory could produce 1.3 million tonnes of cement a year and sealed Quinn's place in the market, second only to CRH. In the three years from 1997 to 2000, Quinn invested more than IR£300 million in the various businesses, funded by bank debt and reinvested profits.

David Mackey left the group in 1999 to work on other projects, and Liam McCaffrey stepped into the top job. Another Quinn lieutenant, Kevin Lunney, was running Quinn Direct, which was gaining solid market share. Born and bred in Derrylin, Lunney fitted Quinn's liking for hiring and promoting young local talent. In 1996, at the age of twenty-eight, Lunney had been one of the first people in the door when Quinn set up Quinn Direct. He had seven years with Andersen Consulting under his belt at that stage, working on projects in Ireland and overseas. Lunney's brother, Tony, also worked for Quinn, in his building-products division, where he would ultimately hold a senior position.

★

On 1 January 2000, the group expanded its financial services business with the launch of Quinn Life, selling investment, savings and pension products from its call centres. It was the first time investment products were sold over the phone in Ireland. Reports of the move were effusive – an *Irish Times* article was headlined 'Mighty Quinn takes on giant killing role again with life assurance venture'. It noted Quinn had 'a long history of taking on established interests'.

Coinciding with the launch of Quinn Life, Quinn Direct released figures showing it had 100,000 policyholders. Its 1999 accounts were still to be finalized but it expected to report premium income of IR£60 million and pre-tax profits of IR£6 million for the year. The final profit figure for 1999 was later revealed to be even higher, at IR£8 million. The figures were better than many in the industry expected, though sources in the financial sector suggested Quinn could struggle in the life assurance sector. 'He faces an uphill struggle,' one unnamed source told the *Irish Times*. 'The jury is still out on selling advice-led products over the telephone.' Another source suggested the Quinn brand lacked the credibility to attract people making important long-term investment decisions. By the end of the following year, Quinn's critics had plenty of evidence to back up their concerns.

Quinn, always hands-on, personally directed the investment strategy at Quinn Direct. It was an unusual arrangement, in stark contrast to the professional investment committees that made asset allocations at his multinational rivals. He had had some success. In late 1998, the insurance company paid about £4.5 million sterling for a 6.1 per cent stake in Powerscreen International, a Northern Ireland engineering company that was quoted in London and Dublin. The investment prompted speculation of a Quinn takeover, sending Powerscreen's share price up 30 per cent in a single week. Quinn had no interest in acquiring Powerscreen but viewed its shares as undervalued after an accounting scandal. In June 1999, a US engineering group, Terex, bought Powerscreen for £181 million. Quinn's stake was worth more than £11 million, a £6.5 million profit in just eight months.

Through 1999 and into 2000, shares in technology and telecoms companies boomed as dotcom fever took hold. Quinn had made a deliberate decision not to get involved in technology stocks and Quinn Direct had no tech investments at the beginning of 2000. It looked a wise decision. On 10 March 2000, the Nasdaq peaked above 5,000 points, then began a sharp and steady decline. Sean Quinn watched as the dotcom bubble burst, then took an extraordinary decision: betting the tech sector would bounce back, he piled Quinn Direct's assets into tech stocks.

'After the market corrected by about 30 per cent . . . I felt it was an opportunity to get into technology,' he said in an interview in 2001. At the end of 2000, having started the year with no tech investments, almost 37 per cent of Quinn Direct's reserves were invested in equities, a significantly higher proportion than the industry average of 22 per cent.

Quinn's decision to invest aggressively in tech shares backfired spectacularly. The dotcom shares didn't recover as Quinn had predicted; in fact, the collapse in tech shares was the start of a severe retrenchment from which some IT companies would never recover.

The dotcom gamble cost Quinn Direct IR£15.6 million in investment losses in 2000, at a time when other insurers were reporting investment gains. There were further heavy investment losses in 2001 as the insurer liquidated some equity holdings and crystallized significant losses.

The strategy of betting heavily on a single equity sector had been a disaster. 'I myself would be the person who puts their hands up and says that we got involved in some stocks we shouldn't have got involved in,' Quinn said. 'We paid a heavy price for that decision.'

An even bigger red number for Quinn Direct in 2000 arose from an underwriting loss of IR£22.9 million for the year. The firm had not reserved enough money to cover the cost of claims during its first three years in business. The insurance industry as a whole was suffering from 'claims inflation': claims were coming in higher than expected. Quinn Direct, with its high proportion of risky customers, was affected more severely than most. In total, Quinn Direct lost IR£38.5 million in 2000, wiping out all the profits the insurer had made since its foundation several times over. It was a massive sum given the company's revenues of about IR£100 million for the year.

Amazingly, there was no formal regulatory fallout for Quinn Direct. The Irish government had agreed in principle in late 1998 to establish a single regulatory authority for all financial services, including insurance. But the process of setting it up was agonizingly slow. In fact, it would be May 2003 before the new regulatory regime, the Irish Financial Services Regulatory Authority, was launched as part of the Central Bank.

In the meantime, insurance regulation remained the responsibility of the Department of Enterprise, Trade and Employment. It was the department's role to make sure that insurers were solvent and to protect policyholders. Though the department had the power to censure Quinn or revoke his licence if Quinn Direct's solvency was considered doubtful, he escaped unscathed from his dotcom adventure. In fact, Quinn's growing customer base only learned of the risky investment strategy almost a year after the fact – not from the department's regulatory staff but through newspaper reports on the company's annual accounts in December 2001.

Analysis of the figures in the *Irish Times* described the losses as 'pretty staggering', lambasted Quinn's asset-allocation strategy, and speculated about the possibility that he would sell the insurance business. 'It's hard to see Quinn Direct growing to the extent where it can realistically challenge the likes of Hibernian, Allianz and Axa,' the newspaper said.

It emerged then that Quinn Direct had to increase its reserves by IR£16 million. And, as a result of the 2000 loss, the insurer needed IR£55 million in new capital to stabilize its operations and keep trading.

In 2001, Quinn's bankers provided the necessary cash. To fund his group interests up to that point, Quinn had worked mainly with a small core of banks, including Northern Bank. In 1999, when Anglo Irish Bank acquired Smurfit Paribas Bank, where Quinn was a client, he became a client of Anglo. Headed by Sean FitzPatrick, a thrusting banker with a taste for risk, Anglo was expanding aggressively and becoming the lender of choice for up-and-coming property developers. Anglo led the funding deal for Quinn Direct in 2001, its first major involvement with Sean Quinn.

Quinn's rivals in the insurance business seized on Quinn Direct's investment losses and the shortfall in the insurer's reserves to highlight the company's shortcomings to the regulatory authorities. But Mary Harney – then the Minister for Enterprise, Trade and Employment, and the de facto Regulator – backed Quinn. The entrepreneur was bringing down prices in the insurance sector, which had endured huge price hikes. In the pro-enterprise, free-market approach of Harney, a Progressive Democrats TD, Quinn was part of the solution, not the problem.

In the aftermath of the episode, Quinn fired himself as Quinn Direct's fund manager. Paddy Mullarkey, a former secretary-general of the Department of Finance and a fellow Fermanagh man, joined the board of the insurer to oversee investments. John O'Hanlon, a former chief executive of the Irish unit of Allianz, the global insurance company, was hired to make investment decisions. Officially, they were Quinn appointments, but it was rumoured the changes were prompted by the Department of Enterprise. By the end of 2001, the insurance company had altered its investment strategy fundamentally, holding about 20 per cent of its reserves in equities, more in line with its peers.

In a rare interview with the *Sunday Business Post* in December 2001, Sean Quinn said that Quinn Direct was a young business and he was happy to nurture it. He also emphasized the depth of the connection between the company and its founder. 'Quinn Direct is not in trouble. The only time that Quinn Direct will be in trouble is when Sean Quinn is in trouble. And Sean Quinn is in no trouble.' Though Quinn Direct was formally a separate business from Quinn Group, Sean Quinn spoke openly about the insurer, the group and himself as though they were all the same. 'Quinn Direct needs support in the same way as any other business that we started needed . . . Any new business needs a three- or four-year nursing period, and we are very happy to give that to Quinn Direct.' It was a blunt admission that money could flow between the companies, and it went virtually unnoticed.

'Maybe we made mistakes. Maybe we could have done better the first two or three years, and certainly we could have done better in our investments. But overall I would go as far as to say that Quinn Direct will be the best investment that we ever made,' said Quinn. He was facing 2002, he said, 'in the most confident mood that our group was ever in'.

The defiant tone of the interview seemed to silence Quinn's critics and knock the issue on the head. In a later article, the *Sunday Business Post* described the appointments of Mullarkey and O'Hanlon to run Quinn Direct's investment strategy as a 'vote of confidence' in the insurance company. It noted that Quinn Direct's underwriting performance was likely to improve because all insurers were increasing premiums after the terrorist attacks on the USA on 11 September 2001. 'Sources close to the company said that the company's business was now growing "extremely well",' the newspaper reported.

Speaking to the *Sunday Times* in June 2002, Quinn was again bullish about the insurance company. 'Quinn Direct is fully compliant with all regulations and is trading well, very profitably. We're expanding our book by 30 per cent to 35 per cent this year,' he said. 'We've invested IR£100 million in the glass factory and IR£100 million in the cement factory and I'd be happier with the IR£100 million we invested in insurance than either the glass or the cement,' he said. Despite the insurance setback, he was resolutely upbeat.

In March 2002, the Ardagh glass factory at Ringsend in Dublin closed, rendered uncompetitive by Quinn's lower costs and pricing. Quinn was already planning a second glass factory, at Elton in Cheshire in the north of England. It would be the largest glass factory in Europe and the first in the UK with its own bottling lines, an innovation that would allow customers to fill their bottles onsite, saving time and money. In 2002, having recovered from the Quinn Direct hiccup, Quinn Group recorded revenues of €542 million and operating profits of €76 million. Its total debt was less than €200 million, a low level of borrowing relative to its fast-growing profits.

As part of its investment portfolio, Quinn Direct held a 4.5 per cent stake in Alphyra, a payments business listed on the Dublin and London Stock Exchanges. The company provided phone top-ups and bill payment services, but its founder, John Nagle, felt that it was unfairly viewed as a tech stock and that the business was undervalued. In autumn 2002, Nagle started plotting a management buyout of the business, backed by Barry Maloney, a venture capitalist who had previously run Esat Digifone, Ireland's second mobile phone operator.

Nagle and Maloney were being advised by Conor Killeen, an investment banker who had set up his own corporate finance business, Key Capital, a year earlier. Killeen met Quinn and Liam McCaffrey to see if they would use their 4.5 per cent stake in Alphyra to support the buyout plan. A meeting with Nagle was arranged within days. Quinn liked Nagle's entrepreneurial style and told Killeen he would back the buyout bid.

Quinn's small but strategically important stake would help Nagle to fight off a rival bid for Alphyra from FirstData, a US payments giant. In April 2003, Nagle took the business into private ownership in an €88 million deal. 'Quinn did everything he said he would do. You felt he was a guy you could do business with,' said a source involved in the Alphyra deal.

Killeen, a former head of equities with Dresdner Kleinwort Wasserstein in London, had been impressed with Quinn and kept in touch with the businessman. In the summer of 2003, Killeen was trying to engineer a deal of his own, the buyout of NCB Stockbrokers, then owned by Ulster Bank. The bank was selling non-core assets and Killeen, himself an ex-NCB executive, saw an opportunity to do a deal.

Dermot Desmond, the financier and NCB founder, was willing to support the buyout with a €2 million loan but wanted a buyer lined up for his debt, which would allow him to quickly exit the deal. Quinn seemed an ideal candidate. Killeen arranged a meeting. After rapid negotiations, Quinn agreed to put up €4 million for a 20 per cent stake in NCB, to be held by Quinn Financial Services, the unit that included Quinn Direct and Quinn Life. It was less than the €5 million Killeen was seeking, but it was enough to repay Desmond and invest a substantial sum in NCB.

The investment gave Quinn more than just a stake in a broker. It gave him a more direct route to NCB's wealth of investment knowledge, its analyst research and insight about investment trends and what deals were being done by whom. For Quinn, who prided himself on being one step ahead of his competitors, that kind of access was potentially invaluable.

Killeen liked what he saw in Quinn, too. Announcing the Quinn investment in NCB in November 2003, he said, 'The people at Quinn are similar to ourselves. They are free-thinkers and independent, and like challenging the establishment.' Quinn Group, Killeen noted, was likely to make an operating profit of €150 million in 2003 as revenues headed for €650 million.

Flush with cash, Quinn's next move was an audacious attempt to buy Ardagh, which had 38 per cent of the glass market in the UK. The bid pitted Quinn against Paul Coulson, the Dublin financier who chaired Ardagh and was trying to buy the business himself. Coulson prevailed, with the backing of his banks, led by Anglo. However, Quinn had shown his appetite and ability to take out even well-known quoted businesses. Within months, he would do just that.

In early 2004, Barlo, a radiator and plastics company, was languishing on the Irish Stock Exchange. The company's value was stuck around €45 million, held back by poor economic conditions and pricing issues that were out of its control. Barlo management, led by chief executive Tony Mullins, agreed a buyout of the business for €70 million, a generous premium to its market value. It looked a done deal until Quinn emerged with an €84 million offer.

Quinn trumped the management deal by buying a key stake from Dermot Desmond, whose NCB stake Quinn had acquired in 2003. In the space of five weeks, Quinn went from owning just 2.4 per cent of Barlo to 88.2 per cent, enough to make his offer unconditional. It was one of the quickest takeovers of an Irish plc in history. NCB, now chaired by Conor Killeen, advised Quinn on the buyout. Quinn, the outsider, was easing himself into the inner circles of the financial world.

The Barlo purchase was a coup for Quinn, who could act quickly because he didn't have to report to shareholders. 'The decision-making process within the organization is extremely quick,' said one source close to the company at the time of the deal. 'It is a hallmark.' The takeover brought Quinn into twelve countries and provided a base for future growth. Quinn installed his own managers in the businesses and tasked them with expanding them. Liam McCaffrey, the Quinn chief executive, would later say the potential of the Barlo business was 'much greater than we realized when we took it over'.

After the deal, Quinn haggled with Killeen over NCB's fee, before settling with a spit handshake. He was like a farmer sealing the purchase of an animal instead of a multimillionaire buying an international business. There was a party in the Slieve Russell, which ran well into the small hours of the morning. The NCB dealmakers celebrated with Quinn and his managers. 'He was good to be around; he was inspiring,' said one person involved in the Barlo deal. 'Everyone felt they were around something real, a real industrialist and entrepreneur who cared for people and doing the right thing. He was tremendously smart but also really centred and fair to people.'

Not long after the Barlo deal, Conor Killeen parted company with NCB after his ambitions to internationalize the business were thwarted. With the Irish economy booming, NCB was enjoying a huge domestic expansion and the international strategy was parked. Killeen returned to Key Capital with several NCB colleagues, focusing on capital markets and more complex financial products. The exits gave Quinn an opportunity to increase his NCB stake to 25 per cent, though he remained close to Killeen. In the midst of the upheaval at NCB, he called Killeen and asked him to join the board of Quinn Group as a non-executive director, a position Killeen was happy to accept.

There were other additions to the Quinn board. Paddy Murphy, a former Bank of Ireland banker, was appointed a non-executive director. A new finance director, Dara O'Reilly, also joined the boardroom. A Belturbet boy, raised just a few miles from the Slieve Russell, he was following a virtually identical path to Liam McCaffrey. A Coopers & Lybrand accountant, with some experience in the internal audit department at Aer Lingus, O'Reilly joined Quinn at the age of twenty-five. By the time he was twenty-eight, he had been appointed group finance director. The new appointees joined a board that included Sean and Patricia Quinn, Peter Quinn, Liam McCaffrey and Paddy Mullarkey. They were barely in their seats when Quinn began a fresh flurry of deal-making.

He bought a 13 per cent stake in Airtricity, the wind energy business run by Eddie O'Connor, for €36 million, complementing his own wind interests. In 2004, Quinn Direct entered the motor market in Britain, using the same low-cost strategy it had in Ireland. The insurer's 900 Dublin staff moved into an eleven-storey landmark building, the Q Centre, on the Cavan road out of the capital. A new Quinn Packaging plant opened at Scotchtown, outside Ballyconnell. A Quinn Therm factory opened down the road. A roof tiles factory that had only opened in 2001 was expanded in 2005.

In Britain, the group was spending a total of €400 million on two giant projects: the glass bottling plant in Cheshire and the world's biggest radiator factory at Newport in Wales. Plans were in train too for a chemical factory near Leipzig in Germany to make MMA, a raw material for the plastics business.

By 2005, Sean Quinn was an extremely wealthy man. The family business, a strong group of companies with relatively little debt, was valued at up to €3 billion. The group, headquartered in a modest office block beside Quinn's mother's home, employed about 4,500 people in one of the most economically disadvantaged parts of the country. Its prospects were bright. The construction sector was booming, which meant more business for Quinn's cement and building-products divisions; and greater prosperity meant there were more cars and businesses for Quinn Direct to insure.

'It was like everything he touched turned to gold,' said a former Quinn Group executive. 'All the stuff that people said was mad – the cement plant, the insurance, the glass factory – had succeeded. It was as if he was indestructible.' The 2005 accounts for Quinn Group would show an almost 50 per cent surge in pre-tax profits to €326 million. Revenues rose 38 per cent to €1.2 billion. Both revenues and profits were split almost evenly between Quinn's manufacturing and insurance enterprises.

Quinn Direct had bounced back from the heavy losses of 2000 to build a lucrative 14 per cent market share in motor insurance. It was a tightly run business and Quinn took a very active interest, particularly in the larger claims coming through the system. He attributed the company's success to his fast-track claims model; as soon as a policyholder informed the company of a claim, a regional claims manager was appointed to investigate it.

Quinn Direct would ultimately have a panel of 600 regional claims managers – 300 in Ireland and 300 in Britain. Unlike the staff at conventional insurers, all of Quinn's claims managers were self-employed; a large proportion were retired police officers. They were incentivized to settle claims early and cheaply, keeping them outside the costly courts process. The insurance company developed a reputation for aggressively querying claims and settling with claimants on the steps of the courts to avoid legal fees. It was unorthodox but it was proving highly lucrative for Quinn.

On the back of the surging profits, the Quinn family took a dividend of €120 million out of Quinn Direct in 2004. The next year, Sean Quinn drew a €1.1 million salary from Quinn Group and topped it up with a €6.5 million contribution to his pension fund. The Quinns were well on their way to being Ireland's richest family, outstripping the likes of Sir Anthony O'Reilly, the Independent Newspapers and former Heinz executive.

For more than twenty years, despite the growth in his businesses and his wealth, Sean Quinn had lived in the same relatively modest house overlooking Aghavoher Lake, beside the Slieve Russell. He had bought the land there, he told Colm Tóibín, because his father had owned it in the 1950s and he remembered going to look at it on an ass and cart.

In the summer of 2004, Quinn and his wife, Patricia, sought planning permission for a new home on the old family land. The old two-storey house would be demolished. In its place, Quinn would build a four-storey mansion. At 14,700 square feet, the new house would be more than ten times the size of a good-sized family home.

The house would have seven en-suite bedrooms, a swimming pool and leisure area in the basement, a cinema, bar and snooker room, a golf simulator and indoor putting green.

The garage, linked to the house with a covered walkway, would accommodate nine cars. The property was surrounded by landscaped grounds and enclosed by a high fence and intercom-controlled gates. 'Sean Quinn is a well-known businessman in the Cavan area,' read the planning application submitted by Paul Joyce Architects, a Dublin practice. 'This present application seeks to demolish their existing house and replace it with a new family house which is more fitting to their needs.'

2

'Sean Quinn does risk'

From the early years of the millennium, Sean Quinn had talked openly about stepping aside from Quinn Group and finding the best way to secure its future. It wasn't a foregone conclusion that he would pass the running of the business on to his five children. He knew that family businesses tended to suffer when they were passed from a single founder to several members of the next generation.

In his 2001 interview with the *Sunday Business Post*, Quinn said he would reduce the family's shareholding in the group to less than 50 per cent within four to seven years. 'The Quinns don't have a divine right to make decisions on the company over the next few years, because the Quinns wouldn't have the company if it wasn't for the support that we got from our staff,' he said. 'It's important that we make the right decisions, so that when Sean Quinn is dead and gone, the group survives and the two thousand jobs we created are sustained.'

Despite the enormous wealth their father had created, the Quinn children didn't lead ostentatious lifestyles. Apart from expensive cars, they had few of the trappings of growing up with a billionaire father. They were educated at local schools and kept a low profile. With the exception of Brenda, the youngest, the children all worked in the family business.

Colette was working in Quinn's hospitality division, heavily involved in decisions about the Slieve Russell and other properties. Ciara, Sean and Aoife all had jobs in Quinn Direct. There was no suggestion they were on an accelerated management track or getting much preferential treatment. Quinn wanted them to see the nuts and bolts of business before they made decisions about their futures. Sean Junior, for example, had gone into the insurance company at twenty-one, straight from college, learning the ropes of selling insurance, then moving into claims. He had followed in his father's footsteps in other ways, playing Gaelic football for Teemore Shamrocks and the Fermanagh county team. He was a keen golfer, too – with a single-digit handicap honed on the Slieve Russell championship golf course.

'They were very decent people,' says a person who was close to the family during that period. 'The children were raised in a very cocooned environment. Their access to money was controlled, where they went was controlled.'

But the children weren't just employees of Quinn Group – they were its owners. Behind the scenes in 2002, Sean Quinn had handed the shares in the group to his children through a corporate restructuring. They had equal 20 per cent stakes in the group and an agreement that their father would run it for them until he was ready to step down.

As far back as 2001, Quinn had sought trade partners for his various businesses. A prospectus was even drawn up for a sale of the cement business and circulated to potential buyers. Seven companies made approaches but Quinn baulked when he realized each one of them had higher borrowings than Quinn Group. 'We should be buyers rather than sellers,' he said.

Since then, his plan to avoid a messy succession had solidified around a decision to formally split the group into manufacturing operations and insurance, and float the two divisions separately on the stock exchange. By 2005, newspaper reports suggested that implementation of the plan was three to five years in the future. 'A flotation would be the easiest way to pass on the business,' Liam McCaffrey said in a 2005 interview, adding, 'at least, that's the current plan.'

If the plan went ahead, the stock market listings would crystallize huge wealth for the Quinn children, though they would no longer own the companies that bore their family name. Quinn was not hung up on any of his children running the group, according to sources close to the businessman at the time. But having started with nothing himself, he was increasingly determined to leave his children with fabulous wealth. 'I intend to live poor and die rich,' he said in 2001.

While the flotation plan remained notional, Quinn took steps aimed at making his children super-rich in another way: through ownership of a sizeable property portfolio that would deliver consistent, strong income. What Quinn envisaged was, essentially, a family of billionaires, with wealth on a scale not seen in Ireland.

The property plan swung into action in 2004, boosted by the €120 million dividend paid to the family out of Quinn Direct. Late that year, Quinn launched an audacious bid to buy the exclusive Wentworth Club in Surrey, with its three championship golf courses, for £135 million sterling. After a protracted and testy takeover battle, he lost out to Richard Caring, a colourful multimillionaire who was then Britain's biggest clothing supplier.

Just months later, Quinn consoled himself by buying the Belfry hotel and golf resort, a similar asset to Wentworth, for £186 million sterling. Bank of Ireland led the funding of the deal, with some secondary loans coming from Anglo Irish Bank. Buying the Belfry, the four-time venue for the Ryder Cup, wasn't just a property purchase. He was announcing his presence in the British market as a man of substance. Like the Slieve Russell, the Belfry would be a base to entertain Quinn Group customers and advisers. 'Because he had lost out on Wentworth, he really wanted the Belfry and was willing to overpay for it,' said a source close to the purchase. The ownership of the property was registered in the name of Sean Quinn Junior, who had just turned twenty-six.

The Belfry, despite its international reputation and hefty price tag, would be one of the less exotic purchases for Quinn's International Property Group (IPG). 'He did a lot of investigation and analysis and felt there was value to be had in Eastern Europe, in Russia, and India,' according to a former colleague.

In late 2004, Quinn paid €145 million for the Prague Hilton and an adjoining Ibis hotel. The Hilton was an enormous property, a 791-bedroom hotel with the biggest conference facilities in Central and Eastern Europe. It was a record price for a hotel deal in Central Europe, but Quinn was confident of steady growth in the Czech Republic, a new entrant to the European Union. (Several years later, Quinn and his wife would be photographed at the Prague Hilton with US President Barack Obama and his wife, Michelle.) Anglo provided the finance for the Prague deal, the first time the Sean FitzPatrick-led bank funded a major Quinn deal. Continuing the new strategy of putting properties in the names of his children, Colette Quinn would own the Prague hotels.

From there, Quinn accelerated his property plan. The Quinn Group already had a dedicated hospitality division, which ran the Quinn hotels and pubs. It was headed by Alan Hynes, an accountant who was, like many of Quinn's senior executives, in his mid thirties. Quinn bolstered the hospitality team with the addition of a new financial controller, Paul Morgan, an accountant from Dundalk in Co. Louth. Morgan had worked for more than ten years at ABB, an international engineering company, before going into Kirk & Associates, a Dundalk accountancy practice.

Quinn's acquisitions director, Patrick Masterson, was also drafted in to join the property venture. Masterson, a former employee of the telecoms entrepreneur Denis O'Brien, had joined Quinn in 2004 and project-managed the Barlo takeover and the investment in Airtricity. Hynes, Morgan and Masterson would be centrally involved in the early part of Quinn's IPG strategy.

Quinn presented them with an ambitious target. He wanted to spend €1 billion a year on property over each of the next five years. That way, by the end of the five years, each of his children could have a €1 billion property portfolio. It had to happen fast and he wanted good returns, double-digit yields. Those kinds of returns weren't available in the UK or continental Europe; by default, Quinn was setting his sights further afield.

The property team travelled widely. In mid 2005, they spent a week in Paris considering a deal with Vivendi Universal, the publishing group. Vivendi was selling its stakes in Hilton hotels in Sofia, the capital of Bulgaria, and Bucharest, the Romanian capital. The directors reported back that the Sofia Hilton looked like a good prospect, an impressive 245-bedroom hotel that was generating a lot of cash. There were issues with the Bucharest property, however. The title to the land wasn't entirely clear and there had already been some litigation. A purchase there looked risky.

'Sean Quinn does risk,' Quinn reprimanded them, characteristically referring to himself in the third person. 'You don't have to worry about risk; I worry about risk.' But he passed on the Bucharest deal. He bought the Sofia hotel in a two-stage deal reported to be worth about €40 million.

The property ventures were taking up more and more of Quinn's time and money. To focus his energies abroad, he disposed of several of his Irish hotels and pubs. In some cases, he sold hotels to their managers in order to keep ownership in the locality. In at least one case, say sources, he even took the highly unusual step of guaranteeing the bank loan raised by the hotel buyer to do the deal.

The Prague Hilton was given a €20 million overhaul and the Slieve Russell, now registered in Brenda Quinn's name, was expanded with the addition of new bedrooms and high-end spa facilities. Colette Quinn was heavily involved in the refurbishment projects, picking fabrics and overseeing the work. 'Sean was pushing very hard all the time and Colette was right in the middle of it, with a direct route to Daddy,' says a former employee of the group.

Quinn's dogged approach could cause friction. He had bought the Belfry from De Vere Group, a respected British hospitality group, with an agreement De Vere would continue to run the property. Within weeks of the purchase, however, Quinn was unhappy: he felt the property was not being run 'the Quinn way'. Having just spent £186 million, he discussed knocking the Belfry down and building a new 500-bedroom hotel. In the end, Quinn reached a deal to buy out De Vere's management contract as the hotel operator. Ditching De Vere cost a reported €36 million on top of the original cost of the deal.

The property team by now employed about twenty people, based at Quinn Insurance's modern head office outside Cavan town. They would split into smaller groups, research a market heavily and then have a short, intensive visit packed with meetings with local property developers and estate agents. They visited Hungary, the Czech Republic, Slovenia, Slovakia, Lithuania and Latvia. In Azerbaijan, a deal to buy a hotel and apartment complex, which would have delivered a 15 per cent yield, was halted by the local government. A deal to buy a hotel in the Russian city of St Petersburg also fell through.

As word spread about the Irish billionaire on the hunt for property, Quinn's property team were inundated with unsolicited offers. 'There was no strategy to it, expect we weren't allowed to look in the UK, France or Germany,' said a former employee. 'It was very scattergun. We were being forced east all the time, and there was huge pressure to deliver.'

At the end of 2005, it was apparent Quinn wasn't happy at the pace of property purchases. Over the course of a weekend just before Christmas 2005, he took matters into his own hands and completely overhauled how the property business was run. Hynes, the hospitality division director, would move to Dublin, making it easier for him to travel internationally and pursue deals. A new development team would be set up to run the international investment strategy. Kevin Lunney, the general manager of Quinn Direct, would be parachuted in as its boss. Paul Morgan would return to running the hospitality business, reporting to McCaffrey.

On Quinn's instruction, the international property unit would move from Cavan to the group headquarters at Derrylin. It would become a Northern Ireland company and the staff, many from the Cavan area, would be shifted to Northern Ireland tax and payroll. Morgan, facing a longer commute to work and with another job offer on the table, decided to leave the group. He parted on good terms with Quinn and the management team.

The remaining staff faced a serious practical issue. There was no spare office space in Derrylin, so the property unit had to swap their comfortable Cavan office for Portakabins beside the group headquarters until permanent accommodation was sorted out. It didn't make much sense, but it was what Quinn wanted – and Sean Quinn got what he wanted. He soon found a solution to the accommodation problem. Quinn's mother, Mary, had died in May 2005, aged ninety-two. The family home, where Quinn's whole business had its roots, was demolished to make way for an office block for the new property unit.

Under Lunney, the property team went on a spending spree. Quinn bought the Sheraton Hotel in Krakow for about €45 million and a shopping centre close to Istanbul. In Kiev, Quinn paid more than €80 million for a high-spec office block, the Leonardo Business Centre, and €50 million for a shopping centre, the Univermag Ukraina. Unusually, he invited Quinn Group staff to invest in the Leonardo deal, and their investment was managed through a Quinn Life fund. Quinn's management team also invested directly in the Leonardo. The heaviest investment was in Russia, where Quinn acquired the twenty-storey Kutuzoff Tower in Moscow, and paid about €40 million for the Caspiy Business Centre, which was still under construction. The Russian purchases also included a logistics centre in Kazan, capital of Tatarstan, and a retail, leisure and logistics development in Ufa, capital of Bashkortostan, 1,175 kilometres east of Moscow. In India, he bought land earmarked for a high-tech park and hotel in Hyderabad, home to many multinational technology companies.

'Some people go for a safe return – we go for a bigger return,' Quinn said in 2007. 'We don't like the 3, 4 or 5 per cent returns. Any of the properties we ever bought, we only bought them on the basis that we'd receive a 10 per cent return, with one or two exceptions. In Prague, Bulgaria, Poland, Russia, wherever we went, we always got those double figures.' For tax reasons, the Quinn International Property Group was run through a complex structure controlled by a Swedish company, Quinn Investments Sweden.

The family dividends went into the property purchases, which were viewed as personal investments on behalf of the Quinn family rather than group assets. As such, the property deals were not generally discussed at Quinn Group board meetings, according to people with knowledge of the situation. 'It wasn't considered to be on the company account so there was nothing to be concerned about,' said one source. Another source, a former staff member, said, 'We weren't privy to where funding was coming from. It was very tightly managed in Derrylin by Sean, Liam [McCaffrey] and

Dara [O'Reilly]. If a deal was done, the funding was available. That was the way it was.'

With the country enjoying a long economic boom, Quinn's businesses were thriving. Conor Killeen suggested to Quinn that he should take advantage of low interest rates to restructure Quinn Group's finances. In October 2005, the group finalized a restructuring of all its existing bank loans, by now about €700 million in total, into one facility from a bank syndicate led by Barclays. The refinancing streamlined Quinn's various loans and gave him more capital for expansion. As a bonus, the new loan facility was at a lower interest rate than the average rate of the original borrowings.

There was another advantage for Quinn. He had given personal guarantees over some of the group's original borrowings, drawn down for specific factories or investment projects. There was no personal guarantee on the new debt package. The financial restructuring removed Quinn from any personal guarantees over group debts, despite his protestations that he was comfortable with the borrowings. 'If I borrow money, I'll pay it back,' he told the Quinn board. Killeen strongly advised against giving guarantees, a source said.

'You shouldn't put yourself in a position where they can make life more difficult for you,' he told Quinn. 'You'll live to regret it.' The banks decided they could take the risk, lending the money without any guarantees from Sean Quinn or formal security over the Quinn Group. It was an unusual arrangement, leaving the lenders with less security than would have been common, particularly in a deal of that size.

At the same time, Quinn made his first foray into the debt markets, raising $300 million by issuing bonds to international institutions. The loan terms ranged from five years to ten years, and carried interest rates of 5 to 6 per cent. Again, the rates were low for such sizeable corporate borrowings, reflecting the eagerness of lenders to get involved in financing Quinn's operations. He was seen as a safe bet. 'The banks and bondholders loved him,' said one director of the group from that period. 'They all wanted to be involved.' After his years of aggressive expansion and surging profits, Quinn was seen as a blue-chip borrower.

Quinn was comfortable with the debt structure. The bondholders would be passive backers of the company with no real input into strategy or how he spent the money. The loan terms, or covenants, were concerned mainly with the repayment arrangements rather than any draconian restrictions on Quinn. As long as he did not breach the covenants, the lenders were happy.

In April 2006, six months after the first bond offering, the group raised almost $200 million more from bondholders. A year later, it raised another $230 million. Its total debt to bondholders was now $730 million, or almost €600 million, on top of the €700 million owed to the Barclays-led banks. Quinn had plenty of uses for the money.

In Britain, Quinn Group was spending €400 million between the new bottling plant in Cheshire and the radiator factory in Newport. There were plans, too, for a new plastics factory near Leipzig, due to come on stream in 2010 and likely to cost between €200 million and €300 million. It would be the first factory of its kind built in Europe in more than three decades. Cheaper materials from low-cost countries had rendered European plastics manufacturing uncompetitive, but Quinn was undaunted.

'We don't lose any sleep over large capital investment projects,' Liam McCaffrey, the Quinn chief executive, said in an interview with the *Sunday Times* in late 2005. 'There is a fundamental belief that runs across the entire group: if we do it right, and we do it well, then the business will make it through the [economic] cycles.'

Unknown to the outside world, however, Sean Quinn had embarked on another type of investment – a below-the-radar programme of buying shares in publicly quoted companies. On a flight to Italy in early 2005, he had chatted with another passenger about a financial product known as a Contract for Difference (CFD). Though he had been buying shares and commodities from the mid 1980s, as Colm Toíbín had seen first-hand, Quinn had never invested through CFDs.

By buying CFDs, an investor could bet on the price of a share without actually owning the shares. Quinn could bet on the movement in a share price by taking a CFD 'position' with a broker. He would enter a contract with the broker at a set price. At the end of the contract, the two parties would settle the 'difference' between the opening and closing prices of the share. If the share price rose, Quinn got the benefit of the gain; if the share fell, however, he would have to pay the broker the difference between the closing price and the price at the start of the contract.

There were advantages to investing through CFDs. To get started, Quinn would have to pay only a small percentage of the value of the underlying shares. This down payment, often as little as 10 per cent, is known as the 'margin'. This created the potential for much greater rewards than could be reaped by using the same sum to buy shares. At a 10 per cent margin, for example, €10 would 'buy' an investor a CFD stake in €100 worth of shares. If the shares rose in value to €110, the investor would get the full benefit of the rise. Of course, the leverage worked in the other direction, too: if the shares lost value, the investor faced a greater loss. Because they did not involve buying an asset, CFDs did not incur stamp duty. And, unlike share purchases, CFD positions did not have to be disclosed – an appealing consideration to a publicity-shy businessman.

The dotcom investment fiasco of 2000 had not dulled Sean Quinn's appetite for stock market investing. Whenever he was in the Cavan office of Quinn Direct, he would stop by the desk of Mark McNamara, the insurer's investment manager, to see what shares were performing well, according to former Quinn employees. Investing through CFDs would usher in a whole new period of stock market involvement for Quinn.

He consulted PricewaterhouseCoopers (PWC), the global accountancy group and auditors to Quinn Direct, for specialist tax advice on his investing. The accountants advised setting up a company in Madeira to handle the CFD investments. Madeira was a thriving offshore financial centre. Under a scheme approved by the EU to boost business on the island, international investment companies based there paid just 3 per cent corporate tax. Dividends paid back to a parent company in another EU country were exempt from tax. Madeira also had strong bank secrecy legislation.

Using PWC in Portugal, Quinn established a Madeiran company,

Bazzely V Consultadoria Económica E Participações, Sociedade Unipessoal LDA, or Bazzely for short. PWC advised that, for maximum tax efficiencies, the company should be owned by the five Quinn children: Colette, Ciara, Sean, Aoife and Brenda. But the company was theirs in name only; Bazzely's investments would be managed solely by their father, and they took no part in the investment decisions.

In October 2005, Bazzely did its first deals through Davy, the Irish broker, and Cantor Fitzgerald, a London broker that was an early promoter of CFDs. Quinn used CFDs to take positions in Anglo Irish Bank, AIB, Bank of Ireland, Ryanair, Paddy Power and Tullow Oil. He even bought CFDs in FBD, a rival to his Quinn Insurance. Through Bazzely, Quinn also invested in international firms, buying into Royal Bank of Scotland, oil giant BP, chemicals firm BASF, financial services firm BBVA, Deutsche Telecom, Nestlé, pharma firm Sanofi Aventis and some Japanese companies.

It was a diversified portfolio, though the stakes in Anglo Irish Bank and Ryanair were by far the largest, reflecting Quinn's particular admiration for those companies. At the end of 2005, Bazzely's Ryanair position covered shares worth about €60 million. The Anglo stake was even larger, with shares worth more than €100 million, though Quinn had had to put up a margin of only €20 million. If the share price rose 20 per cent, he doubled his original investment, with no stamp duty due.

The CFD investments were entirely hidden from the public. Even the companies whose shares Quinn was betting on had no way of knowing about them. The investor's identity was no secret to the brokers behind Bazzely, however: the Bazzely account at Davy, for example, was registered at the address of Quinn Direct's head office at Dublin Road, Cavan.

Quinn arranged funding for the trades through Quinn Finance and Quinn Group Family Properties, two companies outside the main group structure. The directors of each of the companies were Quinn and his three closest lieutenants: Liam McCaffrey, Kevin Lunney and Dara O'Reilly. There were no independent directors or advisers involved.

'Liam, Kevin and Dara were the Holy Trinity,' said a former senior executive with the group. Another source who had dealings with the group said, 'They were good listeners, good operational guys. Liam was patient and unflappable. He was well capable of standing up to Sean.' Lunney and O'Reilly were considered keen to impress Quinn and less likely to question the boss. 'Lunney,' said one source, 'idolized Sean.'

In March 2006, the Revenue Commissioners announced plans to start applying stamp duty to CFDs. Ireland's financial community mobilized to oppose the plan. Tony Garry, chief executive of Davy, emailed a senior civil servant in the Department of Finance saying the broker was getting 'hugely negative feedback from overseas investors' on the stamp duty proposal. On 24 March, executives from PWC met department officials about the issue. A department record of the meeting mentions an unidentified person from PWC saying that CFDs are used by hedge funds, 'not private clients', and that positions are usually held for just two to three weeks. The description certainly didn't fit Sean Quinn, whom PWC had helped set up in CFD investing. The Irish Stock Exchange also lobbied the department and the Revenue Commissioners against the CFD tax plan. On 30 March, Brian Cowen, the Minister for Finance, announced a review of the measure. In the end, the stamp duty plan was quietly shelved and no tax was introduced.

Through 2006, Sean Quinn aggressively ramped up his CFD investing. By the end of 2006, he held CFDs over Anglo shares worth more than €650 million, roughly 5.4 per cent of the bank's €12 billion market capitalization at the time. If Quinn had owned 5.4 per cent of the bank's shares outright, he would have had to disclose his holding. With the secrecy of CFDs, however, no one outside his inner circle knew about his investment.

Quinn was investing out of admiration for Anglo, according to sources from that period. He had got to know some of the senior Anglo bankers from his property deals and was impressed with their rapid decision-making. 'He did a lot of analysis on Irish banks and he concluded that Anglo stock was cheap,' said one source. 'It was a new bank, with no legacy. It had half the cost base of its competitors, per euro of net revenue. He loved that, he identified with it.' Another said, 'He was enamoured with them; he said the Anglo guys were guys to watch.'

One Quinn associate recalled a conversation at a charity dinner in the Four Seasons Hotel in Dublin, a luxury hotel funded by Anglo loans. Quinn pointed to another guest. 'Do you know who that is?' he asked. 'That's one of the smartest guys in the country. He thinks way out ahead of everyone else.' It was Joe O'Reilly, a property developer who was building a massive shopping centre in Dundrum, a mature Dublin suburb. The Dundrum Town Centre would become the country's biggest shopping centre, with almost a million square feet of space. O'Reilly was one of Anglo's biggest clients.

'He would be in my four-ball,' said Quinn, outlining his perfect golfing partnership. 'There would be Joe O'Reilly, Michael O'Leary, David Drumm and me.' O'Leary was the chief executive of Ryanair, whose obsessive focus on costs Quinn admired. Drumm was the youthful chief executive of Anglo Irish Bank. A former head of Anglo's American operations, he had replaced Sean FitzPatrick as chief executive of the bank in January 2005, when FitzPatrick moved on to become chairman.

At a European banking conference in London in March 2006, Drumm showcased Anglo's strengths, using a presentation titled 'Managing for growth in a complex environment'. The bank could offer 'certainty of execution and confidence for customers', he told the attendees. Its funding had risen 43 per cent to €42 billion between September 2004 and September 2005. It had more than 350 interbank relationships and expected 'no surprises on asset quality'. The presentation concluded with the Anglo slogan: 'Experience the Difference'.

Anglo's strong performance during Ireland's property boom had attracted international recognition. In early 2006, Mercer Oliver Wyman (MOW), one of the world's top financial-services strategy and risk-management consultants, named Anglo as the world's top-performing bank in terms of shareholder returns from 2001 to 2005. The bank's share price had quadrupled, from €3.14 to €12.90, during the period. No other Irish bank featured in MOW's top twenty.

'Anglo Irish Bank owes much of its success to a concentrated focus on business lending, treasury and wealth management in the Irish, UK and US markets,' MOW said, noting that Anglo's business lending had risen 38 per cent annually over the previous ten years. 'A centralized loan approval process has helped the bank maintain high asset quality and minimize the risks of portfolio concentration.'

By late 2006, Sean Quinn's CFD investments had yielded tens of millions of euro in paper profit. Anglo's shares finished the year at €15.71, but Quinn, who had bought his first Anglo CFDs when the share price was around €11.30, did not cash in any of his contracts. Instead, he started disposing of his non-Anglo stakes, breaking up his diverse portfolio.

Shares in robust companies including Ryanair, Tullow Oil and Deutsche Telecom were sold and the profits were used to pile further sums into Anglo. Quinn retained only small non-Anglo stakes, including CFD investments in McInerney, the publicly quoted Irish housebuilder. It was an extraordinary strategy, leading Quinn into an even more concentrated gamble than his disastrous punt on tech shares in 2000.

As MOW had pointed out, Anglo had already enjoyed dramatic share price appreciation. That kind of growth would be hard to sustain. By buying CFD positions in shares now valued at almost €16, Quinn was gambling they could and would rise even further. If the shares fell below the record prices at which Quinn was buying, of course, he would face calls from his CFD brokers to cover the difference.

The slogan of the Quinn Group was 'Strength through Diversity', but Quinn was making a huge concentrated bet on one share. His approach was at best blindly illogical; at worst, it was pathological, fitting a pattern common to extreme and problem gamblers.

At the start of 2007, Quinn bought the Irish operations of Bupa, the health insurer, for an estimated €30 million. Bupa had decided to quit the Irish market, blaming unfair competition from VHI, the state-owned health insurer. The company was preparing to lay off its 300 staff when Quinn bought the business, saving the jobs and adding 500,000 health insurance customers to his business.

As part of the takeover process, the Office of the Financial Regulator, by now established as a stand-alone entity, sent a team of people to Cavan to examine Quinn Group's books. The Regulator's office, headed by Patrick Neary, a career civil servant, wanted to see that everything was in order and that Quinn's group was properly capitalized to run the health insurance business. The probe did not extend to the Quinn family investments outside the group structure, however, so the Regulator had no insight into Quinn's CFD buying. The share gambles would remain a secret and the Regulator gave the group a clean bill of health.

Quinn dispatched his son, 28-year-old Sean Junior, to the relaunch of the former Bupa business, rebranded as Quinn Healthcare. At the same time, Quinn Direct became simply Quinn Insurance. The Bupa deal would make Quinn the second-largest insurance company in the country after barely a decade in business. 'It was white-knight stuff; everyone was thrilled with the outcome,' a source from the health insurance business said about its purchase by Quinn. A helipad was installed with great speed at the health insurance offices at Fermoy, in Co. Cork, to receive visits from Quinn.

There was a late-night party at the Slieve Russell to celebrate the deal, and the former Bupa managers who were staying on at the company played a round of golf with Quinn. The morning after the party, Quinn showed the health insurance bosses around his manufacturing operations on the Cavan–Fermanagh border – starting with the furnace in the glass factory. As they sweated out the previous night's alcohol intake, he proudly pointed out technical features of the installation.

It was an exciting time to be involved with Quinn. In 2006, Quinn Group had bought farmland near Swanlinbar on the Cavan side of the border. It would be developed as a quarry, supplying limestone for the cement factory. To link the quarry and the factory, Quinn negotiated with local landowners to build a ten-kilometre private road. It was built in six months by Quinn workers using Quinn materials. The workers nicknamed it 'the Runway' because it was smoother than the local roads built with government money and maintained by the council. The quarry would produce 100,000 tonnes of rock a month for the cement production, with capacity to feed Quinn's cement factory for another twenty-five years.

'It was a fascinating and rewarding period,' said one former senior executive with Quinn. 'It was in his nature to really push people.' Another said, 'Everything you did was influenced by "What's Sean going to think?" He is a very charming man but there was a fear factor around him. You had to know how to behave around him, how to speak to him. If you were comfortable with it, it was great fun. But if you were different – if you didn't like GAA or didn't quite fit in, you wouldn't last long.'

Quinn was a hands-on boss. After the Bupa buyout, he would invite Quinn Healthcare employees to meetings, 25 or 30 people at a time, and pepper them with questions. 'He wanted to meet customer service people and get to grips with the business,' said the health insurance source. 'He was into the nuts and bolts, and he came up with initiatives of his own. It was the difference between a corporate entity owning a business and a man owning a business.'

When the health insurer needed new premises in Cork, Quinn personally inspected the potential properties. Rather than dealing with estate agents, he quizzed the building developers and architects about minute details of their construction, their insulation, even their car parking spaces. He settled on a building in the Eastgate Business Park, owned by Michael O'Flynn, a Cork developer, but not before haggling over the details.

With the group growing so fast, things were sometimes 'a bit Quinny', said one source. 'Because of the speed he pushed things through at, not every "t" was crossed and "i" dotted.' Quinn wasn't afraid to bend the rules either. In 2000, it had emerged that Quinn had secretly funded a residents' group that was objecting to a cement factory being built in Kinnegad, Co. Westmeath, by rival Lagan Cement. In a related court case, Quinn, who had experienced the dirty tricks of CRH in the 1980s, was accused by a High Court judge of acting in 'a cynical, calculated and unscrupulous fashion' to get commercial advantage over Lagan.

When the glass factory in Cheshire was in the process of being built in 2005, Quinn submitted an application to increase the size of the plant by 20 per cent. Though the application was subject to a public inquiry, he went ahead and built the larger factory. The factory was later approved but not before a planning row that would involve John Prescott, the British Deputy Prime Minister, and a legal challenge to the local council by Ardagh, Quinn's old rival in the Irish glass market. In the legal action, a High Court judge said Quinn had taken a 'calculated risk' by building the factory without full planning permission. Taking calculated risks was in Quinn's nature. Whether he recognized it or not, his stock market plays were moving him into a whole new dimension of risk.

In the first three months of 2007 – leading up to the Slieve Russell speech in which he described his 'simple life' – Quinn took on almost €800 million more in CFDs in Anglo, more than doubling his already enormous stake. In the following three months, he added another €655 million in Anglo CFDs. On 31 May 2007, the bank's share price hit a record high of €17.56, buoyed by the publication of strong results. It was firmly established as the third-biggest bank in Ireland, behind only AIB and Bank of Ireland.

On paper, Quinn's profit on his investment in the bank was in the region of €200 million. Still, he did not sell any of his holdings.

One of the reasons why the Anglo share price continued to rise was because Quinn's CFD brokers were buying so much of the stock to facilitate his deals. Behind the healthy share price, Anglo was vulnerable. The credit crunch was becoming apparent in international markets; scepticism was setting in about the property boom and the banks that had fuelled it. Anglo, with its customer base dominated by property developers with huge borrowings, was the biggest lender to the most dramatic property boom in Western Europe.

By this time, too, there was public speculation about Quinn's CFD position. In January 2007, the *Sunday Times* reported that Quinn had taken at least a 5 per cent stake in Anglo through CFDs. It was the first time Quinn's stake-building was referred to publicly, though the paper underestimated the size of his holding. In fact, by that stage Quinn's position covered at least 15 per cent of the bank's shares, something even Anglo did not know.

Publicly quoted companies like to know about their biggest share-holders, particularly whether they are investing for the short term or the long term. Having a large chunk of shares tied up with one share-holder whose intentions are unclear breeds uncertainty. If that shareholder suddenly decides to change strategy and sell out, it could flood the market with shares leading to a collapse in the share price of the company. On the other hand, a shareholder building a large stake, even though CFDs, could be a prelude to a takeover.

Just as Quinn was betting Anglo's shares would continue to rise, however, there were other investors betting they would fall. Some hedge funds, aware of Quinn's CFD buying – though not its full extent – had started to short-sell Anglo stock, betting that the share price would fall. Quinn's huge CFD position was actually directly facilitating the short-sellers: the brokers who sold CFDs to Quinn held the Anglo shares involved and could lend out the stock to hedge funds that wanted to profit by shorting Anglo. The short-sellers could borrow the shares and sell them, expecting it would be cheaper to buy them back in the future.

Though he may not have realized or cared, for each CFD invest-ment Quinn made, betting Anglo's share price would rise, there was potentially someone on the other side of the transaction speculating the bank's shares would fall.

Through the summer of 2007, the short-selling took its toll on Anglo's share price. By mid September, it was down to less than €12. The slump put significant pressure on Quinn. He had entered into some of his later Anglo CFDs at near-record prices and they were now firmly in negative equity. To keep his margin at the agreed level, he would have to stump up more cash. If he did not meet the margin calls, the brokers could sell the shares underlying his investment. As well as crystallizing losses on the CFD positions that were sold, there was another factor to consider: a sale of a significant chunk of Anglo shares would only weaken the share price further, causing Quinn's remaining CFD holdings to lose value.

Quinn decided not merely to attempt to ride it out, but to increase the size of his Anglo position. Between June and September 2007, he took on another €343 million exposure. Quinn now held CFDs relating to more than 20 per cent of the bank's shares, an enormous position for one investor to hold.

Within Anglo, management could see that the proportion of its shares out on loan to brokers was rising steadily, a sign of increasing CFD activity and also potentially a sign of short-sellers at work. In the late summer of 2007, media reports estimated Quinn's Anglo stake at 11 per cent. There was even speculation in the market that Quinn could be preparing a bid for Anglo, with the intention of adding the bank to his financial services interests. He already owned major general and health insurance businesses, a life assurance company and a chunk of NCB Stockbrokers, so it was not beyond the bounds of possibility.

Even if Quinn's interest in Anglo was benign, it was potentially destabilizing for the bank to have so many of its shares tied up with one investor. If Quinn had to unwind his holding for any reason, it could lead to Anglo shares being dumped on the market. A sudden, uncontrolled sale of a big stake could cause Anglo's share price to plummet. David Drumm and Sean FitzPatrick, the bank chief executive and chairman, decided to confront Quinn to see what they could find out about the size of his stake – and his intentions towards Anglo.

On 11 September 2007, Quinn and Liam McCaffrey met FitzPatrick and Drumm at the Ardboyne Hotel in Navan, Co. Meath, a property owned until three years earlier by Quinn Group. Drumm had arranged the meeting after phone conversations with Quinn about the rumours linking him to a large CFD position in the bank. FitzPatrick, speaking to the journalist Tom Lyons, later described Quinn as a 'real 1960s Irishman'. FitzPatrick said, 'He was very human but . . . I didn't easily like him.'

After initial small talk in a hotel meeting room, Quinn revealed to the bankers that his CFD position encompassed 24 per cent of Anglo shares. 'I was physically shocked. I wasn't expecting that,' FitzPatrick said. 'I said: "What!" David said afterwards to me that he looked at [Quinn] and he just saw the surprise in Quinn's eyes at my reaction. How negative I was.'

Quinn told Drumm and FitzPatrick he was losing money on the CFD stakes and quizzed them about how the bank was performing.

He wanted to be reassured that the market was wrong about Anglo. The bankers made it clear they were very uncomfortable with a single investor, particularly one who was also a large customer of the bank, holding such a large stake. 'We just said it is unhealthy, and it is wrong, plus the Central Bank will go wild,' said FitzPatrick.

If word got out about the size of Quinn's stake and Anglo's share price collapsed, there could be serious consequences for the bank's funding and deposits. With a global credit crunch starting to bite, the situation could scarcely be more serious. Quinn told the bankers he had no intention of buying Anglo but admired its style and way of doing business. He intended to be a long-term investor and seemed inclined to continue to handle the investment on his own terms. Even after the negative reaction at the Ardboyne meeting – and despite the Anglo share price falling further – Quinn did something extraordinary: he bought more CFDs in Anglo, ultimately bringing his total stake to 28.5 per cent.

From October 2005 to September 2007, the money to fund Quinn's CFD investments came through loans from companies owned by the Quinn family and companies in the Quinn Group. By the second half of 2007, however, with global equity markets under pressure, Anglo's share price sharply in decline and Bazzely, the CFD trading company, facing regular demands to fund the loss-making CFD positions, Sean Quinn had burned through the group's resources.

He turned to Anglo.

At this point, the interests of Sean Quinn and Anglo Irish Bank were inextricably linked. If Quinn started selling shares, something he did not want to do, he faced large losses. From Anglo's point of view, a fire sale of shares could force the bank into a downward spiral from which it might not recover. After talks with Quinn, the bank devised a system by which it would provide the funds to cover the margin calls from Quinn's CFD brokers. That way, the CFD stake could remain under wraps while the bankers figured out what to do about it.

Dara O'Reilly, the Quinn finance director, would have regular dealings with Anglo executives to establish how much Quinn needed in order to fund the margin calls. O'Reilly would give an Anglo manager a rough calculation of the latest call and the bank would approve loans to cover it. Documents were drawn up saying that the loans were for property development, and O'Reilly would then obtain the necessary signatures so that the funds could be transferred. In late 2007, new Anglo loans of hundreds of millions of euro were issued to Quinn family companies in this way.

In early December 2007, Quinn and Drumm had a phone conversation. Quinn indicated to Drumm that €400 million was needed to pay margin calls and to repay loans from Quinn Group companies that had been used to buy CFDs. If the loans could not be repaid, the 2007 accounts for the Quinn Group would show the outflow of funds and potentially draw attention to the extent of the Quinn Group's funding of the CFD position.

To avoid that situation, Anglo advanced Quinn another €500 million, in the guise of a gearing-up of the property portfolio of a group company. To complete the deal and protect its position, the bank sent an official to the five Quinn children, the official owners of Bazzely, with boxes of documents to be signed accepting the loan agreements. They signed the paperwork, though they would later say they did so without any interaction with Anglo management or professional advice. As Sean Quinn's bet on Anglo shares continued into 2008, the five children signed more documents sent by the bank. The usual practice, according to sources, was to receive only the signature page, which would be signed and returned to Dara O'Reilly or other Quinn Group staff and then passed on to Anglo.

It was in the interests of both Quinn and the bank to keep these dealings under wraps. Quinn Group already had its borrowings of €1.3 billion, owed to the Barclays-led consortium and the international bondholders. In addition, Quinn had significant borrowings from Anglo and other lenders to fund the International Property Group purchases. The disclosure of his loss-making CFD bet would certainly cause those other lenders to ask serious questions and could compromise those loan agreements, potentially putting his entire group in jeopardy.

For Anglo's part, the effect of a disclosure of Quinn's CFD

shareholding could be terminal. From late 2007, Anglo management had been fighting rumours that the bank was in serious difficulty. There was speculation that large corporate clients including Ryanair were pulling their deposits from Anglo, and that international lenders were withdrawing their funding lines to the bank. The share price remained under pressure into early 2008, despite Anglo announcing that its profits for the 2007 financial year topped the €1 billion mark for the first time.

At Anglo's AGM on 1 February 2008, FitzPatrick strongly denounced a research note from UBS, the international investment bank, which downgraded all Irish banks one notch. Predicting that commercial property values could fall 30 per cent and banks would face massive impairment charges, UBS recommended investors should sell shares in Anglo and AIB. FitzPatrick came out fighting, saying the bank was not worried about property prices, only the ability of its customers to repay their loans. Nothing could stop the falling share price, however, and its biggest victim was Sean Quinn.

In the spring of 2008, accountants from PricewaterhouseCoopers (PWC) arrived in Cavan to carry out their audit of Quinn Insurance's 2007 figures. There would be plenty for the auditors to consider. The takeover of the former Bupa business had made Quinn the second-biggest insurer in the country and pushed its revenues above €1 billion. The Financial Regulator would want to see it was meeting solvency requirements and reserving enough money to cover future claims. In the Quinn books, however, the PWC auditors made some extraordinary discoveries.

In mid 2007, Quinn Insurance had sold a sizeable chunk of its equity portfolio, generating large amounts of cash. Sean Quinn had then borrowed money from the insurer to pay his CFD debts through a complex arrangement. Using a series of financial manoeuvres, the insurance company agreed to place deposits with the Quinn Group, which immediately loaned the money on to family companies outside the group structure. The funds were then used by Quinn to meet the margin calls on his CFDs.

The arrangement was described in Quinn Insurance's books as a 'treasury agreement' with Quinn Group, and the transactions were referred to as cash deposits in Quinn Insurance's accounting. It was clear to the PWC auditors they were nothing of the sort. They were loans from one Quinn company, the regulated insurance business, to the wider group. The sums of money involved were huge. In early 2008, the auditors found, Quinn Insurance had advanced €398 million to Quinn Group and then on to Quinn's other companies. They were clearly intercompany loans, for which prior approval ought to have been sought from the Financial Regulator.

The auditors also discovered the insurance company had paid €300 million to Quinn Group and a related Quinn company in October 2007 for a number of property assets. The properties, including hotels and office blocks, were now part of the insurance company's asset reserves. But they had not been independently valued before they were bought from the Quinns, and the Financial Regulator had not been informed of the deal.

Between the two transactions, just shy of €700 million had flowed out of Quinn Insurance and into Sean Quinn's hands. PWC immediately informed the Financial Regulator about what it had found. With the backing of the Regulator, PWC established independent valuations for the properties. Their value was put at €211 million, €89 million less than had been paid out to Quinn. The money would have to be repaid; the €89 million was listed in Quinn Insurance's 2007 accounts as a debt owed to the business by the Quinn family.

After PWC's audit, the cash advances from Quinn Insurance to Quinn Group would also be properly reclassified as intercompany loans. There was still €288 million of the €398 million intercompany loans outstanding, and a schedule was put in place for Quinn, through Quinn Group, to repay it in full. The Financial Regulator agreed to a repayment plan, though Quinn Insurance was required to make a provision in the event it could not be repaid.

The regulatory breaches uncovered by PWC were serious, much more serious than Quinn's ill-considered investment in tech shares at the turn of the millennium. Quinn had been able to carry out the transactions because he totally dominated his companies, including Quinn Insurance. There had been no board discussion or approval for the transactions uncovered by PWC. Paddy Mullarkey, the former civil servant, had resigned from the boards of Quinn Group and Quinn Insurance in August 2007, citing 'personal family reasons'.

Mullarkey had been chairman of the investment committee at Quinn Insurance at the time of his departure. In his absence, the committee – which was supposed to meet formally five times a year and report monthly – simply did not meet. After the PWC audit, Mullarkey was asked to rejoin the board of Quinn Insurance, which he did on 28 February 2008. Beyond the speculation he read in the newspapers, however, Mullarkey did not know about the extent of Sean Quinn's investment in Anglo CFDs, according to sources. Like virtually everyone else, he did not have the full picture of Quinn's financial commitments.

The Office of the Financial Regulator, headed by Patrick Neary, was reluctant to censure Quinn. Through his office's dealings with Anglo, Neary knew about Quinn's huge CFD stake in the bank. If it was revealed that Quinn had used insurance company funds to fund his CFD position, it would destabilize the bank as well as Quinn Insurance (one of the country's biggest insurers) and Quinn Group (one of its biggest employers).

As the country's top regulator, Neary had adopted a light-touch approach, practising 'collaboration' with financial institutions rather than hard-line regulation. In a speech at a conference of the Institute of Bankers in the International Financial Services Centre on 5 March 2008, Neary lauded the 'huge importance of the financial services industry to our economy' and the need for it to prosper. 'While there had been and should be healthy tension between a regulator and the industry, we believe that this collaborative model is one that very much helps guide our approach to regulation,' he said. The other conference speakers included Sean FitzPatrick, the Anglo chairman.

The day after the IFSC conference, Anglo, amid speculation about its financial health, issued a detailed trading statement to the stock exchange. 'Anglo Irish Bank is strongly positioned with an unwavering commitment to asset quality, a robust funding franchise and excellent liquidity,' said David Drumm. He said the bank was 'actively managing' a limited number of 'smaller relationships'. There was no mention of Sean Quinn.

Within the bank, however, dealing with the Quinn situation had become a priority. Between December 2007 and March 2008, a number of discussions took place between Anglo and Quinn about the businessman's CFD interests and his intentions. The bank was anxious that Quinn should close out his CFD positions. Anglo hired Morgan Stanley, the international investment bank, to advise on its options. On 11 March, Drumm led an Anglo delegation to the Middle East to try to find buyers among the region's sovereign wealth funds for at least some of Quinn's CFD stake. That effort, and a subsequent effort by Morgan Stanley to place shares with some of Anglo's institutional shareholders, failed.

In early March 2008, the share price of Bear Stearns, the US investment bank, collapsed. The bank was seriously exposed to risky sub-prime mortgages, and investors were spooked. Over the weekend of 15–16 March, J. P. Morgan struck a deal to buy Bear Stearns for $236 million, just 1.3 per cent of its value a year earlier. When the markets opened on the Monday, 17 March, the reaction was instant – and the reverberations were felt right across the Atlantic. The so-called St Patrick's Day Massacre wiped €3.5 billion off the value of the companies listed on the Irish Stock Exchange. Anglo's already suffering share price lost another 15 per cent. The shares finished the day at €6.96. Spooked, FitzPatrick went so far as to call Brian Cowen, the Minister for Finance, who was in Malaysia on a trade mission. The two men talked about the rumours stalking Anglo and the Quinn CFD issue.

The collapse in the share price caused panic at Anglo. Between 17 and 19 March, the board of the bank had five conference-call meetings to discuss the share-price collapse and its impact on the bank's funding and liquidity. Quinn's CFDs were also on the agenda. The falling share price had triggered demands for cash from Quinn's CFD providers. In four transactions between 14 and 19 March, Anglo loaned Quinn almost €375 million to cover the margin calls, bringing his total loans to nearly €1.6 billion. Highlighting the urgency of the situation, one loan was dealt with by a Quinn company in Britain because St Patrick's Day was a bank holiday in Ireland. Though the loans were all to meet CFD margin calls, they were described as being for property developments in Russia and India. Within Anglo, they were described as 'working capital' for Quinn Group, an entirely inaccurate description.

The St Patrick's Day Massacre would mark the point of no return for Quinn. International sentiment had turned firmly and viciously against banks with big property exposure. There seemed no prospect of Anglo's shares recovering to the levels at which Quinn had bought the CFDs. No matter what happened from here on in, he was facing huge losses on his investment.

On 18 March, Liam McCaffrey wrote on behalf of Sean Quinn to Michael O'Sullivan, the Anglo executive who managed Quinn's account at the bank. In return for the latest batch of loans, the Quinn Group chief executive, with Quinn's approval, granted the bank charges over the shares held by the Quinn children in the group holding company. Quinn had effectively signed over control of the group to the bank in return for the borrowings.

To cover the new loans, he also offered personal guarantees in his name and the names of his children. 'I can confirm that as additional comfort in relation to the security on this facility, the Quinn family are prepared to support their personal guarantees by giving Anglo Irish Bank Corporation plc physical custody of their shares in Quinn Group ROI Limited,' McCaffrey said in his letter. It was an extraordinary move – Quinn was giving the bank the power to take control of the group he had built up over more than three decades. If he couldn't repay his loans, he would lose his business.

After St Patrick's Day, there was a shift in the relationship between Quinn and Anglo. The bank was now actively putting Quinn under pressure to reduce the CFD exposure.

At a meeting in Buswells Hotel around 27 March, FitzPatrick and Drumm spelled out the urgency of the situation to Quinn and McCaffrey. A subsequent meeting was also attended by Colin Morgan, the general manager of Quinn Insurance. The bankers raised the prospect of unwinding Quinn's CFD position by buying the shares underlying the CFDs and placing them with the Quinn family and a third party. This would crystallize a loss of at least €1 billion for Quinn – on an investment that most people didn't know he even held.

A 'memorandum of agreement' outlining the plan was drawn up between Anglo and Quinn Group on 31 March 2008. A copy was sent to the Financial Regulator. The agreement said that a 15 per cent stake in Anglo would be split evenly between Patricia Quinn and Quinn's five children, thus avoiding rules about public disclosure of individual stakes greater than 3 per cent. The bank said it would fund purchase of the shares by the family members.

The remaining 10 per cent of the Quinn Anglo stake would be placed with an outside investor or investors. The agreement specified that the aim of the share placing was to 'ensure the market price of the company's shares [would] not be destabilised'. The terms of the agreement, approved by the Regulator, would be kept confidential from the other shareholders in the bank.

Quinn was unhappy. Even though Anglo's shares had lost more than half their value between June 2007 and March 2008, he still did not want to sell out. He felt he was being pressured by Anglo to dump his shares, shares that might yet rise in value. His protests were academic, as it turned out – the share placing could not be arranged because of lack of demand for the 10 per cent of Anglo's shares that were offered to investors.

The complications with the PWC audit at Quinn Insurance had pushed the signing-off of the 2007 accounts past a date agreed with the Quinn Group banks and bondholders. They wanted to know what was going on. Quinn was now finalizing a detailed presentation to the lenders on the group's financial performance and what it described as 'recent developments'. His movement of money out of Quinn Insurance would have to be disclosed, but Quinn wanted to keep full details of his personal investments secret from the lenders who were owed €1.3 billion. To do that, he needed to be released from a guarantee he had given covering €250 million in loans from Anglo. After discussing the matter with officials from the Financial Regulator, Anglo agreed to the move.

The 88-page confidential presentation was circulated to the Quinn Group lenders in May 2008. It detailed the group's financial performance in 2007, reporting revenues of €2.1 billion and earnings of €492 million. The group forecast revenues of nearly €2.4 billion for 2008 and €2.65 billion for 2009. The presentation referred to the transactions that had unsettled PWC during their audit. The report said Quinn Group had made 'tax-efficient intercompany loans to related companies over time to invest in property and equities'. But 'certain equity investments outside Quinn Group' had incurred losses, 'triggering margin calls' during the second half of 2007 and the first quarter of 2008.

The losses were funded through the 'treasury arrangement' with Quinn Insurance but the loans had been treated as cash deposits at the insurer. The presentation document continued: 'The group's auditors disagreed with this accounting treatment and instead held that they should be accounted for as intercompany loans and that on this basis they should have been notified to the Financial Regulator.' Quinn had come around to the auditor's way of thinking, the document said. 'Management now accepts that the decision to enter into the treasury arrangement (now intercompany loan) was not undertaken with proper due diligence on the regulatory impact of the transactions.'

The presentation also informed the lenders about the overvalued €300 million property deal between the Quinns and Quinn Insurance. It blamed the mismatch in valuations on 'the impact of falling property valuations in late 2007 and early 2008'; yet the group had added €78 million to the accounted value of other properties, including its international hotels. The property deals meant the amount of property held as reserves by Quinn Insurance had more than doubled to €575 million between 2006 and 2007. At the end of 2007, with the property market collapsing, property made up 35 per cent of the insurer's reserves, an unusually high proportion.

The presentation document noted that 'the Financial Regulator has given the company a derogation to use more of its property assets than is normally allowed for the purposes of meeting its technical reserves if it needs to'. The investment strategy for 2008, the group said, was focused on 'unwinding positions in certain inadmissible assets' and investing in cash and bonds, more normal assets for an insurer.

PWC had signed off the 2007 figures only after the group agreed to make a provision of €692 million against the intercompany loans in the accounts. 'A significant amount of this relates to unrealised losses on the family's equity portfolio,' it said. It was a huge number, more than half the €1.3 billion that the group owed to its banks and bondholders. The group warned that it might require an unspecified 'temporary amendment' to the covenants attached to its senior debt. It said, however, that it was comfortable with its overall debt load, a situation helped by the recent release of the €250 million Anglo guarantee. The significance of the guarantee being dropped was downplayed in the presentation but Anglo's move, approved by the Regulator, had spared Quinn from making a more damaging disclosure that could have destabilized his entire group.

To reassure the lenders, Quinn Group said it had committed in writing not to provide any more loans, dividends or subordinated guarantees to entities outside the group. Importantly, the Regulator had allowed PWC to sign off the 2007 accounts without any qualification.

'As part of the audit sign-off process PWC received comfort from the Financial Regulator that it will not take any action against the company that would affect its ability to continue as a going concern,' it said. It was an extraordinary statement, all the more so because the Regulator was still considering what action it might take over Quinn raiding the insurance company's cash.

In the bondholder presentation, Quinn committed to apparently sweeping changes. 'The company accepts that the corporate governance structure of the company did not work as it should have in relation to these transactions,' it said. After 'input' from the Financial Regulator, it had agreed to more intensive involvement from non-executive directors in monitoring its cash balances and intercompany dealings. A formal board resolution was passed requiring all decisions of a 'material nature' to be agreed at board level.

'Recent events had identified a requirement to review the

effectiveness of the group board, particularly in relation to activities outside of the group and the flow of group funds supporting these activities,' it said. 'In this regard, the group board will in future oversee investments outside of the group with particular regard to any funding requirement they could impose on the group.'

At Quinn Insurance, the investment committee was reconstituted, with Paddy Mullarkey as its chairman. KPMG was appointed to carry out a detailed review of corporate governance at the insurer. 'The board of the company is committed to discussing the result of this review with the Financial Regulator and implementing any recommendations in full,' Quinn Group said. The presentation did not make pretty reading but it succeeded, with the assistance of Anglo and the Financial Regulator, in concealing the scale of Quinn's CFD gamble from lenders who were owed €1.3 billion by Quinn Group.

Despite the close shave, Quinn struck a defiant tone about holding on to his investments. The CFD losses had 'no significant impact' on Quinn Group's capital expenditure plans, the presentation said. Quinn was suggesting his group was effectively insulated from the Anglo share disaster, which was going to cost at least €1 billion. He also indicated there was 'substantial equity' in the investment portfolio and he was unwilling to see it liquidated.

'Unwinding the positions in short order is not the current preferred option to the family . . . If required to meet any other cash requirement outside the group, then these positions could be liquidated in an orderly process and over time to avoid undue disturbance to the market,' the presentation said. At Anglo, the bankers were grappling with two parts of that equation – how to unwind the Quinn position in short order without precipitating the collapse of the bank.

In the meantime, the bank's share price continued to fall and the margin calls continued to roll in. The bank continued lending to Quinn to cover the calls. In June 2008, it loaned him a total of €232 million in nine transactions. Quinn's Anglo loans now stood at €1.9 billion.

Just a month after the bondholder presentation, Quinn faced potential disaster. Quinn Group's cash flow was falling as the recession took hold, and it was in danger of breaching the ratio of cash flow to debt agreed with the banks and bondholders. Before they would agree to waive the loan terms, the lenders wanted an independent review of the Quinn family's assets and liabilities. If that happened, the group would be compelled to make a detailed disclosure of the family's investments – including the Anglo gamble.

After discussions between Quinn Group management and Anglo executives, it was agreed that such a revelation would be detrimental to both sides. Anglo loaned another €200 million to a Quinn company, which paid it on to Quinn Group. The loan pushed Quinn's borrowings to €2.1 billion, a staggering figure that was still unknown outside a circle of people in Anglo, Quinn Group and the Financial Regulator.

An email from David Drumm to Pat Whelan, the managing director of Anglo's Irish operations, on 9 July showed that the bank's patience with Quinn was wearing thin. 'He has zero options because he is almost bust,' wrote Drumm. 'If he persists with his messing, then the next [margin] call won't be funded and he's dead.'

In return for the latest loans, the bank wanted something – power of attorney over Quinn's CFD positions. That would give Anglo the power to unwind Quinn's stake as it saw fit. It would be a crucial tool in taking control of the situation.

Quinn's insurance company breaches remained unknown to Quinn customers or the general public, but there were other clues that all was not well. On 7 July 2008, Moody's, the ratings agency, revised its outlook on Quinn Insurance downwards. At the same time, Moody's said its Baa2 insurance financial strength rating on Quinn would be withdrawn 'for business reasons'. The agency's criteria said Baa-rated insurers 'offer adequate financial security' but 'certain protective elements may be lacking or may be characteristically unreliable over any great length of time'. Now Quinn didn't even have that distinction.

The development was unusual. Moody's and other ratings agencies judge the strength of financial institutions, such as banks and insurers, on a range of criteria from financial performance to asset quality, product risk and the adequacy of their reserves. For insurers, a solid rating is needed to attract investment and to gain business from brokers.

The development was benignly reported in most Irish media. The *Irish Times* said Sean Quinn had 'pulled out of his company's credit rating contract' with Moody's because there was little prospect of Quinn Insurance's rating being upgraded. 'We've no debt in issue so we've no requirement for a rating,' a Quinn spokesman told the paper. The report did note that Quinn was reported to have a 5 per cent interest in Anglo back in January 2007. The bank's shares had since fallen from almost €16 to €5.47. There was no way of knowing the real extent of Quinn's stake or the efforts that were going on behind the scenes to unwind it.

In the *Sunday Business Post* the weekend after the Moody's rating withdrawal, journalist Kathleen Barrington noted that it wasn't clear whether Quinn had dumped Moody's or Moody's had dumped Quinn. 'In the current uncertain financial climate, a credit rating from a leading credit rating agency should surely be seen as a plus, particularly if you are an insurance company and you want everyone, including your customers and the business community, to know about the blue-chip financial credentials of your business,' she wrote.

Despite months of effort, Anglo was still no closer to sorting out the Quinn share situation. Attempts to place shares with Bain Capital, a US investment firm, and with the Dutch lender Rabobank, were unsuccessful. In early July 2008, David Drumm, the bank chief executive, came up with an alternative strategy – to ask some of the bank's biggest and longest-standing customers to buy the shares. Morgan Stanley and Matheson Ormsby Prentice, Anglo's Dublin-based lawyers, would advise on the transaction.

Drumm and Pat Whelan narrowed a list of possible participants down to ten based on three criteria: loyalty to the bank, discretion and financial muscle. The ten would each be asked to buy a 1 per cent stake in the bank from Quinn's CFD dealers. The Quinn family would buy the remaining 15 per cent. Anglo would lend the ten cus-tomers the €450 million – €45 million each – needed to buy the shares. In return, it would only ask for recourse over one-quarter of the value of the loans. Morgan Stanley had code-named the Quinn-

Anglo situation 'Maple'; the ten customers would become known as the 'Maple Ten'.

Drumm and Whelan spoke to Sean Quinn and Liam McCaffrey to brief them on the plan. Quinn was unhappy; Anglo's share price had almost halved since the share placement arrangement was first discussed in late March. At a price of €4.85 a share, he faced massive losses on the unwinding of the CFD stake. Drumm told Quinn he had little option; the Financial Regulator had cleared the planned transaction and warned the bank not to lend any more money to Quinn under any circumstances. The bank board had approved the CFD unwinding and had the power of attorney to do it, even against Quinn's wishes.

After the conversation with Quinn, the bank moved to square off the deal with the Maple Ten. The ten were Gerry Gannon, Seamus Ross, Paddy McKillen, John McCabe, Sean Reilly, Gerry Conlan, Patrick Kearney, Gerry McGuire, Brian O'Farrell and Joe O'Reilly. They were, for the most part, big property developers and investors.

The Maple Ten transaction was initiated over the weekend of 12–13 July 2008. On the morning of 14 July, Quinn, grudgingly, gave his go-ahead in an email sent from McCaffrey to Pat Whelan. The next day, the Quinn family issued a statement through Brian Bell, a public relations executive at Wilson Hartnell PR. It said they were unwinding their CFD stake in Anglo and taking a direct shareholding of almost 15 per cent.

'In recent years, we have been highly impressed with Anglo's ability to outperform the banking sector in terms of profit growth and we are confident this trend can be maintained over the longer term notwithstanding the current difficulties being experienced in international banking,' Quinn said in the statement. There was no mention of the Maple Ten or the fact Quinn had held 28 per cent of the bank at one point. After the announcement, Anglo's share price slipped further – to €4.08, valuing the bank at €3.1 billion. It had lost €10 billion in value in just over a year. The 15 per cent stake held by the Quinns was worth about €465 million, less than a quarter of what it would have been worth 12 months earlier.

Anglo loaned the five Quinn children and Patricia Quinn the

money to buy their 15 per cent stake in the bank. The loans were channelled through six Cypriot companies formed to hold the shares on behalf of the Quinns. Patricia Quinn guaranteed the liabilities of a Cypriot company with more than €102 million in borrowings from Anglo, while each of the children guaranteed the liabilities of a company with €77.3 million in borrowings. In addition to the existing billions of euro in borrowings owed by their father and the family companies, the Quinn children and their mother were now on the hook for €488.5 million.

After the 15 July statement, there was extensive speculation in the media about the extent of Quinn's losses and the possible impact on Quinn Group. The group had more than 6,000 staff and supported thousands of other related jobs; any impact on Quinn could affect a lot of people. Based on the 15 per cent figure in Quinn's statement, media reports estimated he had lost about €1 billion. In fact, his losses were almost double what people thought – and he had borrowed more than €2 billion from Anglo in his desperate attempts to shore them up.

Quinn did not comment on the losses, but he was privately furious at Anglo, and at Drumm in particular. In a letter to Drumm on 26 July, he said he had been forced to sell the shares 'regardless of market price' while the buyers, the Maple Ten, benefited at his expense. 'I feel that the bank's insistence on a sale was detrimental to our position and the longer-term development of this [Quinn] group,' he wrote. The process seemed to be driven by 'a degree of panic' and there was no 'proper considered action plan'.

Quinn said he had asked to meet the Anglo board but his request was 'disregarded'. Furthermore, 'I strongly believe the actions of the bank were ill-advised and will have a considerable impact on our wider group for many years,' he said. After sending the letter, Quinn consulted White & Case, a London law firm, about the possibility of suing Anglo.

According to sources, Quinn's anger was real. He felt Anglo and the Financial Regulator had 'ganged up' on him to force a resolution to the situation. It was an unusual standpoint, to say the least. By lending to support his margin calls, Anglo had allowed Quinn to maintain secrecy about his CFD gambles and avoid a catastrophic situation that could bring down his Quinn Group. Time and again, the bank had helped him avoid full disclosure to his group's lenders. The Maple Ten transaction was potentially the most benign solution for Quinn.

Through the late summer and early autumn of 2008, Anglo's share price fluctuated. The global financial system was under strain and rumours were flying about Ireland's financial institutions. On 15 September, Lehman Brothers, the fourth-largest investment bank in the USA, collapsed, stunning the international markets. The money markets, where Irish banks got about half their balance sheet funding, shut down. Deposits flooded out of any institution regarded as risky. Anglo, with its huge concentration on property lending, began losing deposits on a massive scale; within days it was losing up to €1 billion a day in funding.

With its cash about to run out and the Central Bank unwilling to provide emergency credit, Anglo was soon on the verge of collapse. The result was the state's extraordinary blanket guarantee on the assets and liabilities of the Irish banks, worth an astonishing €440 billion. It was introduced in the early hours of 30 September 2008 after late-night meetings between bank bosses, the Finance Minister Brian Lenihan and his officials, and Patrick Neary, the Financial Regulator. Government officials briefed journalists that the guarantee was intended primarily to protect Anglo.

On Friday 24 October, just over three weeks after the bank guarantee, the Financial Regulator announced it had fined Quinn Insurance €3.25 million and Sean Quinn personally €200,000 for breaching the Insurance Act. The Regulator did not say what the specific breaches were, but said it had 'reasonable cause' to suspect Quinn had failed to notify the Regulator before providing loans to related companies. It soon emerged they related to the €288 million Quinn had taken out of Quinn Insurance. The Regulator had known for six months about the movement of the money but had kept it under wraps. It was the largest fine ever levied by the Irish financial regulatory authorities. As part of the sanction, Sean Quinn would step down as chairman of Quinn Insurance and Jim Quigley, an existing Quinn director who was a veteran of Axa, the international insurer, would be appointed chairman.

Despite all that had happened, Quinn issued a defiant statement: 'While I accept that I made mistakes, I feel that the levels of fines do not reflect the fact that there was no risk to policyholders or the taxpayer, but are a result of the pressures existing in the current environment. However, we will pay the fines and move on.' It would not be that simple.

The bank guarantee had provided an initial respite but the pressure was continuing to mount on Ireland's banks. In early October, Iceland's two largest banks, Kaupthing and Glitnir, had gone bust. Concerns were high that at least one of the Irish banks, with their large exposure to property lending, could follow suit. Bank shares were under tremendous pressure, a reflection of the view in the market that they needed more capital. The issue was no longer liquidity, it was solvency.

By early December, with the Anglo share price at 67 cents, Sean Quinn's 15 per cent stake in the bank was worth not much more than €75 million. On 18 December, Sean FitzPatrick resigned from Anglo after informing the bank's board that his personal borrowings from the bank had been concealed by transferring them to another lender, Irish Nationwide Building Society, at the end of each financial year. Drumm followed suit the next day.

To keep Anglo afloat, Finance Minister Brian Lenihan announced the government would invest €1.5 billion in the bank and take preference shares, giving the state control over 75 per cent of the voting rights. It was nationalization in all but name. Lenihan said the 'misbehaviour of management meant that, even with a state guarantee, there was uncertainty about the viability of the bank'.

On 9 January 2009, Patrick Neary, who had approved many of Anglo's dealings with Sean Quinn, announced he would retire as chief executive of the Financial Regulator at the end of that month. A government inquiry had found the Regulator's office knew about FitzPatrick's loan transfers, though Neary insisted he had personally

only just become aware of them. He retired with a payment of
€636,000 and an annual pension of €143,000.

A week later, when details became public of transactions between
Anglo and Irish Life & Permanent intended to mislead the markets
about the state of the Anglo balance sheet, the government withdrew
its €1.5 billion funding offer and moved to nationalize Anglo. With
its weak funding position and what the department described as 'un-
acceptable corporate governance practices', the bank had no future as
a publicly quoted company.

The nationalization decision, taken by Taoiseach Brian Cowen
and Finance Minister Brian Lenihan after consultation with the
Central Bank and the Financial Regulator, was revealed at a rowdy
extraordinary general meeting of Anglo shareholders on 16 January
2009. It meant Anglo shares would be delisted from the Irish and
London Stock Exchanges.

For Sean Quinn, the game was up. The Quinn family's 15 per cent
stake in Anglo, all they had to show for their father's spectacular CFD
gamble, was finally, undeniably worthless. There was no going back
from that fact. 'I think if anybody had said ten years ago, you're going
to invest in glass, radiators, plastics, packaging, Russia, India, Ukraine,
the Irish banks, some people would say you're safe in the Irish banks
but I'm not too sure if you're safe in Russia,' Quinn told RTÉ.

It was a good sound bite but it ignored a crucial fact. Quinn's
group had enjoyed thirty-five years of success at least partly because
of the diversity of his interests – the glass, radiators, plastics, packaging, insurance and property investments. In little over two years,
he had taken the combined value of all of those businesses and bet it
on Anglo Irish Bank. Entirely unnecessarily, he had put all of his
phenomenal number of eggs into one basket.

'The money we lost is hurtful, and we do not like it and I'm not
trying to dismiss it or downsize it, but at the end of the day a lot of
people in Ireland have lost a lot more in share dealings and in their
value than we have,' Quinn said. This was patently untrue. Quinn
was not only Ireland's biggest loser in the crash; he was one of the
biggest globally.

Quinn made no mention of the almost €2.4 billion he and his companies borrowed from Anglo in the doomed effort to shore up the CFD situation. He owed the bank another €455 million, borrowed to fund his international property purchases. With the bank nationalized, the full €2.8 billion was now owed to the Irish public.

Just another set of bankers

In March 2009, an idea took root in the mind of Mike Soden.

A former chief executive of Bank of Ireland, Soden had resigned from his role almost five years earlier when it emerged he had accessed the website of a Nevada escort service on his office computer. Soden tendered his resignation a day before details emerged publicly in the *Sunday Business Post*.

Soden's departure meant he was out of the banking industry for the years of most dramatic growth, the spectacular explosion in lending between 2004 and 2008. Now he was watching the implosion of the financial sector with grim fascination. His own investments in the Irish banks lost some €3 million in the crash. But the crisis had a silver lining for Soden: the details emerging of shocking mismanagement of the banks during the boom years put his own internet misdemeanour into context. His reputation was rehabilitated and the government routinely sought out his opinion.

It was nearly six months since the government had rushed through the blanket bank guarantee and three months since Sean FitzPatrick and David Drumm had resigned from Anglo Irish Bank. The bank had sought to install Declan Quilligan, the head of its British operation, as chief executive, but the Financial Regulator and the government vetoed the ascension of an insider to the top job. In the meantime, Donal O'Connor, a former PWC managing partner, was holding the fort as acting executive chairman at Anglo.

It had fallen to O'Connor to face hundreds of angry Anglo shareholders at an extraordinary general meeting at the Round Room of the Mansion House in Dublin on 16 January, the day after it was decided the bank was to be nationalized. The government was insisting Anglo had a future, but by March the bank was still operating with the senior accountant, rather than a banker, at the helm. It was an untenable situation. So Mike Soden decided to play matchmaker. In March, he picked up the phone and called an old colleague.

The *Australian Financial Review* once described Arthur Michael Royal Aynsley – he signed himself 'AMR Aynsley' – as a 'respected but not particularly unusual mid-level banker and consultant'. This was, perhaps, a slight injustice, given the variety and scale of positions he had held within international banking. Aynsley was educated at Barker College, an Anglican private boarding school on Sydney's North Shore, before picking up a degree in commerce.

He spent one year on a cadetship programme with the Commonwealth Bank of Australia, where his grandfather had worked as a banker before him, before moving to the Sydney office of the Banque Nationale de Paris in 1978. Three years later, he moved to Amsterdam-Rotterdam Bank as a senior manager in its treasury department. In 1983, Aynsley moved again, to Security Pacific – a bank that had, ironically, co-funded Sean Quinn's first cement plant – and its Hoare Govett stockbroking subsidiary.

During the Japanese boom, Aynsley was sent to Japan to open a trading desk for Hoare Govett. When the bubble burst, he was asked to shut it down again. He then went to Europe and closed the company's European trading desk, working as an executive director of Hoare Govett in London, where his career overlapped with that of Mike Soden. Aynsley had become the man that Security Pacific called when it wanted something closed or wound down – a sort of banking undertaker. In the early 1990s, he returned to Australia and closed its operations there.

In 1992, Aynsley moved to National Australia Bank, then owner of National Irish Bank in Ireland. Two years later he was reunited there with Soden. Both men did well. By the time Aynsley left in 1998, he had worked his way up through the NAB ranks to group general manager of the global markets division; when Soden left for

Ireland in 2001, he was effectively second-in-command at the Australian bank.

Aynsley's next stop was the lucrative world of consulting, and a five-year stint as a global partner in the banking and financial services practice of Deloitte. In 2004 he returned to banking as a senior executive with Australian & New Zealand Banking Group (ANZ), working in both Wellington and Sydney.

Then, in 2006, when he was just forty-five, a heart attack put a halt to Aynsley's gallop. The heart attack forced him to re-evaluate, and he swapped a smoking habit for hiking, though he retained a taste for good wine. He left banking and returned to the more sedate world of consultancy, specializing in advising on risk. He went back to education as well, gaining an MBA in finance and strategy at the graduate school of business at Macquarie University in Sydney.

Soden reckoned Aynsley was the ideal candidate for the top job at Anglo, and he asked his old colleague if he would be interested in moving to Dublin. Aynsley seemed agreeable, so Soden dispatched a letter to Donal O'Connor outlining Aynsley's credentials and recommending him for the job. Based upon the recommendation, O'Connor instructed Anglo's headhunters to contact the Australian banker.

The interest from Ireland came at an ideal time for Aynsley. He was working as a consultant with the Asian Development Bank, advising on banking reform in Thailand. It was interesting work but it required him to spend six out of every eight weeks in Asia. By 2009, with his three sons grown up and his daughter about to go to college, he was ready for a new challenge, ready for a return to something more demanding.

Having been approached by the Anglo headhunters, Aynsley flew to Ireland to meet O'Connor, as well as Frank Daly, a former head of the Revenue Commissioners who was a public-interest director on the Anglo board, and Kevin Cardiff, the head of financial services at the Department of Finance.

There were downsides to the Anglo job. The bank was a basket case: Anglo had just disclosed a €4.1 billion loss for the six months to the end of March 2009 and relied on a state bailout to plug the deepening hole in its finances. The latest review of the bank's loan book suggested losses could spiral to €11.5 billion. Anglo was over-staffed, had a dreadful reputation, and was at odds with bondholders over repayments. No one seemed to know how bad the balance sheet actually was, but everyone agreed it was getting worse by the month.

Did Mike Aynsley really want to move halfway around the world to take over a nationalized zombie bank? If he was to take the job, Aynsley would need to be handsomely rewarded for it. Eventually, he settled on a package with the Department of Finance. He would be paid an annual salary of €500,000 – the highest available under new government regulations on pay to executives at nationalized banks. Adding in pension contributions, relocation expenses and payments for eight flights home per year, however, the overall value of his package would be €974,000 in 2010, his first full year in the job. Aynsley also insisted on being allowed to recruit his own team, people he trusted, to help him run Anglo.

Aynsley's first day as chief executive was 7 September 2009, a Monday. He would be based at Heritage House, close to the bank's main headquarters building on St Stephen's Green in Dublin city centre. He set about briefing staff, telling colleagues their initial job was to 'stop the bleeding' and 'manage the crisis' at the bank. With a full in-tray, Aynsley quickly set about bringing in reinforcements.

His first recruit was Tom Hunersen, an American consultant who had worked at National Australia Bank for fourteen years. A lean, athletic New Yorker, Hunersen was nicknamed 'the Gunner' by Anglo staff because of his no-nonsense approach. Hunersen was made head of corporate development. Among other tasks, Aynsley asked him to manage the outstanding loans of former Anglo directors, including Drumm and FitzPatrick, and help handle the exits of a number of remaining executives from the old days.

It was not Hunersen's first time in Ireland; he had actually been poached by Mike Soden to work in Bank of Ireland when Soden was chief executive there. Hunersen had left the bank when Soden departed in 2004, and his short spell in Ireland did not even merit a mention on the biography released by the bank to mark his appointment. (Neither did Hunersen's brief period in 2001 as chief executive of Slingshot Game Technology, a tech firm that had pioneered an online snow-boarding game.)

In his first week at Anglo, Aynsley wrote to David Drumm about repaying four outstanding loans from the bank totalling €8.3 million. This included €7.7 million loaned to Drumm to buy Anglo shares in January 2008, part of a concerted effort by the directors to show their confidence in the bank at a time when its share price was under severe pressure. A lot had happened since then and the loans were due for repayment.

Since leaving the bank, Drumm had relocated with his family to Cape Cod, where he still owned a house he had bought during his years running Anglo's American operations. The banker had put his Irish home, in the upmarket Abington development in Malahide, north Co. Dublin, on the market for €2 million. The new chief executive wanted an undertaking from the old chief executive that the proceeds of the house sale would remain in Ireland until the bank's claim for the €8.3 million was resolved.

After a number of meetings failed to resolve the situation, Hunersen issued legal proceedings against Drumm. In early November 2009, the bank also demanded repayment of €110 million in loans due from Sean FitzPatrick and members of his family. The bank needed every penny it could get, of course, but the pursuit of Drumm and FitzPatrick was also part of a deliberate strategy to distance the clean 'new' Anglo from the men who had run the 'old' Anglo.

The new management team was not coming to Ireland merely to chase outstanding debts and liquidate a bust bank. Right from the beginning, they started hatching plans to reinvent Anglo as something other than a commercial property lender and to develop a new strategy for the future. The government had to be convinced, however.

At the first meeting between Aynsley and Brian Lenihan, the Finance Minister said the government had still to decide whether the bank would be shut down. This came as news to Aynsley: from his meetings with the recruiters and the Anglo board before taking the job, he had come to believe he was being charged with rescuing and rebuilding the bank. Aynsley told Lenihan he had taken the Anglo job because he believed a good bank could be built out of the debris of old Anglo. He later raised Lenihan's comments with Donal O'Connor. The government's view was news to the Anglo chairman, too.

It wasn't just the government who would need convincing that Anglo was worth saving. Aynsley and his management team would also have to convince the European Commission that the bank had a viable future and deserved the €4 billion in state aid it had received from the government in May 2009. If Anglo couldn't present a viable plan to stay in business and repay the state, it would have to outline plans to shut itself down.

Aynsley and his team had decided the best option was to focus on transforming Anglo into a business bank, specializing in providing loans to small and medium-sized enterprises (SMEs), as the state-owned Industrial Credit Company (ICC) had done in the past. They thought this would appeal to the Irish government, as it would help get a flow of credit into small Irish firms. There was widespread scepticism about the Aynsley plan, with several economists and analysts questioning whether Anglo was in any way salvageable. Opposition politicians openly wondered if it was not merely a ruse to ensure that the bank received the €4 billion in state aid. There was a strong body of opinion which held that the bank should be dismantled immediately.

As the authorities debated Anglo's future, Aynsley went about his job, convinced his plan to create a new SME lender from the ashes of Anglo could work. The man Aynsley wanted to help him do this job was another former National Australia Bank colleague, Richard Woodhouse.

Woodhouse looked and sounded the quintessential British banker. The grandson of an English submarine commander, he sported a pocket handkerchief in his sharp suits, spoke in an upper-class accent and had a taste for fine food and wine. He had spent nine years at National Australia Bank, holding senior roles, including head of acquisitions and leveraged finance and head of corporate banking for its European operations. After leaving the Australian bank he had taken a job at the London operations of Commerzbank, the German financial services group. Initially head of relationship management for its corporate clients, Woodhouse had advanced to global head of commodity trading, overseeing Commerzbank's international trades in oil, minerals and metals. It was a high-powered, highly paid job, but slightly removed from the rough-and-tumble of corporate banking that Woodhouse had previously enjoyed.

Aynsley approached Woodhouse in November 2009. England were playing Australia in a rugby match at Twickenham in London, and a number of the former National Australia Bank executives attended the game together on 7 November. Woodhouse turned forty-seven the day after the match, but his reasons for celebrating ended there: England had been well beaten by an unfancied Australian side.

At drinks after the game, Woodhouse heard all about Aynsley's new job at Anglo. He heard, too, that Hunersen was on board. Aynsley asked Woodhouse if he would be interested in joining him. Woodhouse was, indeed, interested.

In the days and weeks after the Twickenham reunion, Woodhouse discussed his likely role with Aynsley and Hunersen. All three firmly believed there was a gap in the Irish market for business lending. Aynsley wanted Woodhouse to help devise strategy for the new SME lender he hoped to create, come up with all the lending protocols and manage the corporate banking division under Hunersen.

The role appealed to Woodhouse. The Irish economy was in dire straits but if the country was to trade its way out of it, companies would need funding to do business. It was a compelling prospect – Anglo as a phoenix rising from the ashes, playing an important part in the economic recovery of the nation.

Woodhouse busied himself looking into the old ICC, established by Sean Lemass in 1933 to help finance fledgling Irish businesses. ICC had been taken over by Bank of Scotland (Ireland) in 2000, and the Scottish bank had dropped its focus on small businesses in favour of cheap mortgages and lending for property development. Woodhouse believed there was a chance to replicate what ICC had done. He decided to take the job at Anglo, becoming group head of specialist lending. He began work on 4 January 2010.

★

On 4 January, the same day Woodhouse started at Anglo, a new resident moved into a key office at the Central Bank of Ireland on Dame Street in Dublin city centre. Matthew Elderfield would be the new Deputy Governor of the Central Bank, responsible for Financial Regulation.

A UK passport-holder, Elderfield considered himself English despite an upbringing and career that spanned the Atlantic. Unusually for a financial regulator, he had never taken a finance exam in his life. Instead, his qualifications consisted of a degree in foreign service from Georgetown University in Washington, DC, followed by a master's in international relations from Cambridge. His career was firmly financial, however, with stints at the London Investment Banking Association, the British Bankers' Association and a Washington consultancy firm, the Institute for Strategy Development.

At the age of thirty, Elderfield had established the European operations of the International Swaps and Derivatives Association, a high-powered association of 300 banks and bodies with an interest in complex financial instruments. In 1999, he joined the UK Financial Services Authority (FSA), the regulatory body for banks and insurers in Britain. In an eight-year career there, he held senior roles in several areas, including banking supervision.

In January 2007, Elderfield swapped the FSA for a job as chief executive of the Bermuda Monetary Authority, the financial regulatory authority of the sunny British overseas territory. Within its 20 square miles, more than 15,000 companies have registered to take advantage of Bermuda's relaxed tax regime. There are no taxes on profits, income or dividends in Bermuda. There is no capital gains tax, no estate duty and no death duties. Companies can accumulate massive profits, tax-free and without any obligation to pay dividends. As a result, massive amounts of capital flow through the country, a significant portion of it from companies in the insurance and reinsurance sector.

When Matthew Elderfield arrived in 2007, Bermuda could claim to have the highest gross domestic output per capita in the world. With an economy driven by financial companies and professional services firms, the average salary was $95,000. As head of financial regulation in Bermuda, Elderfield supervised an insurance industry with $442 billion in assets, an investment sector worth $171 billion, a banking industry with assets of $23 billion and the Bermuda Stock Exchange, whose companies had a combined market capitalization of $226 billion.

During his term at the Bermuda Monetary Authority, Elderfield increased the focus on insurance, working to ensure that Bermuda was well positioned when new EU regulations on solvency came into force in 2012. He had also introduced capital stress tests to protect the island's banking system and insurance industry, and implemented wide-ranging reforms to strengthen the island's reputation for international insurance, banking and fund management. Once upon a time, such moves might have been seen as a threat to the island's attractiveness to foreign capital; but in the aftermath of the global financial crisis, regulation was coming into vogue.

Occasionally, headhunters looking to fill regulatory positions would contact Elderfield's office in the port town of Hamilton, the financial centre of Bermuda. The questions were generally the same: Would he be interested in moving? What would it take to lure him away from Bermuda?

He had turned down all the previous offers but, by the middle of 2009, Matthew Elderfield was ready for a change. His first three-year term as Bermuda's regulator was due to expire at the end of the year. Another three-year contract was on his desk, but Elderfield was unsure if he would sign it. Bermuda was small and Elderfield was feeling the effects of 'island fever'. Every two months, he got on a plane and flew to New York or Washington for a big-city change of scenery. Then a headhunter called and wanted to know if Elderfield would be interested in moving to Dublin and becoming Ireland's top financial regulator.

Elderfield looked at the facts. He would be paid less to do much more work, and it would involve swapping sunny Bermuda for rainy Dublin. Still, Ireland was at the frontline of the global financial crisis and the work was sure to be exciting.

Elderfield had visited Ireland a handful of times, visiting Dublin occasionally and holidaying in Kerry. He had been following the country's economic collapse closely. For the highly ambitious Elderfield, aged just forty-three, the job was a step up, bringing him into one of the hot spots of the European financial crisis. All eyes were focusing on Ireland as it stumbled from one financial disaster to another. He knew he would have to rebuild financial regulation in Ireland from the ground up. Brian Lenihan assured Elderfield of his government's support in the task. He decided to make the move.

In December 2009, ahead of his 4 January start date, Elderfield attended a series of briefings in Dublin. All of them focused on the state of the banks; there was no briefing on the insurance sector. When he arrived in his Central Bank office, then, Matthew Elderfield knew little of Sean Quinn and had never heard of Quinn Insurance. Within days, all that changed.

One of the first people Elderfield called when he decided to accept the Irish job was Jonathan McMahon. Elderfield wanted McMahon, a well-built Englishman with floppy hair and a no-nonsense streak, to join him in Dublin as his chief enforcer. Like Elderfield, McMahon had worked in the FSA in London, where his roles included serving as private secretary to its chairmen, Sir Howard Davies and Sir Callum McCarthy.

He started his career as a bank supervisor, but by the end of his seven-year stint at the FSA, McMahon was leading the supervision and research teams, and was actively involved in reforming the regulatory regime for Britain's banks. When Elderfield called him in November 2009, McMahon was working with the Promontory Financial Group, an international consulting firm comprising former senior regulators. Through Promontory, McMahon had carried out a number of projects for Elderfield in Bermuda.

Now, Elderfield wanted McMahon to come to Dublin. McMahon said yes, and then spent the next month trying to talk himself out of it. Like Elderfield, he would be taking a hefty pay cut to work in a largely discredited institution. But McMahon eventually accepted the job. His title was Assistant Director General with responsibility for Financial Institutions, making him Elderfield's point man in dealing with the banks, credit unions and insurers.

At the FSA, it was normal to have ten regulatory staff monitoring one institution. In certain cases in Ireland, there was just one employee of the Regulator tracking an entire institution. With the backing of the government, Elderfield planned to hire 160 extra staff in his first year, bringing staff numbers up to 520. He would then add a further 200 staff over the following two years.

In the middle of January 2010, shortly after they arrived in Ireland, Elderfield and McMahon received detailed briefings on key issues from their senior regulatory staff. One of the first briefings was on the state of the Irish insurance market. As the presentation progressed, one name kept cropping up: Quinn Insurance.

The new regulators already knew that Sean Quinn had lost billions on his Anglo share dealing; as the supervisors of the banking sector, they had detailed knowledge of the scale of his position and his spiralling losses. Now, they were being told of old and emerging problems within his insurance company.

Over at Anglo, Richard Woodhouse was getting a similar education. Before he arrived in Ireland, Woodhouse knew nothing about Sean Quinn's audacious stake-building in Anglo Irish Bank through CFDs. He had never heard of the Maple Ten transaction. He did not know what Sean Quinn had told Sean FitzPatrick or what FitzPatrick had told Quinn. He merely knew that Quinn was once Ireland's richest man, and that he now owed a vast amount of money to Anglo, money Woodhouse would be responsible for collecting.

When Aynsley was pitching the Anglo job to Woodhouse, he had mentioned Quinn as an aside, almost an afterthought. Woodhouse recalls that Aynsley told him, 'This is what we want you to do: write all the protocols; run corporate banking, big and small. And, by the way, you'll caretake this other thing, just for a short period of time, just as we work out what we're going to do with it.' It didn't take Woodhouse long to work out that Sean Quinn's relationship with Anglo needed more than just a caretaker.

With the nationalization of Anglo, Quinn's stake in the bank had become worthless. But the €2.8 billion debt the Quinns owed to the bank still stood. When he first heard the figure, Woodhouse asked

Aynsley to repeat it: 'Did you say billion?' But the number was right, and the chief executive wanted Woodhouse to handle the situation personally. He would be the main figure in all the bank's dealings with Quinn and his family. The task would soon become all-encompassing for Woodhouse.

Besides the €2.8 billion the Quinns owed Anglo, the family's cement and glass manufacturing group still had outstanding debts of a further €1.3 billion to its institutional bondholders and a syndicate of banks. At the same time, as far as Woodhouse could see, the performance of the Quinn businesses was poorer than people realized. Interest was mounting at a rate of €3 million a week on the Anglo debts alone. It was not obvious that Anglo would be able to get its money back.

Within weeks of arriving in Ireland, Woodhouse set about building a relationship with Sean Quinn. He went to Derrylin and ate lunch in the staff canteen with Liam McCaffrey and Dara O'Reilly. He held a number of meetings with Sean Quinn also. Quinn's imposing manufacturing operations were an impressive sight. He had built a tremendous business and Woodhouse couldn't fathom how or why he had gambled it all on a secret investment in Anglo Irish Bank. Quinn had put his whole enterprise, his life's work, on a single share and it had gone badly wrong.

In Derrylin, Woodhouse found Quinn as he portrayed himself – a man of the people, open, direct, apparently simple to understand. But it occurred to Woodhouse that Quinn didn't fully understand the reality of the situation he was in. Woodhouse quickly reached the conclusion that Quinn needed to sell assets to reduce his debts. There were three core groups of assets in the wider group: the manufacturing businesses, Quinn Insurance and the Quinn International Property Group.

Woodhouse considered the insurance company to be the jewel in the crown. The manufacturing group was struggling: the collapse of the property market and general economic slowdown had weakened demand for Quinn's cement, building products and glass. But Quinn Insurance was building market share and generating fantastic numbers – a profit of €211 million in 2007 alone. A sale of the company could generate a multiple of that figure, possibly as much as €700 million.

Further asset sales would be needed, including the disposal of the international properties, which were valued at around €500 million. 'You have to sell something,' Woodhouse declared to Quinn and his lieutenants. They were shocked at his opinion and at the directness with which he expressed it. Nobody told Sean Quinn what he had to do.

On Friday 19 February 2010, Woodhouse and Mike Aynsley sat down with Sean Quinn for formal talks in Dublin. The bankers told Quinn that he should offload Quinn Insurance to recoup cash. Quinn had other ideas. Without a Quinn at the helm, the business-man bluntly told the bankers, the insurance company would fail. Quinn provided no solid back-up or evidence for this extraordinary claim. He had taken a similar tone in a meeting with Donal O'Connor shortly after the nationalization of Anglo, warning that he could be a difficult customer if the bank tried to flex its muscles over the debt.

Now he was laying down a marker to the new regime: they were just another set of bankers, and he had outlasted lots of bankers. The meeting ended politely, despite Quinn's fighting talk. Quinn and Aynsley exchanged correspondence in the following days, thanking each other for their time. Behind the pleasantries, the bankers remained deeply worried. Before they could look to the future, they had to sort out the past, and they still had no strategy for recovering the €2.8 billion owed by the Quinn family. But Richard Woodhouse was sure of one thing: if Anglo was to get a decent chunk of its money back, Quinn Insurance needed to be sold. The insurer was central to Anglo's Quinn strategy.

The day after the bankers' meeting with Quinn, 120,000 people marched in Dublin in protest at revelations of mismanagement at Anglo. At 9 a.m. the following Tuesday, 24 February, officers from the Garda Bureau of Fraud Investigation raided three Anglo offices in Dublin, including its headquarters on St Stephen's Green. Garda search teams went into the bank with investigators from the Office of the Director of Corporate Enforcement, the agency responsible for policing breaches of company law.

The day-long raid was focused on collecting records relating to the three controversies that had engulfed the bank: the concealment of Sean FitzPatrick's borrowings from the bank; the artificial gilding of the balance sheet via the temporary deposit arrangement with Irish Life & Permanent; and the €451 million loans from the bank to fund the share purchases by the Maple Ten.

Just over three weeks later, at 6.30 a.m. on Thursday 18 March, Gardaí arrested Sean FitzPatrick at his home in Greystones, Co. Wicklow. At nearby Bray Garda station, the former Anglo chairman and chief executive was questioned all day under section 10 of the Criminal Justice (Theft and Fraud Offences) Act 2001. It was an unprecedented move, the first high-profile arrest of a major banking figure under the white-collar crime legislation. Brian Lenihan issued a statement, noting there were multiple investigations under way into Anglo's activities. 'I am eager to see justice take its course,' the Finance Minister said. FitzPatrick was released just before two o'clock the following day, after being questioned for the maximum time allowed.

Anglo, already toxic, was now being probed for criminal activity during its extraordinary boom and bust. Only time would tell where that left its biggest borrower, Sean Quinn.

4

'I thought Sean Quinn was a billionaire'

It was one of the things Michael McAteer had noticed since joining Grant Thornton in September 2008: his phone just seemed to ring incessantly. So when his mobile rang around 8 p.m. on the night of Monday 29 March 2010, it was no particular surprise.

McAteer was the co-founder, with fellow accountant Brendan Foster, of Foster McAteer, a small Dublin practice that had carved out a niche liquidating insolvent firms and advising cash-strapped businesses. McAteer had grown up in Artane, a solidly working-class area on Dublin's north side; Foster was from down the road in Cabra. Both trained as accountants at Farrell Grant Sparks, a mid-sized practice, before opting to go into business together. Both were understandably proud of what they had achieved: two north-side Dubliners who had their names over the door of a south-side accountancy office.

By 2008, Foster McAteer had a staff of twenty-six and annual revenues of €4 million. Foster and McAteer regularly appeared in the business pages of the newspapers as liquidator or receiver to some troubled company or another. But their ambitions were limited by their firm's size and resources. The larger accountancy firms had all but ignored the insolvency market during the good times, preferring to help high-net-worth individuals get richer or to advise large corporates on tax strategy. But, with the economy in uncertain territory, they were bulking up their insolvency teams and sniffing around Foster McAteer's bread-and-butter business.

Foster and McAteer knew there would be indebted property developers and large corporates requiring expert assistance. They also knew that developers and large companies would naturally gravitate towards larger accountancy firms. If they really wanted to secure the big jobs during the recession, they realized, they would have to merge with someone.

The partners at Grant Thornton were having similar thoughts. They had the fifth-largest accountancy firm in the country, but they were dwarfed by the Big Four – KPMG, Ernst & Young, Deloitte and PricewaterhouseCoopers (PWC). Grant Thornton had a reputation as the accountancy firm of choice for Ireland's small and medium-sized indigenous businesses, with 410 staff and fee income of €45 million; but with the economy going into meltdown they needed more insolvency specialists on the team.

It was a logical fit. Grant Thornton had the scale and ambition, and Foster McAteer had the expertise. In September 2008, the old Foster McAteer business was subsumed into Grant Thornton, with both Foster and McAteer becoming partners in the newly enlarged Grant Thornton. Foster moved into the corporate finance department, while McAteer moved into insolvency, readying himself for the glut of examinerships, receiverships and liquidations that the recession would surely bring in.

Since then, McAteer's phone had been in overdrive. Now it was ringing again. McAteer was at home, between episodes of *Coronation Street*; one had just finished and the second would begin in half an hour. He looked down at his phone, and saw the name of Paul McCann.

'Paul, what can I do for you?'

'Mick, do we have any conflict with Quinn Insurance?'

Paul McCann was another partner at Grant Thornton, and one of the instigators of the Foster McAteer merger. He was its main insolvency specialist and a corporate restructuring expert. He was just thirty-eight, but he was already the favourite to be the accountancy firm's next managing partner.

McAteer racked his brain for any reason Grant Thornton might not work with or for Quinn Insurance. The firm had investigated a number of mundane insurance claims for the insurer, but, he told McCann, there was nothing that created a conflict of interest.

Then McCann dropped a bombshell. He had just received a call from Jane Marshall, a solicitor who ran the corporate restructuring and insolvency group at McCann FitzGerald, a major law firm. The Financial Regulator was poised to take control of Quinn Insurance, and Marshall wanted to know if McCann and McAteer would act as joint administrators. McAteer fought with the remote control to turn off the television, quickly getting his mind into gear. Details. He needed details.

'When are they going into court?'

'Tomorrow.'

'And they want us?'

'Yeah, they want us.'

Both men knew this was the job of a lifetime. Quinn Insurance was a household name, a €1 billion operation. It had obviously got itself into very serious trouble, and now the two accountants were being asked to run it on behalf of the state. The pair teased out the implications. A job of this size would require tremendous resources and no little expertise. What did they know about insurance in general, and the administration process in particular? And with its two main partners running an insurance company, how would the Grant Thornton insolvency department hold up? They needed to be sure Grant Thornton was big enough to do the job, and that they, as accountants, were up to it.

'Look,' McAteer told McCann. 'This is the reason we merged. We have spent the past year and a half pitching ourselves as the main player in the insolvency market. If we decline it, what does that say about us? Besides, we can do this.'

'Absolutely,' agreed McCann. 'I guess we should go meet them, then.'

'When?'

'Now.'

McAteer got in his car, his head spinning. *Coronation Street* would have to wait.

The administration process had not been used in Ireland since the mid 1980s. Very few people knew what it actually entailed. Fortunately, one person who did was Jane Marshall, and she was waiting in

her office in McCann FitzGerald to give Paul McCann and Michael
McAteer a crash course. She had worked on the administration of
PMPA Insurance, which went into administration in the 1980s amid
solvency issues, and was the closest there was to an expert on the
process.

McAteer left his home in Raheny and drove down the road to
Clontarf to pick up McCann. They drove silently for a large part of
the journey, trying to comprehend the significance of what was
about to happen. Then Michael McAteer turned to Paul McCann,
slightly bemused.

'I thought Sean Quinn was a billionaire,' he said.

McCann responded, 'Me, too.'

There is always a tipping point, a moment when anger leads to action.
Patrick Brady was not quite at that point, but he was close to it. It was
Wednesday 24 March 2010, and Brady was in his office on the quays
of the river Liffey, trying to make sense of things. He had issued
warning after warning after warning. There had been reports, letters,
presentations, promises. As head of Insurance Supervision with the
Financial Regulator, his job was to regulate insurers. Yet, here was
one insurance company that seemingly did not want to be regulated.

What was Patrick Brady going to do with Quinn Insurance?

Within most institutions, there are good guys and there are bad
guys. Patrick Brady was one of the good guys. Talk to anyone at the
Financial Regulator about Patrick Brady and the same description
keeps coming back: fair, tough, honourable. Colleagues refer to him
as almost emotional about the job, taking regulatory breaches as a
personal insult. His hands-on approach was at variance with the
light-touch regulation espoused by Patrick Neary, the former Financial Regulator, and by successive governments.

Brady's unit was located in Spencer Dock, a brisk ten-minute walk
from the Regulator's main office in the Central Bank on Dame Street.
Brady joined the insurance division in 2003 and became head of it in
2006. He had campaigned for more resources, gradually building
his team up from twenty-three to sixty. It was still a small staff by
international standards. Sources within Irish finance say that the

insurance division was the most effective unit with the Regulator, although, given the unfolding events emerging from the banks, this was hardly a ringing endorsement.

Brady had long held concerns about Sean Quinn's insurance company. He liked its business model, a no-frills system that was self-styled as the Ryanair of the insurance market. But unlike Ryanair, Quinn Insurance had to play by the Regulator's rulebook. Brady felt that Sean Quinn overlooked this fact.

Quinn had created something highly unusual, if not unique, in international insurance: a regulated insurance company that was a subsidiary of a wider family business. Most of the world's leading insurers are stand-alone entities; but Sean Quinn's company was just another division within a wide-ranging conglomerate, sitting uneasily alongside radiator plants and bottle factories. Funds could be moved between regulated and unregulated entities on Sean Quinn's instruction; and, as far as Brady could tell, most of the non-executive directors of the Quinn business seemed to know little about the movements. The events of 2001, when Quinn Direct took a big loss owing to Sean Quinn's punt on tech shares, showed the dangers of an insurance company dominated by a single man.

If a new company had come knocking on his door trying to replicate Quinn's family ownership structure, Brady would have cut it off at the knees because of the inter-group structure. However, Quinn Insurance had been authorized in 1996, before responsibility for the sector transferred to the Financial Regulator from the Department of Enterprise. Quinn had his licence and there was nothing Brady could do about that. If the Regulator attempted to force through an ownership restructuring, Brady knew that Quinn could fight it tooth and nail, and probably win. After all, the Regulator was lacking in both regulatory power and political support. Quinn, meanwhile, was a formidable figure, and an enormous job creator. If there was a fight, most people would have banked on the government supporting Quinn.

In the decade since Sean Quinn's dotcom share gamble, in line with government policy, the Regulator had adopted a light-touch approach to insurance companies. General insurers such as Quinn Insurance were required only to provide the Regulator with an annual statement of actuarial opinion confirming that the company had made adequate provision in its reserves. If the signing actuary couldn't give an unqualified opinion, the actuary was obliged to inform the Regulator.

The system meant that even the biggest insurers, including Quinn Insurance, were effectively self-regulating. Though rumours had long circulated about the performance of Quinn Insurance, and some customers raised concerns about its business practices, very few went to the Central Bank to provide any concrete evidence, according to the Regulator's office. Similarly, although the Financial Services Authority in Britain had raised some concerns with the Regulator about Quinn Insurance's aggressive pricing, it had not provided any specific data to back up the concerns it raised.

The Regulator was also desperately under-resourced to deal with the insurance sector. Throughout the noughties, the insurance division had about thirty-five staff who were responsible for regulating all general insurance and life insurance companies operating in the state. At no point in those years did the division employ more than two actuaries, and they were working almost exclusively on the development of new insurance legislation coming from Europe. Brady and Domhnall Cullinan, the two most senior insurance regulators, had sought significantly more resources but to little avail.

It was widely believed that Quinn had been chastened by the 2001 experience and learned his lesson. In 2008, however, PWC discovered that Quinn had used hundreds of millions of euro of the insurance company's reserves to fund his gamble on Anglo shares using contracts for difference. For that breach, the Financial Regulator fined Quinn Insurance €3.25 million, and fined Quinn €200,000 personally. Quinn said he had done nothing wrong but resigned as chairman of the insurer, to be replaced by Jim Quigley.

That was supposed to be a turning point. Quinn would no longer have anything to do with the regulated entity. But nothing really changed at all, and Brady knew it. Ever since then, the company and the Regulator had played a rather tedious cat and mouse game. The Regulator demanded reform, and received nothing but platitudes and pledges from Quinn.

The 2008 raid on its coffers had left a mark on the balance sheet of Quinn Insurance; the company's solvency ratio and solvency margin were well below the required levels, and Quinn was missing deadlines to restore them. For months, Brady had been asking Quinn for a €50 million capital injection to restore some order to the balance sheet, but the money was not forthcoming.

On 23 March 2010, Brady sat down with Quigley, the Quinn Insurance chairman, and Colin Morgan, the insurer's chief executive. They laid out yet another restructuring plan to restore the solvency of the company. Brady had lost patience. He had already warned them that he was prepared to push the nuclear button, and put Quinn Insurance into administration – effectively appointing outsiders to take control of the firm. But he knew that he was talking to the wrong people. He was not talking to a Quinn.

There is always a tipping point, a moment when anger leads to action. For Patrick Brady, that moment came the following day, Wednesday 24 March 2010. The phone rang. Jim Quigley, the Quinn Insurance chairman, was on the other end.

Jim Quigley had succeeded Sean Quinn as chairman of Quinn Insurance in October 2008, after Quinn had been fined by the Regulator and removed from the insurer's board. On a board filled with Quinn lieutenants and former civil servants, Quigley, a former director of Hibernia Insurance, was one of the few directors with any actual experience in the industry. He was the obvious choice to succeed Sean Quinn, perhaps the only plausible choice, and his elevation was quietly sanctioned by the Financial Regulator.

By March 2010, Quigley had been deeply worried for months. Patrick Brady and Domhnall Cullinan, the Regulator's point man on Quinn Insurance, were not backing off. Matthew Elderfield had a no-nonsense approach. Quigley had heard reports of Jonathan McMahon, too – another uncompromising character.

After Sean Quinn's raid on Quinn Insurance's coffers came to light in 2008, Quinn Group had agreed a plan to repay the €288 million to the insurer, with the approval of the Financial Regulator. The repayment plan, conceived in a more optimistic time, was meant to restore the insurer's solvency margin to 150 per cent and its solvency ratio to 40 per cent, in keeping with international norms. It had not happened.

This issue was taking an increasing amount of Quigley's time. Indeed, one of his first jobs as chairman was to sanction a letter informing the Regulator that the Quinn Group, its parent company, was unable to meet its obligations under the plan. In April 2009, the insurer had made the first of what would be a host of presentations to the Regulator. During the presentation, the insurer forecast that its gross written premiums (GWP) – effectively the total of all the insurance policies that it writes – would be limited to €972 million in 2009 in order to improve its solvency. Of this, €610 million would come from its Irish operation, with the other €362 million coming from policies being written in Britain.

In the presentation, Quinn Insurance said it was on course to meet the year-end solvency ratio for 2009 of 40 per cent and that there had been significant improvement in its British operations over the previous twelve months. At a further meeting on 10 June 2009, the insurer reaffirmed the improvement in its British operations. Based on the success in Britain, it informed the Regulator that it was changing its GWP ratio, and would be doing more business in Britain and less in Ireland. The Regulator did not object to the new strategy.

However, at a presentation six months later, in December, the insurer said that it was likely to fall below the 150 per cent solvency margin at year-end. On 18 January 2010, the Financial Regulator asked Quinn Insurance to formulate 'contingency plans' in the event of the failure of Quinn Group. The plans were submitted on 29 January. Even after requesting, and then receiving, further information about the plans, the Financial Regulator was unhappy. During a telephone call with Colin Morgan, the chief executive of the insurer, a regulatory official said the office was 'exceptionally disappointed' with the financial recovery plan. The investment returns quoted by Quinn were very optimistic and the insurer's profit forecasts were unrealistic.

By this point, Quigley was communicating on a daily basis with the Financial Regulator's office. The Regulator was demanding that

Quinn put money into the insurance business, and Quigley kept on hammering home the point to the insurer's management. Quinn had promised to stump up the money, but it had yet to materialize. The Financial Regulator was also looking for a new business plan, having rejected the previous one.

Quigley helped Morgan put a plan together, and it was dispatched to the Regulator on 22 March. A meeting was held the following day between several regulatory officials, led by Patrick Brady, and attended by both Quigley and Morgan. The plan proposed reducing the firm's British exposure through 'a substantial price adjustment'. Again, however, the Regulator was not convinced, stating it was also concerned about 'the insurer's equity exposures and the insurer's continued over-exposure to property'.

If Quigley was wondering what was coming next, he was not left waiting long. Some of the lenders that were owed a combined €1.3 billion by the Quinn Group had been nosing around the group's finances to determine its real financial position. The lenders were worried about their exposure to the group, in light of Quinn's investment in Anglo Irish Bank. The bondholders had a particular interest in the performance of Quinn Insurance: in 2005, they had secured a series of guarantees over Quinn Insurance property assets. Essentially, if Quinn Group did not repay its debts, the bondholders would be able to claim the Quinn Insurance property assets in recompense.

Quigley learned about the existence of the guarantees for the first time on 24 March, the day after the lengthy meetings with the Regulator. It was an explosive development, which raised a whole host of questions. If the guarantees were called upon by the Quinn Group lenders, there would be a material impact on the insurance business: such a move would reduce the insurer's assets by €448 million, leaving a €200 million hole in its balance sheet and thus dramatically weakening its already inadequate reserves.

The guarantees had been signed by Kevin Lunney and Liam McCaffrey, two of Sean Quinn's top executives. Quigley thought about the legal position. Were Lunney and McCaffrey empowered to sign away Quinn Insurance assets without the approval of the board? Were the guarantees legally valid? In the short term, Quigley

reckoned he had to assume that the guarantees were valid and binding.

The Regulator was already making threats about Quinn Insurance; there had even been some talk of the possibility of putting the
insurer into administration. Quigley knew that the existence of the
guarantees would annoy the Financial Regulator still further, but he
had to be told.

Quigley picked up the phone and called Patrick Brady.

If Sean Quinn was worried, he was not letting it show. Jim Quigley
had been on the phone and Colin Morgan, too. They were panicky,
tense. The Regulator was making threats about the guarantees to the
group bondholders, and the chairman and chief executive of Quinn
Insurance wanted its founder to find a solution. Everyone wanted
Quinn to put in more money to bail out the insurer and boost its balance sheet.

The bondholders who had loaned money to Quinn Group had
been giving him grief for months now, making requests and suggestions about how he should run his business. They had told Quinn
they would not give up the guarantees, on the grounds that it was
legitimate security. Yet Quinn reassured his senior team that the
guarantees would never be called in, maintaining that the company
would honour its debts and agree a deal with its lenders. 'It will all be
fine,' he told one senior staff member.

Quinn had always taken a hands-on role with Quinn Insurance.
Every Sunday, after his dinner, he went into his office and started
working through the claims position of Quinn Insurance. He did it
every week, going through all the large payments that his claims handlers had approved the previous week, or were looking to sanction in
the following days. If the payout was too high for his liking, Quinn
made a note and would follow it up with a call to the claims handler
the following day. He knew his staff hated the Monday phone calls
from the boss, but it was his job to make sure that they were keeping
costs down and payments low. Of course, Quinn had agreed with the
Regulator in 2008 that he would no longer have an executive function
within Quinn Insurance. But he had carried on checking the claims.

As far as Quinn was concerned, his personal approach was one of the drivers behind the company's success. Under his stewardship, it had grown market share and harvested rich profits: €134 million profit in 2004, €205 million in 2005 and €282 million the following year. In those three years alone, the Quinn family took €548 million in dividends from the business. In 2009, the company was forecasting profits of €250 million, a nice number given the economic maelstrom.

The regulatory climate might have changed, with Elderfield and McMahon putting an end to the lax, almost whimsical approach of the Regulator's office, but Quinn remained convinced that they would not challenge him or his company. 'Not a chance,' he told one associate. He never believed they would appoint an administrator or seek to take over his company.

Quinn had employed so many people and created so many jobs. He firmly believed that no government would sanction anything that might disturb this, according to several sources close to him. Even in March 2010, with the bondholders up in arms and the Regulator contemplating administration, Quinn remained convinced that it would all blow over.

On Monday 29 March 2010, the regulatory team assembled in a 1980s-style meeting room on the seventh floor of the Central Bank. Matthew Elderfield was there, chairing proceedings, with Jonathan McMahon at his side. Patrick Brady was sitting across the table, with some officials from his office. The Governor of the Central Bank, Patrick Honohan, was not in attendance, but he knew what the meeting was about, and he knew its potential consequences.

The following day, in a series of choreographed announcements, the government and the Regulator were to reveal how much capital the banks had to raise. They would outline how much Anglo Irish Bank was actually going to cost the taxpayer, and the details of loan transfers from the banks to the National Asset Management Agency, a specialist agency set up to assume the devalued property loans from all the Irish banks. Elderfield had been brought in to clean up the banking disaster, and this was supposed to be his big day, the day when some sort of line would finally be drawn under the Irish banking collapse. Yet here he was, discussing Sean Quinn. Elderfield was perplexed. In his short time in Ireland, he had asked other insurance companies to boost their balance sheets with cash. All of them had obliged within days, a week at the most. But Quinn acted as though he was negotiating a deal.

Elderfield had been receiving calls about Quinn even before Patrick Brady had walked in the previous week to tell him about those guarantees. The FSA, Elderfield's former employer, had raised concerns over Quinn's operations in Britain. It was undercutting all its competitors there on price, building up market share but losing significant sums. The FSA wanted to know if the paper billionaire could cover the losses. Elderfield knew enough about Quinn's Anglo position to have his doubts.

He had met Brady and McMahon on the previous Thursday and Friday to discuss the situation. They had talked about putting Quinn Insurance into administration, but Elderfield had decided to wait out the weekend. He knew that representatives of the bondholders were in town, and he asked Brady to meet them and see if there was any chance the guarantees could be lifted, though he knew this was unlikely, in the midst of a crisis for the economy and for Quinn.

Now, Brady was delivering the inevitable news. He told the meeting that the guarantees were not going to be lifted, and that Quinn was not going to inject capital into his company. Brady was advocating administration, and quickly. He had run out of forbearance, Quinn Insurance had run out of time, and Sean Quinn had run out of money. Jonathan McMahon agreed. He reminded the meeting that Quinn had taken money out of the insurer to speculate on bank shares, and highlighted the fact that the insurer did not even employ an internal actuary. This was not illegal, but it was unusual. The company was in breach of its solvency requirements, and it needed to be sanctioned. McMahon told the room that it was a black and white issue, and that the rules were the rules.

No one said it at the meeting, but everyone there knew that appointing an administrator to Quinn Insurance would also be a watershed moment for the Financial Regulator. It would be a bold statement about the independence and the tenacity of this new regime. They were taking on Sean Quinn, a legend of Irish business. Elderfield was savvy enough to know that this could work against him, and that he would face serious criticism. Quinn was a big employer with a long reach. Elderfield knew that many people already perceived him as an ambitious careerist, and that a move against Sean Quinn would fit neatly into that narrative.

Still, he had a job to do and a decision to make. He weighed it up. Quinn was a man who had taken funds from an insurance company in the past, a man who had been subject to enforcement action in the past. Now, he was refusing to sort out a long-standing solvency breach, unwilling or unable to put the required money in. Negotiations had been ongoing for months before the existence of the potentially ruinous guarantees had even emerged.

Elderfield gave Brady the green light. He walked back to his office and placed a call with Brian Lenihan, the Minister for Finance. He was not asking for permission, just telling him out of courtesy. He looked out of his window. It was dark and depressing. Snow was forecast. Meanwhile, Patrick Brady went back to his own office and broke the news to Domhnall Cullinan and another official at his office, Andrew Mawdsley. They were going into the High Court the following morning to seek the appointment of an administrator to Quinn Insurance.

Paul McCann and Michael McAteer got home from the offices of McCann FitzGerald just before midnight on 29 March. They had been briefed on the administration process and given a crash course on Quinn Insurance and its regulatory issues. They agreed to return at 9 a.m. the next morning. Before then, they had some housekeeping to attend to. The partners of Grant Thornton meet at 8 a.m. each Tuesday morning to brief each other on developments. Before taking a job of this magnitude, McAteer and McCann knew they had to tell their colleagues and make sure no one objected.

No one did.

They then made the short trip along the quays to McCann FitzGerald, and their first meeting with Patrick Brady and

Domhnall Cullinan. Elderfield was not in attendance; in preparation for his banking announcements, he was exercising in a gym in Aston Quay, just around the corner from the Central Bank.

Appointing an administrator to an insurance company is a serious task and, under legislation, it must be dealt with by the President of the High Court. Fortunately the President of the High Court, Mr Justice Nicholas Kearns, was available to take the case that morning. The application was ex parte, meaning only one side was represented; as a consequence of this, the Regulator could ask only for the appointment of provisional administrators. The hearing lasted twenty minutes, enough time for the Regulator's legal team to outline the concerns and some of the background to the case. Mr Justice Kearns consented to the application, appointing Paul McCann and Michael McAteer as provisional administrators to Quinn Insurance.

Everyone expected Quinn to object once the news broke, and Brady was lined up to file a responding affidavit revealing more details of the 2008 issue, which had resulted in Quinn resigning as chairman. As part of the deal approved by the previous Regulator at the time, certain details relating to Quinn's involvement and sanction had never been disclosed. Brady was prepared to put those into his deposition.

The administration process had not been used in two decades, so everyone was finding their feet, trying to make sure that everything was done correctly. McAteer knew he had to inform Quinn Insurance, but the question was whom to tell, and how to break the news.

For a number of months, McAteer had been working on a rescue plan for Irish Car Rentals, which held the franchise for the Europcar, Alamo and National Car Rental brands in Ireland. Quinn Insurance provided insurance for the rental cars, and McAteer had engaged with Brendan Moran, the insurer's finance director, on the restructuring. He decided it would be best to break the news to someone he knew.

He rang Moran. 'I know this is going to come as a shock to you, Brendan, but the court has appointed me as joint administrator to Quinn Insurance,' McAteer said. 'Can you get the directors and the management team together? We are on our way up.'

There was a silence. Eventually, Moran responded, 'No problem.' Moran also agreed to McAteer's request not to announce the administrator's arrival to the Quinn Insurance staff.

McAteer knew that the company and the Regulator had been at loggerheads for months, with numerous threats of administration. Yet Moran seemed to know nothing about any of that. Or, if he did, he was doing a good job of hiding it.

Shortly after the court hearing, McAteer and McCann headed for the Cavan headquarters of Quinn Insurance. They left Dublin at 11 a.m., passing the Q-Building, the imposing Dublin office of Quinn Insurance, on their way. By the time they had reached Kells in Co. Meath, it was snowing. By the time they had reached Virginia in Co. Cavan, they were driving at less than 20 kilometres an hour. When they reached their destination at 3 p.m., the secret was out. RTÉ, the national broadcaster, was waiting for them with a mobile broadcasting unit parked outside the Quinn Insurance headquarters. McAteer and McCann had discussed this possibility on the road and decided it would be best to do an interview to explain the situation.

No one sought to block their entrance to the building. The two administrators simply informed security and reception that they were the court-appointed administrators of Quinn Insurance. They spoke to the RTÉ correspondent, Richard Dowling, as soon as they arrived, in the Quinn boardroom. McAteer and McCann repeated, ad nauseam, that it was business as usual and insurance policies were unaffected by the move.

With RTÉ dispatched, McAteer and McCann sat down with the insurance company management, including Colin Morgan, Brendan Moran, financial planning director Shane Morrison, HR head John McGarry, and Sean Quinn Junior, who had recently taken over the running of the UK business. Kevin Lunney joined the meeting by phone. He was acting head of claims, a position previously held by Sean Junior and not yet filled.

The meeting lasted an hour and a half. It was tense but civilized. The Quinn management wanted to know what the administration meant and whether they could challenge it in court. McAteer and McCann explained that they could, adding that there was a good chance the administrators would be removed if the company came to an agreement with the Regulator over the guarantees and the solvency issues. Until this point, most of the people in the room, as employees of the insurance company, did not know anything about the guarantees, which had been designed at Quinn Group level. Sean Quinn Junior did not say much.

As a prelude to the appointment of the administrators, the Financial Regulator had issued a directive instructing Quinn Insurance to stop issuing business in Britain. The Regulator was concerned about the losses and the business model there. It quickly dawned on the Grant Thornton accountants that there were a lot of policy renewals in the system; it would be bad for the company's reputation if customers waiting for routine renewals were left in the lurch. The administrators secured a concession from the Regulator allowing them to process all applications in the system. This issue alone brought home the scale of their task to the two accountants. As administrators, they were responsible for the company. If there was a problem in Quinn Insurance, it was now their problem.

That night, McAteer and McCann made their way back to Dublin and a meeting at an airport hotel. The bondholders were still in town, and they wanted to know what the appointment of the administrators meant for them. The Grant Thornton accountants had agreed to the meeting, but decided to limit the attendance of the other side: the last thing they wanted was full engagement with ten lenders.

They met David Baxter, a lawyer from the Dublin solicitors A&L Goodbody, who was representing the bondholders, and briefed him. At the end of the day, McCann and McAteer talked it through. Neither man was sure how long they would be in place as administrators. Quinn Insurance had problems but, based upon its numbers, it was profitable and solvent. Both men reckoned Sean Quinn could write a cheque at any time and make the whole issue disappear.

Sean Quinn was furious. He had been warned, but he never imagined the Regulator would follow through with the threat to take over the running of Quinn Insurance.

He started calling some of his trusted lieutenants, including David Mackey, one of the few people whose advice he actually heeded. He called Liam McCaffrey and Kevin Lunney. He called his brother Peter. He discussed the situation briefly with his children, four of them Quinn Insurance employees, but he reckoned this was a job for the head of the family. Quinn decided to go political, sending correspondence to all members of the government and to the opposition party leaders. In it, he stated that the administration decision by the Regulator was putting nearly 6,000 Irish jobs in the wider Quinn Group in jeopardy. Much of his ambitious expansion plan for his manufacturing group had been based on forecasts of bumper profits from the insurer. Without those profits, Quinn told his team, it would be difficult to cover the group debts, including the €1.3 billion owed to the banks and bondholders.

He was furious the next day, too, when Brian Lenihan stood up in the Dáil and said he was standing by the decision taken by Elderfield, his new Regulator.

Quinn's press adviser, Brian Bell of Wilson Hartnell PR, was telling him he needed to do something to win public support. So, two days after the appointment of the administrators, Sean Quinn agreed to grant an interview to RTÉ's northern editor, Tommie Gorman.

Quinn told Gorman, 'We can survive without the Anglo Irish shares, we've written it off. It's the five kids and the wife that own the shares in Anglo Irish Bank, so we're not discussing what their losses are – but they are substantial.'

Gorman sought clarity on the scale of the Anglo losses, asking if the figure was greater than €1.5 billion.

Quinn confirmed it was. 'Whether it is today, tomorrow, next week, next year or in five years' time, there has been no impropriety in anything we have done in that bank or any other bank,' he said. 'We are very proud of anything we have done. We are above board. We don't owe anybody anything. We don't owe anybody any great apology. If we owe an apology to anybody, it's our staff; that maybe we slowed up the growth of the company and maybe the reputation was tarnished. From that point of view yes, mistake, but as regards any impropriety, absolutely none.'

Quinn claimed that a 'media frenzy' had built up around the Quinn Group, and that he had no idea why 'the agenda is to get Quinn'. Yes, the lenders had guarantees over Quinn Insurance assets, but he maintained that the Regulator had been informed about them. Given this, he could not see what the problem was. Quinn was adamant that the Regulator had known about the guarantees for a number of years. Through it all, he referred to himself in the third person: Sean Quinn this, Sean Quinn that.

Meanwhile, 300 of Quinn's insurance employees mobilized outside the Dáil in a protest organized by one of his group public relations executives, Mona Birmingham. Quinn also made personal telephone calls to leading members of the Cabinet and other influential politicians. But nothing changed, and there was no movement by the Regulator.

Quinn knew that the Regulator was technically within its powers in appointing the administrators. But he also believed that the threat to jobs at his wider group would outweigh technical breaches on the insurance company's balance sheet. He told his lawyers to mount an appeal to the decision, to challenge the appointment when the full hearing was scheduled. Throughout it all, Quinn portrayed it as an issue of jobs, always highlighting the threat to employment if the company remained in administration. He emphasized the point to Brian Cowen, the Taoiseach, when Cowen called Quinn back days after the appointment of the administrator. Sean Quinn Junior would later claim that Cowen told his father it was best to work consensually with the administrators. 'This will all be sorted out,' Sean Junior claimed Cowen said.

In the meantime, Quinn had to make sure the administrators did not make a mess of his company. He instructed Lunney to contact McCann and McAteer to arrange a meeting. He insisted that the meeting take place in the boardroom of Quinn Insurance, on his home turf. The meeting was arranged for Friday 2 April, Good Friday, just days after the High Court petition. Quinn, accompanied by Sean Junior and a small number of executives, looked McCann and McAteer up and down and then outlined his position.

He said the Regulator had it all wrong; Quinn Insurance was a profitable company with strong cash reserves. It had just had the most profitable quarter ever, and the issue over the guarantees was all a misunderstanding that could be resolved. There was an issue, he said, but it was not a doomsday issue. It was an emotive pitch, but it failed to address the long-standing problems afflicting the insurer's balance sheet. Quinn failed to explain how it had happened, or why he had not injected money into the company to boost its cash reserves.

McCann posed a question: 'If the company is so strong, why are we here?' The administrators told Quinn they felt it was 50:50 they would still be there in a few weeks' time. They did not say it, but they believed Quinn would draw from his seemingly considerable wealth to resolve things. They said they did not want to have an antagonistic relationship, and asked what they could do to work together during the weeks ahead.

Quinn was forceful but cordial, while Sean Junior was largely silent. Quinn said he wanted Kevin Lunney involved in the business as his point man. At the end of the meeting, Quinn got a shock. McCann told him that he would not be involved in the insurance company any more, even if his children were the shareholders. He was not to come into the offices of Quinn Insurance again.

In the days following the appointment of the administrators, Elderfield's phone was hopping. Politicians from the border area were seeking meetings. They respected his independence, they said, but they had concerns. Elderfield agreed to meet some of them, on the grounds that it was a high-profile issue and he had better explain his decision. He had two or three such meetings, and each time he explained the Insurance Act and what it meant, and he explained solvency requirements and why they mattered. McMahon sat in on the meetings, backing up his boss in a forthright manner. Quinn had broken the rules. It was that simple, he said. Quite what the politicians made of McMahon and Elderfield, two young regulators recently arrived from overseas, wasn't clear, but after those initial meetings, they stopped calling.

Elderfield also had a more difficult meeting with employees of Quinn Insurance. Mona Birmingham, by now a vanguard of the anti-administration campaign, had sought the meeting. She turned up with young employees, some of whom were about to get married, or had young children. They said they were worried that the company would be sold and that a new employer would slash jobs. Even if Sean Quinn kept ownership, they were worried about the impact of the administration process upon the company and its employees. Outside the Central Bank, Quinn employees and supporters kept turning up with posters and signs, calling for Quinn to be reinstated.

Brendan Smith, a cabinet minister from the Cavan/Monaghan constituency, rang McAteer looking for a meeting with him and McCann. McAteer told Smith that Arlene Foster, the Enterprise Minister from Northern Ireland, had made a similar request and he suggested they do a joint meeting. McAteer did not realize it, but he was suggesting one of the first meetings involving politicians north and south of the border outside of the official cross-border political process.

It was decided that all political parties would be invited to send representatives to a meeting in the Kilmore Hotel in Cavan, once owned by Quinn, exactly a week after the appointment of the administrators. Politicians of all hues were in attendance, and the politicians, as politicians do, spent the first hour saying what a significant occasion it was to have politicians of all hues in attendance.

That was the way it went for the next two weeks, a phoney war ahead of a highly anticipated courtroom battle between Quinn and the Regulator. There were rallies in Cavan and Enniskillen, two towns that were massively reliant on Quinn Insurance jobs. Anglo Irish Bank, meanwhile, entered the fray with a plan that would see it absorb Quinn Insurance for three years, before selling it on. It could use profits from the insurer to reduce the Quinn family's mammoth debts, while providing Sean Quinn with a mechanism for saving the rest of his group.

McAteer and McCann believed they could be ousted as administrators if Quinn reached agreement with the Financial Regulator to address the solvency issues at Quinn Insurance. If the issue went to court, though, they were confident the Regulator would prevail. Quinn's team had filed a replying affidavit, repeating their contention that the Regulator's office knew about the guarantees. According to several sources involved in the process, however, Quinn's legal team told him that, based upon the evidence, it was not looking good for him.

The Regulator had two files on the businessman: one dating back to his ill-fated foray into tech stocks a decade earlier, and another in relation to the events of 2008, when Quinn took €398 million of the insurance company's reserves to fund his CFD gamble in Anglo Irish Bank. In the 2008 file, there was a letter barring Sean Quinn from any involvement with any regulated company. The letter had never been disclosed. But, if he fought the Regulator, it was made clear that the letter would be released to the court, and to the public.

So instead of coming to court, Quinn retreated. 'In order to resolve this, we need constructive dialogue with the Regulator,' Liam McCaffrey told reporters. 'The court is not the best place to do that. We are where we are – we have to accept the cold reality that we are in administration. We had to allow the administrators get on with finding a solution rather than fighting this in court, because nobody wins there.' In reality, the Regulator had threatened Sean Quinn, and Quinn had retreated.

With no formal objection from Quinn, Michael McAteer and Paul McCann were confirmed as administrators to Quinn Insurance on 15 April. They now had to develop a plan for the business. They continued to talk to the Quinn Group – after all, it was the shareholder, and they reckoned there was still some shareholder value. They still thought Quinn could potentially make a comeback. All he had to do was show Matthew Elderfield the money. Over a sandwich, they discussed the situation.

'I thought Sean Quinn was a billionaire,' McAteer said to McCann, once again.

McCann gave the same response, 'Me, too.'

5

Petey

By May 2010, Peter Darragh Quinn was becoming increasingly unsettled.

Like many people, Sean Quinn's nephew – known to his family and friends as Petey – had dabbled in property during the economic boom. He had not gone in too deeply; just a few investment properties. There was the house on the Navan Road in Dublin 7, and another property along the Royal Canal that he had bought with one of his two brothers. In Cavan, he had teamed up with his sister to buy a property in Ballyconnell, not far from the family home in Fermanagh.

All the properties were mortgaged and, by May 2010, with the Irish market in freefall, they were all in negative equity. But that was not what was bothering Petey. His worries went far beyond a trio of investment properties in Dublin and Cavan.

In any other family, Petey would have been the shining star. But this was no ordinary family, and Petey knew it. The physical proof was all around him. There were the quarries, the wind farms, the factories churning out bottles and radiators and plastics. More than 350 Quinn Group trucks left Ireland each week, carrying products to the UK and Europe.

Petey's father, Peter Quinn Senior, was a local colossus, respected and admired. He was an accountant, a business consultant and a regular appointee to state boards. He had been president of the Gaelic Athletic Association from 1991 to 1994 and was still regarded as one of the intellectual powerhouses of the association, as comfortable talking about balance sheets as on-field tactics. And then there was Petey's uncle, Sean Quinn, the billionaire industrialist who was loved and lauded in the borderlands of Cavan and Fermanagh; a man whose businesses had literally sculpted the locality.

Petey had his own achievements. He had been a fine Gaelic footballer, good enough to represent Fermanagh at both minor and senior level. Those inter-county playing days were behind him, but he was now manager of the senior football team at Teemore Shamrocks, the local club. Petey enjoyed the camaraderie, the responsibility, the sense of place it gave him.

In Ireland, the GAA matters. In rural Ireland, it matters more. And in Northern Ireland, where playing Gaelic games is closely linked with the nationalist identity, it matters most of all. To Petey, it mattered that his own people, the people of Teemore Shamrocks, had asked him to lead. He was respected and liked. The club members looked at Petey and saw a young man going places – they saw the university degree, the nice car and the good job. But also, deep down, they saw the son of Peter and the nephew of Sean. They saw a Quinn.

Petey had lived in Dublin until the age of seven, when his father moved the family back to Enniskillen. As far as he was concerned, however, he was Fermanagh born and bred. It was in his accent and his demeanour. After school, he went to Queen's University in Belfast, graduating in 1999 with a BSc in Accounting. From there it was back to Dublin and a two-year stint at an accountancy firm. He never bothered with his formal accountancy qualifications, though. Instead, like countless members of his generation, he boarded a plane for Australia, another young Irish lad travelling, working, partying on the other side of the world.

When he returned to Ireland in 2003, aged twenty-six, Petey went to work for his uncle. He started as an investment analyst with Quinn Insurance, then moved to Quinn Radiators. In August 2006, his uncle asked him to move again, to property this time. Quinn had started buying international properties, and Petey would be involved in managing the assets for the Quinn Group and the Quinn family. He was to report directly to Kevin Lunney, one of the very few people to have Sean Quinn's ear. A good word from Kevin and Petey would advance.

Lunney had overall responsibility for the International Property Group assets, assembled through a flurry of activity from 2005 onwards, though he focused mainly on the properties in Ireland and the UK. They included the Slieve Russell Hotel, Dublin's Buswells Hotel, a string of Dublin pubs and several hotels in England.

Petey had no real title, but by 2009 he had effectively become general manager of the Quinn property assets in Russia and Ukraine, working with a tight-knit group of Quinn staff. He also took an active interest in the Indian property portfolio. Lunney left Petey largely to his own devices. Court documents would later show that he was trusted to negotiate leases, secure clients and keep the family's overseas portfolio ticking over. Despite his hands-on role and the fact he was a Quinn, however, Petey did not have a shareholding in any of the properties; he was merely managing them on behalf of his cousins, Sean and Patricia Quinn's five children.

It was a demanding job. Petey Quinn spent much of his time on the road and in the air. His uncle was a hands-on manager and he expected the same from his staff. It was not enough to buy a property and leave it in the hands of a local manager. Not out in Russia, and certainly not in Ukraine. Local lawyers had explained it to Petey in simple terms: on Monday, you may own a building; on Tuesday, someone else controls it; on Wednesday, you are advised to leave.

Petey visited Moscow every fortnight, working from his office in the Kutuzoff Tower, a $188 million office block. The twenty-storey Kutuzoff, completed in 2007, was the jewel in the Quinn IPG crown, bringing in $20 million a year in rent from tenants including Coca-Cola, Dunlop, Mitsubishi and Computershare. The official opening of the tower, in 2009, had been conducted by Billy Kelleher, the Fianna Fáil minister of state for trade, who was on a trade mission to Moscow. Petey had held the ribbon for the politicians. The Quinn family kept an office in the Kutuzoff, which acted as a headquarters for the international real-estate business.

In all, Petey managed eight Russian properties on behalf of his cousins. The portfolio included the Caspiy Business Centre, a six-storey high-tech business centre, also in Moscow. There was a parcel of development land in Kazan, the capital of Tatarstan, valued at about $51 million. Kazan, 800 kilometres east of Moscow, would be the location for the first in a network of giant warehousing and logistics centres planned by Quinn.

A deal to build ten stores for StroiArsenal, a Russian DIY chain, took Quinn into ever more remote regions. There was a $21.4 million site in Nizhny Novgorod, Russia's fifth-largest city and a central cog in the country's sprawling transportation network. If you wanted to move goods across Russia between east and west, you had to travel through Nizhny Novgorod. There was a $13 million, 10,000-square-metre DIY store in Yekaterinburg, an industrial city located just to the east of the Ural Mountains. In Naberezhnye Chelny, a city 225 kilometres further east than Kazan, closer to Mongolia than Moscow, the Quinn IPG spent $1.9 million on a development site for another DIY centre. In Ufa, capital of the Republic of Bashkortostan, a city that started as a fortress for Ivan the Terrible, Quinn planned a shopping centre that would also house a health centre and spa.

At first, the bureaucracy of Russian property dealings had astounded Petey; there was so much paperwork, so much red tape. He joked to friends that it would be easier to get elected to public office in Russia than to buy a house. Gradually, he got used to the paperwork, to the vagaries of the system. Every week, he had to devote four or five hours just to signing documents. At first, Petey had sought translations and legal advice on each and every one. Most were in Russian, impenetrable to everyone but fluent Russian speakers with law degrees. But by 2010, he had fallen into the habit of just signing them.

Petey did not visit Ukraine as frequently as Russia, but he went there several times a year, usually to check on the Univermag Ukraina, a shopping centre in the heart of Kiev, the capital. Valued at $77 million, it had four cinemas, restaurants and a tenant roster that included Esprit, Ecco and Massimo.

Quinn had bought the centre in November 2006, the same year he bought Kiev's Leonardo Business Centre. The Leonardo had a different ownership structure – Sean Quinn had allowed friends and senior employees to participate in the purchase, while Quinn Life, the life assurance arm of Quinn Insurance, had also taken a stake. The family had a small shareholding.

Petey generally stayed on top of events in Ukraine via telephone, working with Larisa Yanez Puga, a local who managed operations in Kiev. The Univermag Ukraina was a solid performer, but Sean Quinn was cautious about making major investments in Ukraine. The political climate in the country was uncertain and he also believed that Russia or India would offer a better return for his investment, according to sources involved in the property portfolio. He had bought a $26 million office development in Hyderabad, a city of 6.5 million people considered to be the Indian equivalent of California's Silicon Valley. A development site had also been acquired for $4.2 million and earmarked for a hotel. The plan was for a development of IT parks that would cover almost 14 acres in Hyderabad's HITEC City. The first phase alone of what would be known as Q-City would be 67,000 square metres, about seven times the size of Quinn Insurance's offices at Blanchardstown in Dublin. The second phase would be another 92,000 square metres. Quinn saw potential to repeat the Hyderabad plan in other Indian regions, and set about hiring local people for a Quinn branch office in Hyderabad.

All told, the IPG properties across Russia, Ukraine and India had a peak value of €600 million. The recession had shaved off some of their worth, but by 2010 they were still valued at somewhere north of €500 million, according to the latest estimates Petey had been given. Sean Quinn tended to group these three countries together – they were the new frontier for his property business, offering higher returns than his older assets in Ireland, the UK and Central Europe.

Regardless of where in the world he was, Petey Quinn travelled home every weekend during the GAA season. He had thought long and hard before he took the manager's job at Teemore Shamrocks. Having accepted, there was no way he was going to let the team down. So he came home with an enthusiasm that surprised most people involved with the club. In Fermanagh, this mattered most of all.

By May 2010, Peter Darragh Quinn did not know everything about his uncle's massive debt problem, but he knew enough. In June 2008, before Anglo Irish Bank had collapsed into nationalization, Petey had attended a few meetings with Anglo bankers to review the performance of some of the IPG assets. Anglo's interest in the properties had puzzled him at the time, since the bank had lent only a relatively small sum for the property portfolio. It was not the main banker of the IPG deals by any means.

But since then, Petey had pieced together some of the pieces of the puzzle. From his conversations with the bank, he knew that Anglo had taken some form of security over the assets as collateral for other funds the Quinns had borrowed from the bank. With Quinn Insurance in administration and the Quinn Group creditors on high alert, the landscape had now fundamentally changed.

Anglo was now in state ownership and the new management team – Mike Aynsley, Richard Woodhouse and Tom Hunersen – were obviously not in the business of appeasement. They were being paid to recoup as much money as possible, not to nurture long-lasting relationships with highly indebted clients. The rhetoric was changing, within the bank and within the Irish establishment. Politicians of all persuasions were now referring to debts the Quinns owed to Anglo as money owed to the taxpayer. Alan Dukes, a former Finance Minister who was now chairman of the bank, was repeatedly explaining how Anglo was trying to get money back from errant borrowers on behalf of the men and women of Ireland.

From what Petey could see, it was only a matter of time before Anglo would come looking at the €500 million of international property he managed on behalf of his uncle and cousins in Russia, Ukraine and India. He felt the portfolio could be kept out of the hands of the bank – but only if the family acted quickly.

Within weeks of the Quinn Insurance administration, Petey decided to raise his concerns with his uncle. He did not do this lightly. Sean Quinn still believed the Anglo bosses would come to their senses and do a deal with him to save the insurance company. But Petey believed that it was only a matter of time before Anglo took everything from the family, including the nest-egg IPG properties. He would later tell the Irish courts that his uncle gave this view short shrift. There was no discussion, no debate; he would not even entertain any conversation. That was how the boss operated – he formed a view and that was it.

But Petey persevered. At every opportunity, he raised the prospect of Anglo seizing the assets, even the whole Quinn group. If his uncle would only listen to him, Petey would explain that he could at least secure the international assets and put them out of Anglo's reach.

Petey turned to Sean Quinn's children, his cousins, starting with Sean Junior. The pair were close in age, and they were friends. They had played football together for Teemore and Fermanagh. But Sean Junior did not want to know either. Petey moved on to Ciara, Aoife and finally Colette, without success. He never got around to discussing it with the youngest sibling, Brenda.

By the summer of 2010, Richard Woodhouse was insisting on monthly meetings with Petey about the International Property Group. The banker sought full disclosure on the performance of every asset within the IPG. The meetings took place in Connaught House, the plush Dublin 4 offices Anglo had moved to from its former home on St Stephen's Green. Petey didn't like that very much, according to sources close to the bank. It was the bankers' home ground: given that Petey was a GAA manager, he would have understood the importance of playing on home turf.

At the meetings, Petey gave Woodhouse only cursory details, refusing to be drawn into divulging the properties' specific ownership structures. But the meetings heightened his anxiety. Eventually, Petey came to understand that, to Anglo, the overseas properties were perhaps the likeliest means of getting some money back from the Quinns.

Enough was enough, Petey decided. His job was to manage the valuable property assets in the best interests of the family. One way or another, that was what he would do. He knew that the Anglo security applied to shares in the companies that owned the IPG assets – not to the actual bricks and mortar. On a trip to Moscow in late summer 2010, he met lawyers from Cameron McKenna, a firm with thirteen offices across Europe, which specialized in international tax and legal structures. From there, Petey went to Kiev and met Baker & McKenzie, another blue-chip firm with expertise in tax.

Petey outlined the situation to the lawyers. He was looking for a way to ensure Anglo Irish Bank could not get hold of the property assets, despite the fact it had security over shares in the companies that owned particular buildings. Was this possible? And if so, how exactly should he proceed? He was not asking the lawyers to set a scheme in motion or participate in it. He was just looking for a hypothetical solution.

The specialists at Cameron McKenna and Baker & McKenzie quickly realized Petey had a significant advantage – he had a head start. The Quinn Group already had a complex corporate structure: companies all over the world, with countless subsidiaries and overlapping shareholdings. In the Quinn manufacturing group, for example, the main holding company was incorporated in the Republic of Ireland, but had subsidiaries dotted all over the world.

There were companies in Luxembourg, the Netherlands, Spain, Belgium, the Czech Republic, Slovakia. There were French and German companies, which owned Irish companies, which in turn owned companies in Northern Ireland. It was a maze of corporate structures, devised largely by accountants at PWC to minimize the company's tax bills. It was ridiculously byzantine but all perfectly legal.

The structure for the overseas assets was even more convoluted. At the top of the ownership pyramid were the Quinn children, who owned shares in a string of Swedish companies. These Swedish companies owned another Swedish company, called Quinn Investments Sweden. The five children also held further shares in this company through a number of firms registered in Jersey. Quinn Investments Sweden was central to the whole structure, and it had ten Swedish subsidiaries. Each of those Swedish subsidiaries owned a company in

Cyprus, which in turn owned a company in the country in which each individual asset was located. This structure applied chiefly to the assets in Russia, Ukraine and India.

Petey's other advantage was the fact that the bank had security only over the shares in the companies behind the properties, not over the assets themselves. Cameron McKenna and Baker & McKenzie advised Petey to establish a string of new companies. By transferring shares, voting rights and liabilities between the old companies and the new ones, he could keep the assets from Anglo's clutches. It was like a three-card trick, played simultaneously with multiple decks of cards on different tables.

Towards the end of 2010, Petey took the plan further, meeting accountants from PWC in Belfast. He never told the accountants of his intention, but sought hypothetical advice on how one might void security held by a bank. Based on all his conversations, Petey reckoned he could create enough confusion to hide the assets from Anglo.

All he needed was a green light from Sean Quinn.

6

'The company is insolvent'

Within days of the installation of the administrators at Quinn Insurance, Sean Quinn called David Mackey, his old friend and the former chief executive of Quinn Group. Mackey had left Quinn Group in 1999 to lead an aggressive expansion of P Elliott, a Cavan building company. By early 2010, P Elliott had its own troubles, struggling to repay hundreds of millions of euro in bank borrowings it had used to fund boom-time property deals. Despite that, Mackey agreed to come back on board at Quinn Group and help his former boss.

Mackey could see that the Quinn Insurance administration was a serious blow to Quinn's morale. 'He doesn't feel good about it at all,' Mackey told associates at the time. 'He feels he has done forty years of good work and is being penalized for one bad mistake.'

Quinn's lieutenants Kevin Lunney and Dara O'Reilly had meanwhile cajoled Pat O'Neill, a former boss of Glanbia and a relatively recent addition to the Quinn Group board, to open his contacts book and lobby on Quinn's behalf. The same request was made to Brendan Tuohy, the former secretary-general of the Department of Communications, another recent board appointee. They were given a clear instruction: 'Call anyone who might be able to help Sean.'

Quinn had watched as Michael McAteer and Paul McCann, the Grant Thornton administrators, had moved into Quinn Insurance full-time. The High Court had confirmed their appointment on 15 April, giving them executive powers at the insurer – including the power to sell the business. The legislation used to install the administrators obliged them to put in place a plan to return the business to a sound commercial and financial footing. That meant restoring its solvency to the level required by the Regulator; if Sean Quinn was not willing or able to stump up the cash to do that, then it was the job of the administrators to find someone who would. The business had started losing customers when the administrators were appointed, so keeping the company in administration long-term was not an option.

Quinn still believed, however, that he would regain control of Quinn Insurance. He could close a deal with the Regulator, or even seek to buy the business out of administration. According to people close to Quinn, the businessman believed he had a key ally in this regard: Anglo Irish Bank. At a meeting on 19 February – nearly two months before the administrators were appointed – Mike Aynsley, the Anglo chief executive, had suggested to Quinn that Quinn Insurance be restructured so the bank could recoup some of the €2.8 billion it was owed. Richard Woodhouse had also raised the prospect of Quinn Insurance being sold before the administration, but Quinn had rejected any such suggestion at the time. Now times had changed.

The bank hadn't been pleased about the Financial Regulator's decision to put Quinn Insurance into administration, believing a more subtle approach would have preserved value in Quinn's business. But if nothing else, the administration had brought Quinn around to the bank's way of thinking. Quinn and Anglo seemed to be on the same page – keeping a hold on Quinn Insurance and working with Quinn looked like the best plan to get the Anglo debt repaid, retain jobs and keep Quinn Group intact.

The Quinn Group lenders – the bank syndicate, led by Barclays, that was owed a combined €700 million, and bondholders owed a combined €600 million – wanted a representative working with Quinn Group in order to maximize the likelihood that the €1.3 billion would be repaid. Even before the administrators were appointed to Quinn Insurance, the lenders had been nervous; when the Financial Regulator pulled the trigger and seized control of the insurer, their concern quickly mutated into panic. As the administration effectively took control of Quinn Insurance away from Sean Quinn, it represented a material change to the terms under which Quinn Group had borrowed the €1.3 billion. From the moment Matthew

Elderfield appointed Paul McCann and Michael McAteer as administrators, the profits of Quinn Insurance were no longer available to pay the debts of Quinn Group, leaving the group technically insolvent.

The 2008 presentation drawn up for Quinn Group's lenders forecast that the group would make a pre-tax profit of €439 million in 2009. But the economy was tanking, and that projection was looking far too optimistic. A report from FTI Consulting, an international advisory firm, concluded that Quinn Glass was performing well and the radiator division was holding up, but the core building-products division was losing money and market share. There was a solid business in the group, FTI said, but it was saddled with too much debt and would struggle to repay it all in light of the economic downturn.

It was the bondholders who decided to take action first. Shortly after the Quinn Insurance administration, they appointed Barry Russell, a charismatic New Yorker who was a partner in the London office of Bingham McCutchen, a US law firm, to look after their interests. With his bright-red braces, fashionable rectangular glasses and larger-than-life persona, Russell was like a character from a Tom Wolfe novel. He had worked in Bingham's London office for a number of years, but he had never forgotten his American background, and he coached youth ice hockey near his Surrey home. Once asked by a legal trade magazine to name his hero, Russell responded, 'Ken Dryden – Canadian MP, author, lawyer and one of the greatest ice-hockey net minders in the game.' In the same interview, Russell was asked who he would like to play him in a film about his life. 'Michael Douglas,' he replied, 'because he looks good in braces.'

In London, Russell had built a fine practice for Binghams and a fine reputation for himself. He frequently represented bondholders and creditors in massive corporate restructurings. In the aftermath of the Icelandic banking collapse in 2008, when Iceland's currency devalued by 80 per cent and its stock exchange lost 90 per cent of its value, he helped lenders sort out their exposure to Kaupthing, Landsbanki and Glitnir. Russell had carried out a similar role at Northern Rock in the UK, and had helped restructure Leeds United Football

Club. He even had some Irish experience, having advised the bondholders of Waterford Wedgwood, the luxury goods manufacturer
bankrolled by Tony O'Reilly.

Russell worked with FTI to represent the bondholders, who also
had legal advice from Maples & Calder, an international practice
with an office in Dublin. The Barclays-led banking syndicate had
separate financial advice from Deloitte as well as legal advice from
Clifford Chance, a London law firm, and Arthur Cox solicitors in
Dublin. After the approach from the bondholders, Russell had
quickly decided he wanted his own man on the board of Quinn
Group to oversee the restructuring. It wasn't up for discussion.

'The company is insolvent, that is a fact,' Russell told Liam McCaffrey, the Quinn chief executive. If Sean Quinn said 'no' to the
appointment of an independent director, the bondholders would
seek to have Quinn Group put into administration. Faced with such
a choice, Quinn and McCaffrey acquiesced to the demand of the
lenders.

After considering prospective directors for the Quinn job, Russell
settled on Murdoch McKillop, an accountant he had worked with on
the £5 billion restructuring of Marconi, the telecoms giant. The
lawyer and the lenders liked McKillop's pedigree.

He had spent three decades at Arthur Andersen, the global accounting group, where his insolvency assignments included winding up
Leyland DAF, the truck maker, and Maxwell Private Group following the death of Robert Maxwell, the media baron. He had even led
the workout of Andersen's own banking arrangements when the
financial scandals at Enron, the US energy group, took down the
accountancy practice.

From there, McKillop had become a founding partner at Talbot
Hughes McKillop in London, a specialist advisory firm 'working for
companies in stressed and distressed situations'. It was a boutique
consultancy specializing in restructurings and corporate workouts.
McKillop was a man in demand. Like Russell's, his CV included
restructuring Icelandic banks. He had also advised the government of
Brunei and been lead adviser on the £2.1 billion restructuring of the

1. Sean Quinn photographed in the late 1980s (*John McAviney*)

2. Sean Quinn outside his family home, near Ballyconnell, Co. Cavan, in 1986. The plastic covering is still on the seats of his Mercedes (*Tony O'Shea*)

3. Sean Quinn and his only son, Sean Junior, in the family home in 1986 (*Tony O'Shea*)

4. Sean Quinn with his children in 1986: (*left to right*) Aoife, Colette, Ciara, Sean Junior. His youngest child, Brenda, was born the following year (*Tony O'Shea*)

5. Sean Quinn's block-making operation near Derrylin in 1986. He built his first cement factory the following year (*Tony O'Shea*)

6. Sean Quinn overseeing construction of the Slieve Russell Hotel, his 'baby', in the early 1990s (*Sunday Business Post*)

7. Sean Quinn outside the Slieve Russell in 2001

8. Sean Quinn with the Taoiseach, Bertie Ahern, opening the Q Centre in Blanchardstown, the Dublin offices of Quinn Insurance, in September 2004

9. (*above*) The Quinn Group helicopter, pictured in 2003 (*Fergal Phillips / Sunday Times*)

10. (*left*) The Quinn Group Dassault Falcon private jet, bought in 2005; after it was sold, it ended up in Iran

11. Sean and Patricia Quinn's family home, built in 2004, adjacent to the Slieve Russell Hotel (*Lorraine Teevan*)

12. The Giant's Grave, the tomb relocated by Sean Quinn from the slopes of Slieve Rushen to the grounds of the Slieve Russell to make way for a quarry (*Catherine Daly*)

13. Quinn Group headquarters near Derrylin, Co. Fermanagh (*Quinn Group*)

14. Quinn Group cement plant outside Ballyconnell (*Quinn Group*)

15. Sean Quinn pictured in 2009, the year before his empire began to collapse (*Quinn Group*)

16. Sean Quinn and his wife, Patricia, at a function in 2011

Le Meridien hotel group, which had more than 120 hotels in fifty countries.

Most recently, McKillop had been adviser and board member on the £1.7 billion restructuring of the Four Seasons Healthcare Group, one of the biggest and most complex debt processes since the start of the credit crunch. Four Seasons had defaulted on its debts in the autumn of 2008, leaving uncertainty over the future of the group and its 21,000 employees. McKillop and his Talbot Hughes McKillop colleagues had worked on the solution, which halved the group's debt, gave a share in the business to its lenders, and extended the term of its remaining loans. Russell wanted McKillop to see if he could do something similar at Quinn Group.

The Quinn role piqued McKillop's interest and he was keen to take the job. He worked the phones assiduously to convince the lenders he was the right choice. It was a different type of challenge for him – unlike many of his corporate turnarounds, Quinn was a family business with a strong founder still at the helm. With retirement just a few years away, McKillop was relishing a fresh test. Moreover, having spent years working in continental Europe, the Far East and the USA, it was a relatively short hop over to Derrylin from his office in London.

In particularly complex situations, like that at Quinn, McKillop would take an executive role at a company, giving him a strong position in any negotiations. For the Quinn assignment, he was appointed to the board of Quinn Group (NI), the Northern Ireland-based operating company. McKillop's job was to build a consensus between Quinn Group and its lenders on the future of the company – without the messy business of insolvency. For a short period of time, he would effectively take charge of the company and try to fix it from the inside out.

The key issue was tackling the company's debt pile. The lenders knew they might have to write off some money; McKillop was appointed to tell them how much, and what Sean Quinn was willing to do in return. It was an interesting dynamic: once on the board of Quinn Group, McKillop's legal and financial duty would be to the company – which was still owned by Sean and Patricia Quinn's five children – and not to the lenders. But to do his job properly, he needed the respect and trust of the banks and bondholders.

In a parallel universe, Murdoch McKillop and Sean Quinn could have been friends. McKillop was born in October 1947, just over a year after the Fermanagh businessman. Like Quinn, he was broadly built and physically strong, a man with presence, used to taking charge of situations. His thick eyebrows and grey sideburns contrasted starkly with the dark hair around the sides of his head. On top, he was completely bald. Beyond their ages and influence, however, McKillop and Quinn had little in common.

A proud Scot, McKillop retained his native accent despite a career based in London. He was a keen sailor and his yacht, *Lafayette*, was a strong performer in international competitions. He kept *Lafayette* and another racing boat, *Saskia*, berthed at the Royal Northern & Clyde Yacht Club, where he was a well-regarded member. The yacht club is in Rhu, a village north of Glasgow on the shores of the Gare Loch. In the nineteenth century, Rhu was fashionable as the residence for wealthy Glasgow ship owners and merchants. It has one other claim to fame, as the birthplace of Moses McNeil, Peter McNeil and Peter Campbell – three of the four founders of Glasgow Rangers football club.

In the predominantly Catholic counties of Cavan and Fermanagh, the heartland of Sean Quinn's business empire, Murdoch McKillop's name immediately set him apart. 'I'd say you're a Rangers supporter,' Quinn said to McKillop, not long after meeting him for the first time in April 2010. Others picked up on it, too, making occasional barbed comments about marching season, or about orange being McKillop's favourite colour. McKillop knew what it was all about – his name made him sound like a Protestant preacher, and Quinn was an Irish nationalist running a border business with a mainly Catholic workforce. Quinn and his senior staff didn't like the fact that McKillop was on the board of the group at all. The jibes were their way of letting him know he was an outsider. It wasn't subtle, but it wasn't meant to be. It didn't matter that McKillop cared little for Rangers.

His job title, interim executive director, IED for short, wasn't helping either. A different type of IED – improvised explosive devices – had gained notoriety during the wars in Iraq, killing and maiming soldiers and civilians alike. Fermanagh had seen its share of IEDs during the Troubles, and McKillop's job title became a source of amusement for a group of Quinn executives. In their eyes, Murdoch McKillop was the explosive device with the potential to blow up the Quinn Group.

The animosity towards McKillop had very simple roots: he had been foisted on Sean Quinn at the explicit demand of the Quinn Group's lenders. Outwardly, though, Sean Quinn had made all the right noises when McKillop took his seat at the boardroom table in April 2010. Quinn and McCaffrey both told the Scot that they wanted to come to an agreement with the banks and bondholders about the debt, adding that they felt Quinn Insurance would be out of administration and back in the family's control within months.

Quinn Group had always had two boards. Quinn Group (NI) was the main operational entity, the company that held the debts and ran the show. The Quinn family held their shares through another company, Quinn Group (ROI). This latter company had been established to take advantage of the Republic of Ireland's 12.5 per cent corporate tax rate, and most of the group's profits flowed through it. But the €1.3 billion debt and the responsibility for all the manufacturing operations rested with the Northern Ireland company, which McKillop had been dispatched to sort out. The two boards had always overlapped, with membership made up of Sean Quinn, his wife Patricia, and a small number of key executives and Quinn confidants.

When McKillop was appointed to the NI board, Quinn immediately approached the Scotsman with an idea. He said he would resign from the board of the Northern Ireland company. His wife would follow suit, and his brother Peter, too. Quinn told McKillop that the family would 'regroup' on the board of the main shareholder company, Quinn Group (ROI). McKillop was pleasantly surprised by the suggestion, which would surely help to avoid any potential conflicts and confrontations. He agreed. It made sense that the Quinns would remain on the board of the shareholder company, but would step back from the main operating company.

In a statement, announced first to his workers on the company intranet on 18 April, Quinn cited the 'need to concentrate in the short term on Quinn family interests outside of Quinn Group Ltd and, in particular, on the interaction of these interests with Anglo Irish Bank'. The statement concluded, 'After 37 years of sustained development, Quinn Group Ltd has a mature, professional and skilled executive as well as a very experienced and independent board. For now, I want to concentrate on Quinn family interests outside of the group and bring all outstanding matters to a satisfactory conclusion in that regard.'

On 4 May, Kevin Lunney also resigned as a director of Quinn Group (NI). Dara O'Reilly, the finance director, departed the Northern Ireland board a week later. With Sean Quinn and his lieutenants gone from the operating company, McKillop had to find another board of directors. He turned to the three non-executive directors of the shareholder company, Pat O'Neill, Brendan Tuohy and Paddy Murphy, asking them to resign and become board members of the operating company. It was a simple switch that would bring the non-executives closer to the action. As far as McKillop was concerned, it made sense. The three all had knowledge of the group, and would be able to hit the ground running.

O'Neill, the former group managing director of Glanbia, the food group, had joined the board of Quinn Group (ROI) in March of the previous year. A review of the group by KPMG in 2007 had recommended that corporate governance be improved and the board bulked up with independent appointments. Quinn had resisted the changes all through 2008 before finally conceding in early 2009. O'Neill was independent, though not entirely unknown to the Quinns. He had strong GAA credentials and served on a number of influential GAA committees with Peter Quinn, Sean Quinn's brother. It was Peter who had sounded O'Neill out about joining the board of the company.

During their first discussion, in February 2009, O'Neill bluntly asked Peter Quinn about his brother's losses on his investment in Anglo Irish Bank. He had heard the rumours on the corporate grapevine and wanted some clarity before agreeing to become a director of the group. Peter said the losses topped €1 billion, though they were actually close to three times that amount. 'Look,' Peter had said, 'Sean is a gambler, but he can cover his losses.'

O'Neill asked, too, how the group had funded its various capital projects – having spent his own career in a capital-intensive industry, he was curious how Quinn was paying for his ultra-modern factories and equipment. 'Debt, Pat, debt,' Peter had replied. That response had stayed with O'Neill. Before agreeing to join the board, he spent three and a half hours in Derrylin, getting the grand tour of the industrial empire from Quinn and McCaffrey. O'Neill could not help but be impressed by what Quinn had built. Since then, he had been to four board meetings.

The first meeting, in Quinn's own Buswells Hotel, in March 2009, was called to sign off on the group's 2008 results. Quinn did not attend. O'Neill, who knew his way around accounts, asked for some clarity from PWC, the group auditor, about the scale of the family's debts. PWC said it was not in a position to reveal the figure.

Further board meetings followed in June, September and December 2009. At the end of the December meeting, in the Slieve Russell Hotel, Quinn asked his five children to come into the meeting room and meet the board. They were the owners of the business, he explained to O'Neill and the other directors; he was merely keeping it ticking over for them. The four daughters and one son were polite and respectful. It was an informal introduction and Sean Quinn Junior chatted about getting his golf handicap down to low single figures.

The next time Pat O'Neill heard from the Quinn Group was when the Financial Regulator appointed the Grant Thornton administrators to Quinn Insurance in March 2010. O'Neill had been very shocked, and very annoyed. He took his role as a Quinn Group director seriously and felt he had been kept out of the loop. In the aftermath of the appointment of the administrators, he considered resigning from the board. But he felt he owed it to himself and the company to stick around and help straighten out matters, said people with knowledge of the situation. So, when Murdoch McKillop asked O'Neill to take a more hands-on role, he accepted.

Brendan Tuohy had joined the Quinn Group (ROI) board on the

same day as O'Neill, following a similar approach from Peter Quinn. A former secretary-general of the Department of Communications, Energy and Natural Resources, Tuohy had left the civil service in September 2007. He knew Peter Quinn through Quinn's role as chairman of TG4, the Irish-language broadcaster. He had never had any dealings with Sean Quinn but knew his reputation and record of job creation.

Tuohy was regarded as a high-flier in the civil service, becoming secretary-general, the most senior role in a government department, while still in his forties. Within the Irish civil service, this was rare. He was confident with the media and never afraid to voice his opinion. At Quinn Group, though, he had followed the same path as O'Neill towards disillusionment. According to sources within the board, Tuohy was irritated that Quinn had not informed him of the negotiations with the Financial Regulator before Quinn Insurance went into administration.

By Quinn Group standards, Paddy Murphy was a lifer. A veteran of Bank of Ireland, where he had been chief executive of Bank of Ireland Finance and had run the bank's operations in Northern Ireland, he had been on Quinn's board since 2004. Murphy had strong Northern Ireland links, as a former president of the Northern Ireland Chamber of Commerce and chairman of Co-operation Ireland, a charity that supported the Northern Ireland peace process. He had been in demand since leaving the bank, taking on directorships at Choice Hotels, Data Electronics and Boundary Capital, a private equity investment group. At Quinn Group, Murphy had quickly aligned himself with O'Neill and Tuohy when they arrived on the board in 2009, again feeling his appointment had been viewed by Quinn as 'decorative rather than useful', according to well-placed sources.

All three men accepted McKillop's offer to quit the shareholder board and join the board of the operating company to work on the debt restructuring. Just a few weeks into his task, McKillop had his board in place, with Pat O'Neill occupying the chairman's seat that Sean Quinn himself had previously occupied at Quinn Group (NI). McKillop's next task would be bigger – to restructure the group's debt and broker a deal between Quinn and the lenders. He knew it wouldn't be easy. At the next board meeting, in summer 2010, it quickly became apparent just how hard it was going to be.

Liam McCaffrey, as group chief executive, remained an executive director on the NI board and could be Sean Quinn's eyes and ears. Then Peter Quinn, the businessman's brother, rowed back on his intention to leave the NI board, keeping a seat as a non-executive director. Before long, David Mackey, Quinn's friend and confidant, was there, too – not as a director but as a non-voting board observer on Quinn's behalf.

Both Mackey and Peter Quinn were Sean Quinn's men, loyal to a fault. They were vocal at board meetings and had little time for McKillop and his restructuring plans. In the series of hastily arranged board meetings that followed McKillop's arrival, they never tried to hide their animosity. Two years earlier, after being fined and reprimanded by the Financial Regulator, Sean Quinn had resigned from the board of Quinn Insurance, but retained de facto control.

Now it looked like he was trying the same tactic again.

Sean and Patricia Quinn regrouped on the board of Quinn Group (ROI) with Mackey, Kevin Lunney and Dara O'Reilly, and prepared to fight back. There were now effectively two boards for the Quinn Group, with very different agendas. The first task for the ROI board, and Lunney and O'Reilly in particular, was to assemble a plan for Sean Quinn to regain control of Quinn Insurance and resolve his difficulties with Anglo Irish Bank once and for all.

The Quinn Insurance administration had started badly from their point of view. With the company retreating from the British market, the administrators reckoned it was overstaffed. McAteer made the case that redundancies were needed, though Paul McCann was worried about how such a move would be perceived. There was public disquiet about the administration, and McCann thought it might be best to hang on for a few months and let the dust settle. Eventually, however, he agreed. The numbers did not stack up. Sean Quinn had prided himself on never laying off a worker. Now, with the business in administration and leaking customers, there were too many employees and too few customers. It was directly affecting the performance of the company, and the Grant Thornton partners had a mandate from the High Court to restore order to the business.

They worked the numbers, and decided that 900 staff, more than a third of the 2,450-strong workforce of Quinn Insurance, would be let go through a voluntary redundancy process. The announcement was made in early May, just over a month after the Financial Regulator had first installed the administrators. Of the 900 lay-offs, just over 300 would be from the office in Blanchardstown in Dublin. Some 235 would come from the Cavan headquarters, 190 would come from Enniskillen and 110 would be from Quinn Insurance's newest office, in Navan, Co. Meath. More than 50 jobs would be lost in Quinn Insurance's British offices in London and Manchester. The administrators said the cuts would save the business €30 million a year. In a personal statement, Sean Quinn said he was 'devastated' at the announcement.

McAteer and McCann then had to finalize a decision about the long-term future of Quinn Insurance. The administrators believed that Quinn Group, as the shareholder in the insurer, should be involved in any major decision about its future. Murdoch McKillop would be the group's point man in the process, joining the boards of a string of Quinn Insurance-related companies along with McAteer and McCann.

Leaving the company languishing in administration indefinitely was not an option. Customers look for certainty when picking an insurer and each day the business was in administration, the uncertainty around the business was growing. Sales were falling and the administrators did not have the cash to make decisions on capital expenditure. Quinn Insurance needed a new owner, one that could inject funds into the company and manage it professionally.

Despite some public calls for the insurance company to be nationalized, there was no political appetite for such a move. Once it became clear that Sean Quinn was not going to write a cheque to restore the company's solvency, the administrators knew that Quinn Insurance would have to be sold on the open market. In the opinion of the administrators, it should happen as quickly as possible to limit the

disruption to the business and avoid further lay-offs. At the start of
June 2010, McAteer and McCann announced the appointment of
Macquarie Capital Europe, the European unit of an Australian investment bank, to conduct a formal sales process. If he wanted his
insurance company back, Sean Quinn would have to bid just like anyone else.

Quinn went on the offensive, giving a wide-ranging interview to
Prime Time, the RTÉ current affairs programme, on 3 June. He had
been hounded by print journalists seeking interviews but was wary
they would twist his words; he felt a television interview was the best
way to speak directly to the public, according to sources close to him
at the time. Kevin Lunney sat in as Quinn outlined to Paul Murphy,
an RTÉ reporter, his alternative to the planned sale of Quinn Insurance.

He described a scenario whereby Anglo would link up with the
Quinns to run Quinn Insurance. The profits from the insurer and
from the wider Quinn Group, if necessary, would be used to repay
the bank. 'What we would like to see is two things,' Quinn said.
'Firstly the profits of the enterprise go to the reduction of the Anglo
debt, one hundred per cent of it. The second thing we'd like to see is
that the jobs would continue to stay in rural Ireland, as many as possible. The jobs we've established in Cavan, our head office – we'd like
to think that the new arrangement, if it was accepted, would continue to be our head office. And that it clears all the debt. In seven
years' time – we have a projection to 2017 – we would have enough
profit made in the meantime, plus the value of the company in seven
years' time would clear a hundred per cent of the debt.'

Quinn claimed the Grant Thornton accountants knew nothing
about running an insurance company. 'Two months ago, Quinn
Direct was making €3 million a week; now it is losing €3 million a
week,' he said. Quinn Insurance was 'the most profitable insurance
company in Ireland for ten consecutive years', yet the administrators
were laying people off. He hinted that the administration decision
had been a political move by Elderfield and his team, designed to
show their authority after years of lax financial regulation.

Quinn's figures were fanciful. Before the administrators were appointed, the Quinn Insurance board had been in talks with Price-waterhouseCoopers (PWC) about finalizing the audit of the insurer's 2009 accounts. The draft unaudited financial statements indicated a loss of about €47 million, though PWC believed the provision for claims had actually been understated by €68 million. Instead of the €295 million profit forecast in the 2008 presentation, Quinn Insurance was facing a €115 million loss for 2009, even before the administrators were appointed. The 2009 accounts had yet to be finalized or published, however, and for the moment Sean Quinn could throw around figures with impunity.

During the interview, conducted in Quinn's wood-panelled office at Quinn Group headquarters in Derrylin, Murphy asked the businessman about the scale of his borrowings and the security that his creditors held against them. Quinn acknowledged that the overseas property assets had been used as collateral for his CFD gamble on Anglo, but there were few signs of remorse. 'All I can tell you is that we didn't do anything wrong with Anglo or anybody else,' Quinn said.

The interview did not go down well in the Financial Regulator's office. Elderfield and McMahon were willing to do a deal with Quinn if he came up with the money to restore the solvency of Quinn Insurance and acknowledged some wrongdoing. But here he was on national television, accusing them of stroke politics for career advancement.

Lunney and O'Reilly were meanwhile hard at work on Quinn's behalf. Dividing their time between the Slieve Russell and Buswells, they put flesh on the bones of Quinn's plan to repay Anglo. Through the summer of 2010 they worked on the plan, meeting executives from Anglo more than thirty times in total. Sean Quinn Junior contributed his knowledge of the insurance company, crunching the numbers on its reserving policies and loss ratios. Deutsche Bank and Goldman Sachs assessed the viability of the plan, and Mason Hayes & Curran, the Dublin commercial law firm, gave advice on how to structure the deal.

By late summer, they had assembled a 32-page document, effectively a rescue plan for Quinn Insurance. Quinn was proposing that he and his family would establish a new company, which could acquire Quinn Insurance for the nominal sum of €1. Anglo, despite already being owed more than €2.8 billion by the Quinn family, would lend 'the necessary funds' to the new company to restore solvency levels at the insurer and pay the banks and bondholders in order to release the guarantees they held. The 'necessary funds' would be a cool €650 million, a proposal that would push Quinn's Anglo debt – money now owed to the taxpayer – close to €3.5 billion.

The plan acknowledged that the 'injection of new capital, particularly at this difficult economic time, is significant', but argued the money would stay on deposit, purely to meet solvency requirements. Just by having the new capital, the insurer would increase in value, it argued. 'The risk, therefore, to the taxpayer, is effectively zero,' it declared. (It also argued there would be no need for the €650 million injection if the Regulator would just accept the 'prevailing alternative view' that the financial guarantees that prompted the administration process had no effect on the insurer's solvency and that the administration move was wrong.)

The Quinns would step back and the insurer would get a new board of 'experienced and reputable individuals' approved by the Financial Regulator and including government nominees, if necessary. From then on, all profits of the insurer would be used to repay Anglo. Within seven years, there would be a lucrative stock market listing or trade sale of Quinn Insurance, the proceeds of which would also go towards the debt. Quinn calculated that the plan would generate just over €2 billion, after Anglo had been repaid its initial investment of €650 million. To settle the rest of the €2.8 billion debt, he could sell the international properties, estimated in the plan to be worth an optimistic €600 million, and dip into the profits of the Quinn Group's manufacturing operations.

There were holes in the plan. It neglected to mention the €1.3 billion the manufacturing group owed to the non-Anglo lenders, and it made certain assumptions that were not easily explained. For instance, it estimated Quinn Insurance would make cumulative profits of €765 million over the next seven years – but only if the Quinn proposal was accepted. Under any other owner, it said, Quinn Insurance would make just €446 million in profit. As a knock-on effect, the company would be worth significantly less in any future flotation or trade sale.

The explanation given was that Quinn's 'unique operation' of the insurance business had allowed it to make higher profits than competitors in the past – and would continue to do so in the future. 'If the current model is maintained into the future then it is reasonable to expect that this advantage will be maintained. If, however, a TPI [third-party insurer] becomes responsible for the operations of the business, then it is also reasonable to expect that this advantage will be diminished, with returns reverting to those more commonly found in the market,' it said.

Incredibly, Sean Quinn was arguing that no one could run Quinn Insurance as well as he could. Despite his present difficulties, despite his history of regulatory breaches, despite being shut out by administrators, he was saying that he was still the best man to run Quinn Insurance. 'If the plan is not allowed to proceed, then the serious demise of critical employment in historically deprived areas, the loss of indigenous insurance competition and the crystallization of losses to the state from Quinn family debt is almost inevitable, along with an inevitable legal dispute for many years,' the document said.

Right through summer and into autumn 2010, Lunney and O'Reilly worked on the basis that the plan would be acceptable to Anglo. 'They met everyone and anyone who would agree to meet them,' said a source close to the situation. 'There was no Plan B. There was Plan A and Plan A.'

Lunney and O'Reilly presented the plan to McAteer and McCann. To the administrators, it looked bonkers. The financial projections seemed far too optimistic and there were basic flaws, such as the omission of any interest payments on the debt and details of how the €1.3 billion owed to the bondholders and banks would be addressed. Looking for another €650 million from Anglo just seemed delusional. 'The lady down the road is going to buy it – she just needs the bank to give her €650 million,' McAteer would say when people asked him how the sale of the insurance company was going. The way the Regulator felt about Quinn, the lady down the road had more chance of getting the money. Murdoch McKillop, with a lifetime of experience in restructuring, agreed.

Richard Woodhouse, the Anglo banker, was also taken aback by Quinn's grand plan to save his business. 'Look, guys,' he had told Lunney and O'Reilly when they tabled the proposition, 'you're going to require us in this process to add €650 million, and that is a big number on top of €2.8 billion and rising.'

There was another big problem. Quinn wanted the money interest-free and wanted the interest clock to stop on the existing €2.8 billion. Woodhouse was astounded. The bank had to borrow money at a premium on the interbank market, and the Quinns were now looking for it for free. 'We can't just zero-rate everything,' he said repeatedly to O'Reilly and Lunney. Woodhouse ran the numbers on the proposal and concluded it would actually cost the bank €100 million a year. Over the seven-year duration of the plan, keeping Sean Quinn in business would cost the bank – and the state – €700 million.

Apart from the mind-boggling arithmetic, there was another issue putting Woodhouse off the Quinn deal. Anglo was a state-owned bank, and lending new cash to a financially distressed insurance company was likely to be viewed by the EU authorities as state aid. As such, the deal would require clearance from Brussels – and that seemed highly unlikely. Woodhouse raised his concern over state aid with Quinn personally, but his impression was that Quinn either did not understand or did not care. In private, Lunney and O'Reilly persisted in telling people that a proposal with Anglo was close to being formalized.

Despite its serious reservations, Anglo did not completely rule out structuring some sort of deal with Quinn, either publicly or privately. The bank still had to get to grips with how it could recoup the €2.8 billion it was owed and was keen not to alienate the businessman until it had a firm strategy in place. 'It was seen as better to have him inside the tent pissing out rather than outside the tent pissing in,' said one source close to the bank.

Managing the bank's relationship with Sean Quinn was originally supposed to be a small part of Woodhouse's overall brief, a loose end from the days of Sean FitzPatrick and David Drumm that needed resolving. Now, it was fast becoming his full-time duty; his diary was littered with Quinn-related meetings, and his briefcase packed with all manner of Quinn documents.

Concerned Irish Business, a pro-Quinn lobby group, was doing its bit, too, meeting politicians and constantly demanding answers from the Grant Thornton administrators and from Anglo. The campaign got vicious at times, questioning the ability of the administrators and the fees they were being paid. The lobby group had dozens of meetings with local politicians, led by Brendan Smith, the Fianna Fáil TD for Cavan/Monaghan, and wrote to Brian Lenihan, the Minister for Finance. He declined to get involved.

Lenihan had plenty of other issues to contend with. The public finances were in tatters and the banking crisis was worsening by the month. In May 2010, Greece had had to accept a €110 billion bailout from the European Commission and the International Monetary Fund. Market watchers hoped the deal would not only help resolve Greece's financial situation but stop so-called contagion – the spread of the debt crisis to other eurozone nations. If that happened, Ireland was close to the top of the list of endangered countries.

The cost of bailing out Ireland's banks had spiralled beyond expectations – Anglo alone had received €14.3 billion by the end of May 2010 to cover impairments on its disastrous property lending. The transfer of loans from Anglo to the National Asset Management Agency (NAMA), at a worse-than-expected discount of more than 50 per cent, had blown a hole in previous forecasts. In an attempt to draw a line under the banking collapse, the Central Bank had also set new thresholds for the amount of capital a bank had to hold, which were higher than international standards. The total bill for Anglo was likely to be €22 billion and Aynsley admitted that the 'lion's share' of that would 'never be seen again'.

'At every hand's turn our worst fears have been surpassed,' Lenihan had said when details of the NAMA transfers were announced in March 2010. Those fears were about to be surpassed again. On 25 August, Standard and Poor's, the ratings agency, said that the cost of bailing out Irish banks could be between €45 billion and €50 billion. Anglo alone could account for €35 billion of the total, the agency said.

Six days later, the bank announced it had lost €8.2 billion in the first half of 2010, a new record for an Irish corporate loss. In the six-month period, depositors had taken €5.5 billion of their money out of the bank. With the bank and the state tied together by nationalization, the interest rate the state paid on its international debt spiked. Lenders were saying loud and clear that Ireland's banks were a risky proposition. Because of the 2008 bank guarantee and the nationalization of Anglo, this meant that the Irish sovereign was also a risky proposition. Ireland was being frozen out of the international funding markets.

There was worse to come. On 30 September, Elderfield and his financial regulation team at the Central Bank announced details of the fourth recapitalization of the Irish banks. Elderfield estimated that, based on the discounts NAMA was applying to Anglo's loans, the bank would need €29.3 billion in funds from the government. The figure could rise by another €5 billion if the commercial property market failed to recover for a decade. The total bill for all the banks would be €46 billion, and possibly as high as €51 billion. It was 'essentially lost money', Patrick Honohan, the Central Bank Governor, said on the day, dubbed 'Black Thursday' by the media. As a result, Ireland's deficit would be 32 per cent of GDP for 2010, more than ten times the EU limit of 3 per cent. The government would have to find drastic new ways to balance the books.

Still Lunney and O'Reilly claimed their appeals to opposition politicians about Sean Quinn's plight appeared to be bearing some fruit. They claimed support for the Quinn repayment proposal from opposition politicians, including Michael Noonan, the Fine Gael finance spokesman, and Joan Burton, the Labour Party finance spokeswoman. Quinn supporters took every opportunity to highlight the thousands of jobs that relied on Quinn Insurance and the wider Quinn Group. That was a language politicians could understand.

Quinn was assembling other weapons for his fightback. It was much too late to challenge the appointment of the administrators, but Quinn still wanted to prove that the Regulator's reasons for the administration were fundamentally wrong. The Regulator had pinned the administration on the existence of the financial guarantees between the insurance company and the Quinn Group. But PWC, the insurer's auditor, had been aware of the guarantees for several years and had no issue with them, Quinn argued. In filings to the Regulator after the administrators were appointed, PWC stood its ground and rejected the Regulator's view that the guarantees were not accounted for properly: 'PWC is of the view that its audit opinions in respect of the years 2005, 2006, 2007 and 2008 were appropriate.' Furthermore, it said, 'PWC is not aware of any decision having been taken within QIL [Quinn Insurance Limited] not to disclose the guarantees.'

Quinn commissioned the London office of Moore Stephens, an international accountancy firm, to have a look at the guarantees. When the accountants delivered their 45-page report, after three months' work, it was news the Quinns wanted to hear: as far as Moore Stephens was concerned, the guarantees had been properly accounted for and didn't affect the solvency of the insurer. 'In our opinion, prima facie, no disclosures in respect of the guarantees issued by the subsidiary undertakings of QIL needed to be made to the Financial Regulator,' Moore Stephens said. 'The existence of the guarantees did not have an impact on QIL's solvency requirements in its annual returns for 2005, 2006, 2007 and 2008,' it added, though the 2009 figures were 'more complex' because the insurer was in administration.

Moore Stephens pointed out that the Regulator had never sought a group solvency return from Quinn Insurance. Quinn forwarded the report to the Regulator. There was no response. Even if the Regulator was minded to accept the Moore Stephens interpretation, the fact remained that Quinn Insurance had been in regular breach of its solvency requirements even before the guarantees came to light. In the early part of 2010, the insurer's solvency margin was just 107 per cent, well below the 150 per cent level required by the Financial Regulator. Sean Quinn had been given every opportunity to resolve the situation and had failed to do so.

★

Day after day, week after week, Michael McAteer and Paul McCann went about their new job, running an insurance behemoth at the behest of the Financial Regulator. It was a complicated business, and it took them some time to get their heads around it. Upon their appointment, McAteer had solicited advice from industry experts: What should I look out for? What is the key to insurance? If you were in my position, what would you do? Invariably, each answer settled on the issue of reserving, the heart and soul of insurance. If your reserving is right, McAteer was told, you will have nothing to worry about. So, as they prepared to sell Quinn Insurance in the autumn of 2010, McAteer and McCann went on a crash course in insurance reserving.

The administrators knew that all prospective buyers would require independent validation of the company's reserves. Unusually, Quinn Insurance had operated without any in-house actuaries, even despite being instructed by the Financial Regulator in April 2009 to establish an in-house actuarial function. Instead, the company used an outside firm, Milliman, one of the biggest independent actuarial firms in the world, to calculate its reserving requirements. The Milliman figures would then be audited by PWC as part of its annual review of the group. There had been differences of opinion between Milliman and PWC about the reserves in the past, however, including the €68 million figure for the 2009 accounts, and the administrators decided the figures needed a fresh look. McAteer and McCann turned to actuaries with Grant Thornton in London, who set about developing the necessary controls and procedures to make sure Quinn Insurance was being viably run.

When they had been seeking an investment bank to sell Quinn Insurance, all the prospective candidates for the job – including Macquarie Capital – had recommended that the administrators should perform due diligence on the insurance reserves. That way, everyone would know exactly what they were getting. Due diligence would settle a few issues for the administrators as well. During mid 2010, they had noticed a trend of reserve provisions increasing over time, rather than staying steady, as would be expected if the company had fixed, predictable reserving rules. They suspected some staff at Quinn

Insurance had been reluctant to set aside appropriate reserves to cover large cases while Sean Quinn was in charge and were now covering their tracks.

The administrators asked EMB, a British actuarial firm, to do the job. McKillop, the administrators' liaison with Quinn Group, was happy to have EMB on board. EMB had a reputation as the toughest actuarial firm in London, and McKillop told McCann and McAteer it would be better to have them on board working for the administrators rather than have them poking around Quinn Insurance on behalf of a prospective buyer.

EMB started its work in July 2010. As it crunched the numbers, the administrators worked on a sales memorandum with Macquarie Capital. It was almost ready to go when, in late August, EMB came back with its initial results. The results stunned McAteer and McCann. EMB said Quinn Insurance was systematically under-provisioning for future claims and that the reserves needed to be almost tripled. That would leave a €400 million hole in the 2009 accounts.

The EMB review painted a damning picture of unsustainably low pricing, poor claims handling and inadequate reserving. It pointed to a reluctance among Quinn staff to set aside adequate reserves for large cases and took a dim view of Quinn's aggressive claims settlement strategy, even for smaller, everyday claims. If a customer's claim was genuinely worth €10,000 – to replace their car or pay medical costs, for example – and they settled for €7,000 with Quinn Insurance, they were out of pocket by €3,000. That went against the basic principle of insurance, that a customer should be in the same position after a claim was settled as before. It was bad for customers and bad for the insurance industry as a whole. EMB advised the reserves should be bulked up to reflect the full cost of settling a claim according to industry norms.

The review also queried Quinn's pricing, particularly in the UK market. The insurance company had expanded into the UK just as the insurance sector there was in a downward cycle, meaning Quinn was undercutting rivals that were already losing money. The underwriting of professional indemnity insurance for lawyers in the UK was particularly disastrous. The company had offered to insure lawyers in the same way it did in Ireland. In the UK, however, there was a much stronger culture of people suing lawyers and lawyers suing each other, particularly in the economic downturn. The EMB figures and subsequent reviews by the administrators would find that for the €93 million in professional indemnity premiums it took in, Quinn Insurance was facing €333 million in projected claims. If the claims were fully and properly reserved, the company was seriously in the red.

The administrators instructed EMB to double-, triple- and quadruple-check the figures. On 5 November 2010, EMB confirmed its position. After examining EMB's analysis, Milliman and PWC eventually revisited their 2009 figures for the insurer. EMB was correct, they said. It was an astounding development that meant the historical figures produced by Quinn Insurance's actuaries and auditors had been spectacularly wrong. When the reserves were increased to an appropriate level, Quinn Insurance was desperately unprofitable.

McAteer and McCann now had a big problem. Until the EMB review landed, they had been working on the assumption that Quinn Insurance was an inherently profitable company with a temporary solvency problem. Now that assumption had been shattered, and there was little or no equity value in the company. Over the summer months, more than ninety parties had expressed an interest in acquiring Quinn Insurance. By the time of the deadline for formal expressions of interest in September 2010, this number had reduced to eight. With the damning new information about the company's finances, those eight could take fright. It did not help, either, that the extent of the meltdown in the Irish economy was becoming clearer by the month.

Murdoch McKillop was as stunned as the administrators at the development. Quinn Group had been making headway on its financial restructuring on the basis that there was some value in Quinn Insurance. If Quinn Insurance was virtually worthless, Quinn Group, with its €1.3 billion in debts, also had a huge problem.

On foot of the EMB report, in late 2010, the Financial Regulator reported PWC to the Chartered Accountants Regulatory Board, an industry body that polices the compliance of accountants in Ireland, for its audit work on Quinn Insurance. The Quinn Insurance administrators would later launch a High Court legal action against PWC over the issue.

Officials from the Regulator also expressed their concerns to Anglo management. They could not understand why the bank was still toying with the idea of doing a deal with Sean Quinn. Elderfield and his staff made their position quite clear. There was no way Quinn would pass a fitness and probity test, a must under the new regulatory regime, and there was no way he would be allowed to have any involvement with any regulated entity. The Regulator was saying in the bluntest possible terms it would not sanction any Quinn Insurance deal that involved Sean Quinn.

By the end of November, with the public finances completely shot, the government agreed to enter a bailout loan arrangement with the International Monetary Fund, European Union and European Central Bank, subject to strict conditions and oversight. The bailout would amount to €85 billion, with €35 billion earmarked for fixing the broken banking system. Now, not only were Anglo Irish Bank and Sean Quinn's insurance company in the hands of the state, but the state itself had handed its economic sovereignty over to its own creditors.

The EMB numbers put an end to any possibility of Anglo taking a further punt on Sean Quinn. Aynsley, Woodhouse and Hunersen went back to the drawing board. They knew Anglo was still central to any prospective deal at Quinn Insurance. The bank had security over the Quinn Group itself, and the group was the shareholder in the insurance company.

They approached Liberty Mutual, the US insurance giant, which was one of the handful of parties still interested in acquiring Quinn Insurance. Ted Kelly, Liberty's chairman and chief executive, was originally from Keady in Co. Armagh and had made no secret of his desire to buy the firm. Liberty, the fifth-biggest insurer in the world, had an impressive balance sheet and a track record of buying troubled insurers. Plus, Liberty had no existing business to speak of in Ireland, so a Liberty takeover could preserve jobs at Quinn.

On 9 December 2010, senior officials from Anglo informed Quinn's representatives that the bank was submitting a bid with an unnamed third party. The Quinns were out of the picture. At a meeting four days later, the bankers told Quinn's people that they had concluded it was no longer possible for the Quinn family to repay their debts.

The Quinn lieutenants went into overdrive, pleading their case in separate meetings with the secretary-general of the Department of Finance, the chief executive of the National Treasury Management Agency and Michael Noonan, then Fine Gael spokesman on finance. All three listened to the Quinn proposal. None followed up with Quinn's people.

Having championed a link-up with Anglo, Quinn's lieutenants now argued the bank had double-crossed them. In a joint venture with Liberty, Anglo would only have partial ownership of the insurance company and could only recover a fraction of what it was owed, Lunney said. Why was the bank that had driven Ireland to a bailout, a bank that was being wound down, being allowed to take over Quinn Insurance in conjunction with an American insurer? How would that address the repayment of the Quinn debt?

Lunney and O'Reilly continued to tout Quinn's repayment plan, with slight alterations. If there was a problem getting Anglo to recapitalize the insurance company, why not get AIB, Bank of Ireland or even NAMA to do it? 'We're hoping somebody somewhere will allow the Quinn proposal to go ahead, in the interests of keeping the company open and the jobs there,' Lunney said. 'If the Quinns don't own the shares [in Quinn Insurance], how can they repay the debt?' The pleas fell on deaf ears.

By early 2011, the administrators were itching to do a deal. It was more than nine months since their appointment had been confirmed, nine months of reassuring and placating staff, of listening to Quinn supporters attack them and their work. There was no crock of gold, only a damaged insurance business and a bigger mess at Quinn Group, where the refinancing talks were dragging on and repayment deadlines were being missed. Something needed to happen, and fast.

Michael McAteer knew there was nothing more corrosive than uncertainty. He decided to brief staff and lay a few matters to rest.

Despite what the Quinns and their supporters were saying, there was no Quinn bid for the insurance business, he told the workers. Sean Quinn would not be involved in Quinn Insurance in future and everyone should get used to that idea.

The administrators asked everyone involved not to jeopardize whatever chance there was of a deal. McAteer and McCann weren't fooling themselves that this was the endgame. There would surely be a court action, an attempt to injunct the sale. Quinn had never accepted defeat before, and they didn't expect him to start accepting it now.

7

'We have a plan and we think it can work'

There are certain incontestable truths about people like Murdoch McKillop. If they arrive at your business, your business is in trouble. The longer they stay, the deeper the trouble. By the end of March 2011, Murdoch McKillop was approaching his first anniversary as interim executive director of the Quinn Group. Getting to the year mark would be no cause for celebration.

McKillop had helped restructure much bigger companies in much shorter time frames. He had dealt with the biggest banks and bondholders in the world and helped resolve some major corporate tussles. But he could not deal with Sean Quinn. He had spent a year trying, without success. Most of the time, Quinn simply would not listen to him. Even when he did listen, he chose to ignore what was being said. In all his years in business, McKillop had never dealt with anyone quite like Sean Quinn.

In the immediate aftermath of his arrival in Derrylin, Murdoch McKillop's focus was on determining the true financial position of the Quinn manufacturing companies. He sought thirteen-week rolling cash forecasts from accountants at PWC, to see if the group could cover its overheads. Cash generation was a bit of an obsession for McKillop – in his career in corporate recovery, he had seen enough situations where a shortage of cash caused problems for companies whose accounts looked healthy. With €1.3 billion owed to the banks and bondholders and Anglo Irish Bank chasing a further €2.8 billion from the Quinn family, the group was not in a position to borrow any more money. It would have to live within its means.

McKillop was acutely conscious that the Quinn Group was in breach of its banking covenants and, according to the strict letter of the law, insolvent. So, at each board meeting, the directors had to verbally agree that a restructuring was possible. If they did not believe a deal was possible, they would have been bound by company law to wind up the company and install a liquidator.

Quinn, McKillop had been told upon arrival, had a reputation for building the best factories possible and making better products than many of his rivals. He would compete on quality, and he would compete on price, absorbing initial losses until he had amassed a significant market share. 'If I build the lowest-cost product with the highest-quality machines, I'm going to win. It's just a matter of when I'm going to win,' Quinn would tell his directors. For years, it had worked. Now, though, McKillop was seeing signs of strain in the Quinn strategy.

Leuna, an industrial town of barely 15,000 people near Leipzig, was home to the Leunawerke, a large complex of chemical factories. In 2006, Quinn Group had started building a factory in the complex to produce methyl methacrylate (MMA), a clear liquid used in manufacturing plastic. It would be the first MMA plant built in Europe for more than three decades. Quinn planned to use production technology developed in Japan to make 100,000 tonnes of MMA a year at Leuna. It would be a big investment, at least €300 million, but he was certain it would justify itself.

The MMA plant was supposed to be up and running within two years, but it had been mothballed in 2009 at the height of the credit crunch. The venture had eaten up €200 million at that point and was only half finished. McKillop was told it would cost another €200 million to finish, a jaw-dropping amount. That sort of money was just not available to the Quinn Group. Deciding what to do with Leuna would be one of McKillop's many headaches.

Long before McKillop's installation on the Group board, Quinn's lenders had also been concerned about the amount of money Sean Quinn was taking out of the group for personal and family investments.

In 2008, for instance, €200 million had been paid from the shareholders' funds of the group to the five Quinn children. At the time, a spokesman for the company said the payment was made 'to facilitate the development of their independent wealth portfolios'.

McKillop began to go through the books to see what other payments had been made. He was stunned by what he found: approximately €800 million had been taken out for the benefit of the Quinn family, according to a report prepared by the advisers at FTI Consulting. Almost €700 million of the total went to cover losses on Quinn's purchase of the Anglo CFDs. The rest, around €106 million, had been used to fund the purchase of the Belfry on behalf of Sean Quinn Junior.

Having seen so much cash leak out of the business for the direct benefit of the Quinn family, the banks and bondholders determined that no more would follow. At the end of 2009, they ordered Quinn to stop taking money from the business. He agreed and gave the lenders a covenant, a binding commitment, that no further money would be removed without their express permission. There had been no request from Quinn for a derogation in the six months since then, so the lenders assumed he had stayed true to his word. In May 2010, however, just a month after arriving in Derrylin, McKillop was informed that €6 million had been taken out of the group to pay an interest bill relating to the Belfry.

The money had left the group in February, just two months after Quinn had given his commitment to stop raiding company money for personal use. The payment had been sanctioned by Quinn but the lenders had not been informed. They were furious. Barry Russell, the US lawyer who was representing the bondholders, started referring to the Belfry payment as 'Sean Quinn's green fees'.

McKillop's next discovery was a hitherto unknown company called Coill Investments. In his speech at the Slieve Russell in March 2007, Sean Quinn had said he wanted to help his management and staff to share in the wealth he was generating. 'The company has become extremely wealthy and my family has become extremely wealthy,' he said at the time. 'So what we are trying to do now is to involve our management and staff in different schemes and in some of our property investments in China, in India and Russia. We already have them involved in one. We expect to expand that, and some financial instruments as well.'

Now McKillop was finding out exactly what Quinn had meant.

Coill Investments had been established as an investment vehicle for Quinn staff. The investments were chosen by Quinn himself, and Quinn was so confident that he provided each investor with a guarantee he would cover any losses out of his own pocket. It must have seemed like a no-brainer to the Quinn Group staff, who invested more than €7 million via Coill. Every employee who invested got a letter of guarantee signed by Sean Quinn personally.

As McKillop discovered, Quinn had indeed found a home for the employee money – much of it went in Anglo Irish Bank CFDs. He had taken the money from his own employees and invested it in Anglo. As Anglo's share price collapsed and Quinn had to cover the cost of his losses, the €7 million investment morphed into a €21 million loss on CFDs, according to internal company documents.

In March 2011, shortly before Quinn Insurance went into administration, Quinn stuck to his word and paid the employees back the value of their initial investments. But it was not that simple. The letter of guarantee that Quinn gave his employees had the Quinn Group logo on the top but it was not a Quinn Group letter; it did not have the company registration details along the bottom margin or the list of directors, as would be expected. It was simply a letterhead that Quinn frequently used for private and personal correspondence.

While the letter of guarantee was personal, however, Quinn repaid the employees from company coffers. The distinction between company and personal funds did not mean much to Quinn, but it meant a lot to McKillop and the bondholders. When McKillop found out about it in May and told the banks and bondholders, they were infuriated. The issue was not the repayment of the money – the banks would have agreed to a waiver rather than risk the wrath of the employees. No, the issue was that Quinn had once again raided company funds without seeking their permission.

It did not end there. As the Coill Investments payback was

essentially a payment from employer to employee, there was a tax liability owed. The group, already pressed for cash, had to go to the tax authorities and cough up another €7 million to cover outstanding taxes.

McKillop, still digging, discovered a similar situation on an investment deal in Ukraine. Quinn had given his senior staff the chance to invest in the purchase of the Leonardo Business Centre in Kiev. It was reported in 2008 that Quinn Group had bought the 24-storey centre in the heart of Kiev's business district for $95 million. In fact, Quinn employees, friends and family had a 45 per cent stake in the block, while another 40 per cent was held by a fund managed by Quinn Life, the group's investment and pensions business. The Quinn Group owned just 15 per cent of the Leonardo property, though it included it in corporate presentations as a group asset.

Again, Quinn had guaranteed the investment personally; again, the letter carried the company logo. No money had been paid out to date, but it was another potential problem. McKillop decided it was time for someone to take responsibility. He pointed the finger firmly at the man in charge of the money, Dara O'Reilly, the Quinn Group finance director, who had been a director of Coill and was close to the transactions. That was the reason why O'Reilly was ushered off the board of the operating company on 11 May 2010. Still loyal to Quinn, he would cross over to the board of Quinn Group (ROI).

McKillop wanted his own man monitoring the money. He got on the phone to Neil Robson, a colleague from Talbot Hughes McKillop. Robson was on the next flight to Dublin and was quickly installed as interim finance director of Quinn Group.

Through the summer of 2010, McKillop worked on the plan to restructure the Quinn Group balance sheet and rescue the companies. By September, he had developed a plan, a structure to save the Quinn businesses while also placating the lenders. It was a simple proposition. The solid manufacturing businesses would be ring-fenced and placed into a new company. A sustainable level of debt, a figure that McKillop and his team believed the businesses were actually capable of servicing, would be attached to those operations.

The rest of the debt would be moved to a separate company, which would include non-core assets like Quinn's corporate jet and helicopter. The half-built MMA plant in Leuna would also be placed into this non-performing company. All of those assets would be sold off and the proceeds used to pay down the borrowings. The proceeds of the sale of Quinn Insurance would also be used to pay down this debt mountain, though, based upon new information emerging as part of the administration process, McKillop was fast becoming convinced there would not be any windfall there.

Under the McKillop plan, between €720 million and €750 million of the €1.3 billion debt would be left with the manufacturing business. The rest would be attached to the non-performing company with its mishmash of assets. The plan amounted to an admission that much of the €550 million debt linked with the non-performing company would never be repaid. But McKillop reckoned he could sell the plan to the lenders. 'Business is business, and some money is better than no money,' he told colleagues.

He also knew that the lenders would demand concessions from Quinn, so McKillop was asking Quinn to do two things. First, he would have to pay a higher rate of interest on the €750 million debt associated with the new manufacturing company. The initial borrowings had been taken out at a time of historically cheap credit, and Quinn had driven a hard bargain.

The rate of interest he was paying on the loans was just 0.8 per cent above the so-called Libor rate, the rate the banks themselves were paying to borrow it from other banks. The cost of borrowing had jumped in the intervening years, as the credit crunch had hit, and the lenders were now effectively losing money on the Quinn loans. McKillop knew the banks and the bondholders would demand a higher interest rate for refinancing the debt and taking the €550 million hit. In McKillop's estimation, the rate should be between 2 per cent and 2.5 per cent higher than the Libor rate.

McKillop knew too that the lenders would demand a debt-for-equity swap, whereby they would take a stake in Quinn's business in exchange for writing the €550 million off the debt. This was standard practice, similar to the deal McKillop had done at Four Seasons

Healthcare. Banks do not write off more than half a billion euro without getting some shareholding in a business. It was inconceivable to McKillop that the banks would consent to any deal without some debt-for-equity swap.

It seemed like a solid proposition. The Quinns would have to give up some shareholding but the lenders would not want to be long-term shareholders in an Irish manufacturing group – Quinn would be able to buy back their stake over time and regain control. Quinn wouldn't have to look far for evidence that such a turnaround was possible. Larry Goodman, the Co. Louth meat-processing entrepreneur, had done it in the 1990s. In the early part of the decade, Goodman's ABP Food Group had come close to collapse with debts of nearly €700 million, saved only by the passing of examinership legislation in an emergency session of the Dáil.

Goodman had cooperated fully with his creditors, giving them the majority stake in his business and selling all available assets – including an extensive property portfolio – to pay down the debt. In 1995, satisfied that they had recouped as much as they ever would from the business, the banks sold their stake in ABP back to Goodman for just €38 million. Restored to full ownership, the businessman had even bought back the properties he had been forced to sell. Goodman's business had thrived since, with revenues going on to top €2 billion.

If Quinn played his cards right – and McKillop had heard all those stories about Quinn liking a game of cards – he, too, could recover equity in his company as the years progressed. It was the nature of business. The lenders would put in place a buy-back clause, allowing Quinn and his family to purchase equity at a particular price if the company hit agreed targets. The lenders and McKillop both reckoned the process would run more smoothly if Quinn was incentivized, and they believed the best way to keep him incentivized was to offer him the chance of getting his group back.

In the long run, such an approach made sense for the lenders. If they could agree a deal with Quinn, it would provide them with a perfect opportunity to offload their equity at a later date and recover as much money as possible. All Quinn had to do was say yes.

Quinn said no.

He said no to any increase in the interest rate, and he said no to any prospect of creditors taking shares in his family business. He expressed his views forcefully, telling McKillop that he would not agree to what he regarded as the pillaging of his empire. At the board meetings, Peter Quinn and David Mackey had become entrenched, too. As soon as the issue of the debt-for-equity swap was mentioned, they raised objections, refusing to even discuss it or allow it to be discussed.

'It is not on the table and never will be,' Mackey told the board.

'Never. No deal,' said Peter Quinn.

McKillop did some homework on Mackey, a former manager of Cavan County Council and chief executive of Quinn Group. A close friend of Sean Quinn, he had been drafted on to the shareholder board after Quinn Insurance went into administration. He was attending all the meetings of the operating company as well. But Mackey still had a day job as chief executive of P Elliott, a Cavan construction company. P Elliott had mushroomed during the building boom, generating revenues of €300 million a year and directly employing about 250 people at its peak.

Like many builders, it had expanded into property development, buying the offices of the *Irish Times* in Dublin city centre for €29 million in 2006. That same year, the company entered a joint venture with Warren Private, a property investment group, to build a big residential development in Stepaside, south Co. Dublin, on land bought for €77.5 million. By 2010, with the property market frozen for more than two years, work had stalled and P Elliott was suffering heavy losses on writing down the value of its boom-time purchases. A number of Quinn Group bankers had expressed surprise that Mackey even had the time to come to board meetings, given the scale of the problems within his own business.

The trio of independent directors, led by chairman Pat O'Neill, were astounded by the resistance of Quinn and his lieutenants. They knew that the banks would not agree to any deal without being given a slice of the business. They asked McKillop what size of shareholding the banks would look for. They never got an answer. Mackey and

Peter Quinn simply refused to even entertain a hypothetical discussion on the subject. Swapping debt for equity was 'a fucking deal breaker' said Peter Quinn, according to the confidential notes of one meeting.

McKillop had a problem. He was due to present his proposal to the banks and bondholders in London in September. This was a big meeting, and it loomed large in his thinking – he had been on the ground in Quinn Group almost six months and the lenders would need a viable plan. He felt he had one, but the board was divided over it and the group shareholders – the Quinn children – were rejecting it outright. With the shareholders rejecting the prospect of any deal, McKillop had little room for manoeuvre.

The London meeting was a farce. McKillop explained his proposal about splitting the company into performing and non-performing entities and dividing the debt. The audience at the meeting, which included six banks and representatives of the bondholders, liked the general premise of the proposal. 'It was a structure I could live with,' said one person at the meeting.

However, Quinn had blocked McKillop from proposing any debt-for-equity swap or higher interest rate for the lenders. Accordingly, McKillop was proposing the creditors write off half a billion euro and get nothing extra in return. The lenders were astonished. 'Murdoch, do you really expect us to buy this?' asked one person at the meeting. In truth, McKillop did not. But he had been left with little choice.

Unsurprisingly, he went back to Ireland without a deal. Quinn had sent him on a fool's errand, and McKillop did not like it very much. Still, the banks and the bondholders had liked the overall idea of splitting the debt, signalling they were open to a deal if Quinn was willing to give up some shareholding and pay a higher rate of interest. As far as McKillop was concerned, he had the structure ready to go. All he needed was Sean Quinn to see sense. But deep down, he knew Quinn was not the sort of man to back down.

After the London episode, Pat O'Neill immediately called a meeting, at which McKillop relayed what had happened. He told the board there was nothing more he could do. Without compromise from Quinn, there was no deal possible. He was not going to waste his time and damage his hard-won reputation by trying. McKillop proposed that the board of the operating company step back from the negotiations with the lenders and request that Quinn and the shareholders take responsibility for dealing with the bondholders and banks directly. It was a risky strategy, and McKillop knew it, but the board accepted the recommendation.

Around that time, in October 2010, Murdoch McKillop started to receive letters. Lots of letters. Sean Quinn had established a string of subsidiary boards within the group as a way of rewarding loyal staff with directorships. Some members of those boards started writing to McKillop, accusing him of destroying the company and calling his character into question. The letters brimmed with vitriol and bitterness. They questioned why he was unable to strike a deal with the banks. They questioned McKillop's fee, reported by the media to be £795 an hour, making him 'the highest-paid consultant in Ireland'. In all his years in the world of insolvency and restructuring, McKillop told friends, he had never seen such loyalty to one man, or felt such hatred towards himself.

McKillop's meetings with Sean Quinn stopped. His engagement with Quinn's children had always been virtually non-existent. The children were the shareholders, the owners of the company, but it had been explained to McKillop early on that they had little to do with the company. If you wanted to talk to a Quinn, you talked to Sean and only to Sean – but that line of communication had now shut down.

There was one plus, though. The three non-executive directors – O'Neill, Tuohy and Murphy – had also lost patience with Quinn and his posturing. They were non-executives, outsiders who had no particular loyalty to Quinn. Moreover, they felt let down by Quinn's failure to tell them about the scale of the problems within the group or the interactions with the Financial Regulator in the year leading up to the administration at Quinn Insurance.

They had their own reputations to protect, and felt that their duty was to the company, not its founder and his family. They had supported McKillop's plan for restructuring the debt. If something was to happen down the line, such as a sale or lender takeover of the group, McKillop knew he could win a boardroom vote, as he now had the majority on his side.

The phoney war continued right into March 2011. McKillop knew Sean Quinn was now negotiating with the banks and bondholders himself, and that he remained confident of a deal. McKillop, however, knew enough of banks and bondholders to know it would never happen. Via Barry Russell in London, he knew that the bondholders were aghast at what was emerging within the group – the Belfry payment, the Coill fiasco, the emerging black hole within Quinn Insurance. 'So what Friday surprise do you have for me this week?' Russell would ask when McKillop phoned for one of their weekly chats. Invariably, there was some new piece of information that would further aggrieve the lenders.

McKillop was experienced enough to know the bondholders were not going to let the phoney war drag on indefinitely. By the end of March 2011, with the first anniversary of his appointment approaching, Murdoch McKillop knew his time in Ireland was coming to an end.

'Unsecured scum.' That is what Sean Quinn had taken to calling the banks and bondholders that had loaned his businesses €1.3 billion. He used the phrase at a number of meetings with his advisers and associates, highlighting the fact that the institutions had been so keen to lend him money that they never bothered asking for any proper form of security to back up the loans. Now, though, in March 2011, Quinn was increasingly confident that the lenders, these 'unsecured scum', were ready to back down and cut him a deal. 'I can feel it, they are coming to their senses,' Quinn told a meeting of advisers in mid March.

As soon as Murdoch McKillop had stepped back out of the negotiating process, after the London meeting with the lenders, Sean Quinn had stepped in. He had turned to the London office of BDO, the accountancy firm, to advise him. He had cut all ties with McKillop. He had never liked the Scot – 'That Rangers man cannot be trusted,' Quinn had told an associate when McKillop had first arrived.

He was now getting constant updates about the goings-on at Quinn Group from his brother Peter and from David Mackey. Over their regular dinners in the Slieve Russell, Mackey told Quinn how McKillop was going through the finances of his companies with a fine-tooth comb, asking lots and lots of questions. Quinn was told of McKillop's fury when he discovered the €6 million payment for the Belfry and the Coill Investments debacle. He was told the secret transactions had not gone down well with the non-executive directors either.

But Quinn was anything but repentant. 'I would do it again,' he told one person close to the situation. 'I gave the staff my word that I would cover the losses, and I will not renege on it. You can tell that Rangers fan that much, as well.'

Quinn had not liked McKillop's plan to restructure the manufacturing group. Under no circumstances was he willing to pay the banks a higher rate of interest. Throughout his career, he had played hardball with financial institutions in order to secure the best deal; he was not about to start giving in now. After all, they were the ones who had so willingly lent him the money in the first place; so willing, in fact, that they had not even bothered to ask where it was going.

And if he was not going to pay a higher interest rate for the loans, there was no way on earth he was going to cede equity in his business, Quinn told anyone who would listen. It was a family business, its shareholders were his children, and he was not going to allow McKillop and the banks to force him to dilute their birthright. He never imagined the family keeping control of the business forever, but he was not going to have some lender muscle in on what he had spent his life building.

McKillop had caught him off guard when, after the lenders had unsurprisingly failed to bite at a plan in which they would write off debt without receiving any equity, he said that future negotiations would have to take place directly between the lenders and Quinn himself. Quinn had not expected that, and he initially thought

McKillop had been bluffing. After all, getting agreement between
Quinn and the lenders was McKillop's job.

Quinn was open to the idea of stepping back at Quinn Group and
handing over some power to managers. He was even agreeable to letting the lenders put more representatives on the boards, and
implementing greater corporate governance controls. That was his
starting point in the negotiations, and it was also his finishing point.
He had told that to Shay Bannon from the start: some small concessions but no equity, no higher rate of interest. Bannon was head of
restructuring at the London office of BDO, the accountants, and he
was now acting for Quinn in the negotiations with the banks and
bondholders. Technically Bannon was the adviser to Quinn Group
(ROI), the shareholder company that Quinn and his executives had
decamped to when McKillop had arrived. However, Quinn effectively controlled the ROI company, so Bannon was working to
Quinn's orders.

Bannon was used to difficult situations. In the summer of 2008, he
had been appointed by Norwich Union as receiver to the Dawnay
Day group, in what was the biggest insolvency in Britain for several
years. Dawnay Day, a conglomerate of more than 600 companies,
had hit the buffers with £800 million in debt. It had more than £1
billion worth of assets, including prime properties, shares in companies such as Austin Reed, the suitmaker, and even works of art by
Damien Hirst and Andy Warhol. But the group had run out of cash
after losing heavily on speculative share investments.

As receiver, Bannon put together a team that would eventually
number more than 100 people and arranged the sale of the group's
portfolio of 223 UK properties in April 2009. The deal raised £600
million and staved off insolvency, though Bannon's work was not
complete. 'I would guess we could still be dealing with Dawnay Day
in ten years' time,' Bannon said in BDO's annual report for 2009. At
Quinn Group, he would face many of the same issues, with one big
difference: the forceful personality of Sean Quinn.

The first thing Quinn wanted was a meeting with the lenders.
Over the years, he had been the master of the meeting. He liked
to step in to save a struggling deal at the last minute, or drop in

unannounced to get a contract over the line. He knew people liked to meet the boss directly; that they liked to close a deal with the founder of the group. So, having discussed it with Mackey and Liam McCaffrey, the group chief executive, he decided to sit down with his lenders, face-to-face, to try to hammer out a deal.

The meeting was arranged for the first week of December 2010. The venue was the office of Bingham McCutchen, an impressive old building located right in the heart of the City of London. The building, at 41 Lothbury Street, had once been occupied by Nat-West and its façade and ground floor were protected structures. However, architects had designed a modern office complex around the protected area, and the building was now occupied by law firms and overseas financial institutions including Silicon Valley Bank.

Binghams, as the firm was commonly known, had the sixth and seventh floors of the building. The distinctive shimmering skyscraper known as the Gherkin dominates the view from the boardroom, where the meeting took place. Quinn had brought his team with him. Shay Bannon from BDO was by his side, as were Dara O'Reilly, Kevin Lunney and David Mackey. Across the table were Barry Russell, representatives from the six banks and several bondholders. On the table were bottles of Binghams' water and a bowl of Binghams' branded mints.

Quinn, at his own request, was first to speak. He was clearly emotional. 'I have never reneged on a debt in my life,' he said. 'Yes, I have made mistakes, but I want a second chance. Surely I am entitled to a second chance. I want to work to ensure that everyone gets paid back. We have a plan and we think it can work.' He outlined his vision for the business and gave a rallying call to the lenders to support him. When he had finished, his own team asked him to leave the room, and he made his way to a nearby office where he settled in to read a newspaper.

Russell then told Bannon and the Quinn executives that the lenders had lost faith in Quinn. If a deal could be done – and there was no guarantee that this would happen – the bondholders said it would have to involve Quinn stepping back from the business. Quinn's team responded that the founder was willing to compromise and take a more strategic, hands-off role within the company.

Then came discussion on the other aspects of a deal, such as debt-for-equity and the interest rate on the loan. Quinn was still unwilling to budge on either issue. Mackey insisted that if the lenders accepted Quinn's plan, they would get all their money back. There would be no need for a debt-for-equity swap. However, another major issue emerged, and it was one that neither Quinn nor his team could fully address. The lenders wanted to know what Quinn intended to do about Quinn Insurance. The only security they had to support their loans were the cross-company guarantees on the assets of the insurance company, and it was by now patently obvious that Quinn was not going to recover control there. The meeting ended with the Quinn camp agreeing to put their repayment proposal in writing and send it on to the lenders in the coming weeks.

By January, Quinn and BDO had pieced together the specifics of their repayment plan, dispatching a letter to Russell and to Matthew Clarke of Barclays Capital, who was representing the banks. The letter, dated 10 January 2011 and signed by Bannon, gave a firm commitment that Quinn would stand back from the business. Bannon said the composition of the Quinn Group (ROI) board was a matter for the company itself to decide but the board recognized 'it is important to ensure an appropriate transition as Mr Quinn's involvement reduces over the coming years'. The board, it said, 'therefore believes it is essential to have additional executive, as well as non-executive, representation on the company board with appropriate proven manufacturing experience'. The lenders would have the right to veto any proposed director.

The letter noted concerns the lenders had about succession, stating that the company would establish a subcommittee to the board charged with ensuring appropriate succession was in place. 'This would ensure the continued profitability of the Quinn Group for future generations,' it said.

The letter had been carefully crafted by Quinn personally. It detailed how he had been instrumental in the development of the business, and claimed that, without him, it would be a pale shadow of its former self. It was a letter designed to convince the lenders that they needed him on board, that the group was nothing without its founder and architect. At Quinn's suggestion, the letter outlined some of his technical feats, describing how he had developed a unique system for using groundwater to wash gravel. As well as using coal in place of cobalt in the glass division (a change Quinn said was saving the group £700,000 a year), he had been a pioneer of renewable energy, developing one of the first wind farms in Ireland. 'This initiative would not have been possible by any other party in the area due to the need to secure agreement from all local landowners and community groups. Mr Quinn had the necessary relationships to facilitate this.'

The letter put great stock on Quinn's ability to strike the deals other people simply couldn't. 'Local landowners will often insist on having the final handshake with Sean Quinn himself or in some cases will only engage in meaningful discussions if he is present. Most have watched and admired as the company has grown and developed from humble beginnings and like to feel part of it by doing a deal directly with Mr Quinn.'

The letter noted that no other member of the Quinn family had any day-to-day responsibility in the manufacturing operations and that this would continue to be the case. 'However, as a result of the significant loyalty to the Quinn brand in the local area and Ireland generally, the Quinn family have all, to varying degrees, established relationships with the Quinn Group's major and local customers over the years. In this regard it is envisaged that they would all continue to be involved in representing the Quinn Group with customers, whether formally or informally, in maintaining that image of the Quinn Group as a family business at corporate presentations, functions, associated sponsorship agreements, etc.'

Sean Quinn himself, the letter said, would continue to be involved in the business, but would not have any role in corporate governance or financial affairs. Furthermore, he would remain off the board of the operating company, keeping his place on the board of the shareholder company. Management would report not to him, but to the management company, though he would remain the head of the group.

Based on Quinn's plan, the banks would advance a further €120 million over a five-year period to help Quinn Group develop its operations. As far as he was concerned, it all made sense. He was making compromises and offering concessions – something he had rarely done in nearly four decades in business. A follow-up letter went to the banks and bondholders on 24 January.

Quinn assessed the situation – what other option did the lenders have? They had limited security over the loans: they could appoint administrators to some individual business, but such a move might jeopardize the entire group and put all of their €1.3 billion at risk. And if he could get the deal with the banks and bondholders over the line, he felt sure Anglo would fall into line on his plan to repay the €2.8 billion it was owed by the Quinn family. According to several people intimately involved in the negotiations, Sean Quinn was now convinced that his manufacturing group was secure and would remain within family ownership.

Barry Russell had seen men like Sean Quinn before. Over the years, he had come across billionaires and tycoons and business visionaries; men, like Quinn, who had built empires from the ground up. Many, like Quinn, referred to themselves in the third person, a habit Russell had never truly understood.

Russell had taken a cold hard look at Quinn's plan to save his business, and quickly decided it was not for him. There were simply too many unknowns. Was Quinn capable of repaying the money? Would Quinn really stand back and hand over control of the company? What would happen to the insurance company?

In truth, the lenders had given up on Quinn the moment the businessman dispatched Murdoch McKillop to London with the risible proposal to the creditors. The lenders felt duped by Quinn, now believing they had not been given the full picture from the time they agreed to bankroll him in 2005. They had offered him numerous chances to reach a deal; to show some humility and compromise. If he engaged properly with them, the lenders felt he could eventually reclaim control of the business. But he did not want to go down that route.

Before they could cut Quinn loose, however, the lenders and Russell needed a plan of their own. There was only one direction in which they could turn to make it happen. If the banks and bondholders were to bypass Quinn, it required doing a deal direct with Anglo Irish Bank. Russell had first met Anglo officials in late March 2010. Matthew Elderfield, the Financial Regulator, had just threatened Quinn Insurance with the appointment of the administrators, and Russell had come to Dublin on behalf of the bondholders to meet Elderfield.

On Monday 29 March, the day before the administrators seized control of Quinn Insurance, he had met Mike Aynsley, the Anglo chief executive, and Richard Woodhouse and Tom Hunersen, Aynsley's two most senior executives. Russell knew the bank had a staggering financial exposure to Sean Quinn, if not the Quinn Group, and he needed to know what role Anglo might play in the weeks and months ahead. The meeting was cordial and, though nothing concrete arose from it, everyone in the room quickly came to the realization that they should have been talking sooner.

Russell had remained in touch with Woodhouse over the following months. In late 2010, when it became clear to the lenders that Quinn would not play ball, Russell told Woodhouse that the lenders were open to doing a deal with Anglo. He told Woodhouse to come back with a proposal.

Richard Woodhouse did not need to be asked twice. He had been meeting advisers and experts for months, trying to determine what could be done with the Quinn Group. Every option was discussed. The bank considered taking control of certain assets in the group. Another option was to push for examinership, a court-approved process that would give the group up to 100 days to restructure its finances. The group would have protection from its creditors during that period and could possibly reach some sort of settlement to ease its debt burden.

There was a nuclear option: receivership. A straight receivership would involve seizing all the group assets and running them for the benefit of the lenders. But seizing a manufacturing group with dozens of factories and thousands of workers was not something to be undertaken lightly. Another option being discussed was share receivership. Anglo had a charge over the shares in Quinn Group (ROI), the company that actually owned the Quinn Group. Sean Quinn's children had pledged the shares as security over the mammoth borrowings during the panic-stricken days in 2008 when their father sought to resolve the CFD situation. The loans weren't being repaid, so the bank would be within its rights to seize the shares. That would give Anglo ownership of the group and the right to appoint its own board of directors to run it, without having to manage every asset individually. Share receiverships were rarely used, but it looked like a good option to Anglo.

At a series of meetings in early 2011, Woodhouse outlined the share receivership plan to Russell. It was a bold approach, but Russell felt it could work. It was a corporate coup, designed to catch Quinn off guard and take control of his company with a minimum of fuss. Anglo would take majority ownership of the Quinn Group, but the other banks and bondholders would have operating control. The bondholders would release the insurance company from the guarantees, thereby freeing Anglo to strike a deal with Liberty Mutual to jointly acquire Quinn Insurance from the court-appointed administrators.

Once they took control of the group, they would implement Murdoch McKillop's plan of splitting the company into performing and non-performing units and ring-fencing a chunk of the debt. It would be complicated, of course, but it could be done.

Through January 2011, Russell and Woodhouse worked out the finer points of the deal. The Department of Finance and the Minister, Brian Lenihan, were briefed. After all, this was a state-owned bank proposing to seize control of one of the largest employers in the country. At all times, the government had publicly declared that Anglo was operated on an arm's-length basis and made its own decisions. In reality, a decision to take control of Quinn Group and Quinn Insurance would require government approval. Everyone knew that.

But there was one giant hitch. The government, a coalition of Fianna Fáil and the Green Party, was lumbering from one crisis to the next. Having just accepted a bailout from the troika of international lenders – the European Commission, the European Central Bank and the International Monetary Fund – the government had lost any last remaining shred of credibility. The Green Party had announced on 22 November 2010 that it wanted a General Election in the new year. Brian Cowen, the Taoiseach, had no option but to agree. The government was about to fall.

The crisis had deepened in the first week of 2011. A book published on 7 January, *The FitzPatrick Tapes*, by *Sunday Times* business journalists Tom Lyons and Brian Carey, revealed previously unknown contacts between Cowen and Sean FitzPatrick, then chairman of Anglo Irish Bank, at the height of the financial crisis in 2008. Cowen, then Minister for Finance, had taken a phone call from FitzPatrick in March 2008, about the collapse in Anglo's share price. In July 2008, Cowen and FitzPatrick had played golf at Druid's Heath, part of the upmarket Druid's Glen golf resort in Co. Wicklow. The book also detailed for the first time the extent of Anglo's knowledge of Quinn's CFD dealings and the lengths to which the bank had secretly gone to resolve the situation.

The revelation of Cowen's contacts with FitzPatrick had huge political fallout. On 20 January 2011, just days after Woodhouse and Russell settled on the finer points of their plan to de-Quinn the Quinn Group, Cowen called a General Election for 11 March. He had seen off a challenge to his leadership but then botched a cabinet reshuffle. Two days later, Cowen convened a hastily arranged press conference in Dublin's Merrion Hotel. It was a hotel Russell knew well from his trips to Ireland, which were by now so regular that the Merrion had agreed a reduced rate for the Binghams partner.

Cowen's press conference was carried live on RTÉ, the national broadcaster. Flanked by a number of loyal colleagues, including his deputy, Mary Coughlan, the Taoiseach announced he was stepping down as leader of Fianna Fáil. In an emotional address to a crowded press corps, he said he would remain as Taoiseach until the election was held. The following day, the Green Party pulled out of government, forcing an earlier election. On 1 February, the Dáil was dissolved and a General Election called for 25 February.

With the government in limbo, the Quinn plan was put on ice. It was simply too big a decision for an outgoing minister to sign off on. The proposal would have to be put to the new Finance Minister, and there was no certainty who would take the coveted post.

As anticipated, the election produced a coalition government between Fine Gael and the Labour Party. On 9 March 2011, the new Cabinet was unveiled. The Minister for Finance would be Michael Noonan, a former Fine Gael leader and health minister. Noonan had been parachuted back into frontline politics in 2010 after a botched attempt by the party's then finance spokesman, Richard Bruton, to oust Enda Kenny as Fine Gael leader.

In a former life, Alan Dukes, the Anglo chairman, had served in Cabinet with Noonan. Anglo management reckoned that Noonan, regarded as a wily old pragmatist, would see the merits of its Quinn Group proposal.

Their hunch was correct.

Noonan green-lighted the project to seize Quinn's companies in late March, just weeks after being formally presented with his seal of office. With the plan ready to go, Woodhouse made a flurry of calls. He called Barry Russell in London. Then, he called Murdoch McKillop. In advance of any move, Woodhouse wanted Pat O'Neill, Brendan Tuohy and Paddy Murphy, the non-executive directors of the Quinn Group, on board.

Then, he placed a call with a KPMG accountant called Kieran Wallace.

8

Day One

When Kieran Wallace was a teenager, a receiver had been appointed to the company that employed his mother. She had kept working for the company, helping the receiver manage its affairs. For her young son, it all seemed exciting and interesting. While most of his friends wanted to be professional soccer players, Wallace set his heart on becoming a liquidator.

A native of Castlebellingham, a village in Co. Louth, Wallace studied at University College Dublin before training as an account-ant. He joined KPMG, quickly climbing the corporate ladder at the accountancy firm – appointed first as partner and then as head of KPMG's business restructuring and forensic advisory practice in Ire-land.

Soft spoken and bespectacled, Wallace had a passion for movies and a habit of periodically turning off his BlackBerry to help clear his head. However, he remained deadly serious about his job. He was also extremely busy. The economic downturn had brought him a lot of business. When a company decided to liquidate or a bank decided to install a receiver, Wallace was often among the first people they would call. Regardless of the size of the job, Wallace always insisted on visiting the property in question. With the economy in tatters, that meant he spent a lot of time on half-finished housing estates, building sites and empty fields.

His first major insolvency job came in July 2004 when a wholesale business in Co. Cork, Ban Ard Cash & Carry, went bust. It was a contentious collapse – Ban Ard had sold its assets on to another company, despite owing €1.9 million to eleven creditors, including household names such as Coca-Cola, Cadbury and C&C. Wallace, then in his early thirties, was appointed liquidator and given the task of cleaning up what was left of Ban Ard.

It would be more than two years before another big-name liquidation – the winding up of Castlemahon Foods, a Limerick company with 300 staff – came his way. With the economy booming, most companies were thriving and corporate collapses were rare. Specialist insolvency practitioners weren't much in demand.

Things had started to change in late 2007, slowly at first, then with frightening rapidity. Some pinpointed the collapse of William Phelan & Sons, a Kilkenny building company, in the autumn of 2007, as the turning point, the moment when it became apparent all was not well. Phelan was building a gated development of houses and apartments on Kilkenny's Castlecomer Road, charging €870,000 for six-bedroom homes. Then the firm ran out of cash.

ACC Bank, owned by Rabobank, the Dutch financial institution, installed a receiver to take control of the project. The bank later secured a judgment for nearly €15 million against three members of the Phelan family. To casual observers, it looked like an isolated case of a company over-stretching itself. But the insolvency industry sat up and took note.

Through 2008, 2009 and 2010, the trickle of insolvencies became a flood. There were 753 insolvencies of Irish companies in 2008, more than double the 2007 figure, according to data from RSM Farrell Grant Sparks, a Dublin accountancy and business advisory firm. The number more than doubled again in 2009, to 1,570, and came close to 2,000 in 2010. The fallout was enormous – for staff, for creditors, for lenders. There was a grim joke among insolvency experts that they had 'survived' Ireland's long economic boom; now the corporate undertakers were having their own boom.

By April 2011, Wallace was one of the country's busiest – and most high-profile – insolvency experts. He had experience of hundreds of insolvency situations, from small business liquidations to complex examinerships. As the economy slid, Wallace had picked up receivership work from most of the banks, taking over the assets and operations of collapsed builders including Howard Holdings, Ellen Construction and the Conway Partnership. He had handled high-profile insolvency situations at the Hughes & Hughes book chain, the Jackie Skelly gym business, and Futura Gael, a Dublin-based charter airline.

Wallace had even set a precedent in his successful handling of the examinership of the Linen Supply of Ireland. That case had gone all the way to the Supreme Court, which ruled the company could rip up expensive property leases agreed at the height of the boom. The previous month, Wallace had won one of the biggest appointments to date by NAMA, as receiver to seven hotels linked to the developer Paddy Kelly. Kelly had assembled syndicates of investors to fund the hotels, including Clarion properties in Dublin and Limerick, but the investment companies had defaulted on their debts. Wallace was the man NAMA turned to in order to secure the properties and maximize the return to the state agency.

From early 2010, even before Quinn Insurance was put into administration, Wallace had been meeting once a month with Richard Woodhouse at Anglo Irish Bank to discuss hypothetical situations for Quinn Group. During one of their first meetings, Wallace had spelled out his view of the situation to Woodhouse. There were three parties at the table, he said: Quinn, Anglo and the non-Anglo lenders. Any two of them could do a deal and freeze out the other. If the bondholders decided to do a deal with Quinn, Anglo was in trouble. It was vital that the bank and bondholders got together against Quinn.

By late 2010, Richard Woodhouse was seeing the wisdom of Wallace's viewpoint. Woodhouse and Wallace were by now meeting weekly at the offices of William Fry, the Dublin law firm, to bash around the possibilities. Wallace brought Eamonn Richardson and Shane McCarthy, colleagues from KPMG, to the meetings, and lawyers from William Fry sat in, too. Anglo had opened talks with the banks and bondholders, represented by Barry Russell. Their conversations were crystallizing around the idea of a share receivership, whereby Anglo could use its charge over the shares in Quinn Group (ROI) to take control of the business. As the idea gathered steam, the bank gave Wallace the go-ahead to sound out new directors for Quinn Group.

Kieran Wallace was well used to meetings that didn't go anywhere. Since the economy had gone into freefall, the banks routinely called in accountants and lawyers to go through their options. Often, they never acted on any of them. This time might not be any different, particularly given the sensitivity and complexity of moving against Sean Quinn.

Still, he approached Jimmy Menton, a former KPMG partner, about joining the board of Quinn Group in the event of an enforcement move by Anglo. Menton had become a partner in Arthur Andersen in his early thirties and had run the firm's audit and assurance practice. When Arthur Andersen merged with KPMG in 2002, after the debacle over false accounting with Enron, Menton had become senior partner in the advisory practice. His particular focus was on corporate governance and risk management and his clients included semi-state bodies and big private-sector companies.

Menton was well regarded, a long-standing member of the Institute of Directors in Ireland, with a good track record. He had retired from KPMG in October 2009, still in his mid fifties, and was working as a business consultant. Wallace gave him a call in late 2010. There was a possibility a big corporate restructuring project would be coming up – would Menton be available and willing to take it on? Wallace was coy about the company involved and Menton knew better than to ask.

Wallace turned, too, to Ray Jackson, another former KPMG colleague. Jackson had been a partner in the accountancy firm for nearly three decades, heading its insolvency and forensics practice in the Republic of Ireland and Northern Ireland. He had worked on some of the biggest insolvencies Ireland had seen, including the liquidation of Irish Ispat, the former Irish Steel, which had closed in 2001 with €45 million in debts and the loss of 400 jobs. Jackson had also navigated the tricky relationship between the government and the private sector as liquidator to Irish Fertilizer Industries, which had been 51 per cent state owned when it went bust in 2002 with the loss of 620 jobs. Wallace had learned a lot from Jackson. His experience could come in useful if Anglo decided to push the button on a Quinn receivership.

Another former KPMG partner, Robert Dix, could also play a role, Wallace felt. A keen sailor who represented Ireland at the 1976 Olympic Games in Montreal, Dix had 20 years' experience in auditing and transaction services. He had left KPMG in 2008 and gone to work for Barry O'Callaghan, a Cork-born investment banker whose star had risen during the economic boom. O'Callaghan had floated Riverdeep, a Dublin-based educational software company, on the Irish Stock Exchange and the Nasdaq in 2000, at the peak of the dot-com boom. When the internet bubble burst, he took Riverdeep back into private ownership and used cheap credit to fund multi-billion-dollar buyouts of two giant US publishers, Houghton Mifflin and Harcourt.

By 2008, O'Callaghan was estimated to have personal wealth of $500 million. He recruited Dix to set up a philanthropic foundation and manage his personal investments. Then the downturn hit. US states, the main buyers of O'Callaghan's products for their school systems, slashed their budgets, causing the company to miss its profit targets. O'Callaghan's lenders had taken control of his business in 2010 and Dix parted company with the entrepreneur.

Dix's most recent work had been as acting finance director of a private mining company, Zamin Ferrous, which was owned by an Indian businessman who had been a client of Dix's at KPMG. The company was based in London but had iron ore interests in South America and Asia. In 2010, Dix was asked to lead a flotation of Zamin Ferrous on the London Stock Exchange, a transaction the *Financial Times* reported could value the company at up to $2.5 billion. However, the flotation plans flushed out a buyer for the company's main asset, a 50 per cent stake in a mining venture in Brazil, which Zamin Ferrous opted to sell for $735 million. Dix was just wrapping up the Zamin Ferrous assignment when Kieran Wallace came calling about the Quinn Group role, in late 2010.

All told, Wallace had approached about twenty people in the hope of finding ten suitable candidates, people with good commercial experience who were considered suitable – and willing – to be alternative directors of the various Quinn companies. By now, many of those involved had guessed the identity of the company in question. However, all were sworn to secrecy. In the run-up to Christmas 2010, they had briefing sessions in the offices of William Fry and KPMG's own offices, just off St Stephen's Green in Dublin city centre, where they outlined to the candidates what their roles would involve. Anglo had approved the final shortlist. Now all they needed was for something to happen.

Menton was skiing in Austria in January 2011 when his mobile phone rang. It looked like the Anglo project would go ahead the following week. He should be prepared. Then another call: false alarm. It would take a little longer to get everything lined up. January became February, and February became March. By March, it was clear in Anglo headquarters that Sean Quinn could not pay his debts, and was in no mood to keep talking to the bank. The relationship between the bank and the businessman was dead.

Woodhouse increased the meetings with Wallace to several times a week, then every day. There would be no deal with Quinn, so drastic action would be needed to secure the best outcome for Anglo. The bank upped its contacts with Barry Russell on behalf of the banks and bondholders. There were bilateral talks, too, between Anglo and the banks and bondholders, meeting at the offices of William Fry to hammer out the details of a deal. Michael McAteer and Paul McCann, the Quinn Insurance administrators, were also brought into the loop.

Wallace and the bank also met key directors of Quinn Group (NI), the main operating company that Sean Quinn and his executives had quit the previous year. They outlined to Pat O'Neill, the chairman, Paddy Murphy, the former banker, Brendan Tuohy, the former civil servant, and Paul O'Brien, the latest addition to the board, what was coming. O'Brien, a native of Co. Louth, knew the border region and had a feel for the sensitivities around Quinn. He knew, too, how international banks and bondholders operated – he had been finance director at IWP, the publicly quoted industrial group, during a restructuring that had seen lenders and then private equity take control.

The meetings, in the offices of A&L Goodbody, the lawyers for the Quinn Group, were tense. The directors had all worked with Quinn, some of them for several years. They were nervous Quinn and his family would find out that Anglo was about to shut him out once and for all. 'They had lost confidence in him but did not want him to know. They were the existing directors and they came onside with the banks and bondholders. They had turned,' said a source involved in the process.

The Central Bank and the government had to be kept up to date, too. There were a couple of meetings between Wallace, Anglo and Matthew Elderfield. The Regulator wanted to make sure nothing the bank had in mind would affect the regulated insurance entities. Anglo gave an undertaking not to unilaterally do anything that would affect the administration process at Quinn Insurance.

Michael Noonan, the newly appointed Minister for Finance, quickly gave his seal of approval to the Anglo enforcement plan. The briefing he had from the bankers was that no jobs would be affected in the restructuring. If the Quinn situation was resolved, it would be one less thing for the new minister and the new government to worry about. Noonan would say later that the Quinn situation was a priority for the new government. 'It was one of the first files I looked at when I came into government,' he said. 'We moved it along pretty quickly. My priority was to maintain the jobs, because it has been a priority of [this] government to maintain jobs and create jobs.' The minister added, 'I think the worst thing that hammers confidence is decisions hanging around not being taken. That's why we moved so quickly.'

Jimmy Menton was visiting one of his daughters, who was studying at the University of Virginia, when the next call came. There was no false alarm this time. The project was on: 14 April 2011, the 99th anniversary of the *Titanic* hitting an iceberg, would be Day One.

At 5.30 a.m. on 14 April, a grey Thursday morning, the plan swung into action.

The enforcement team gathered at a hotel at Dublin Airport, where they prepared for the journey north to Cavan and on to Derrylin.

There were about 115 people in total: bankers from Anglo Irish Bank; the new Quinn Group board directors; lawyers from A&L Goodbody, William Fry and Arthur Cox; advisers from Deloitte and Clifford Chance; even PR people for Quinn Group and the bank. Kieran Wallace was the central figure. After months of deliberations, he would be appointed share receiver to the Quinn Group (ROI), on behalf of Anglo. Everyone present knew the seriousness of what they were about to do. By lunchtime they would be headline news.

It would be a carefully controlled operation. The plan of action was laid out, step by step, in a 65-page document. By 13 April, the so-called 'Day One Sequencing' memo was on its sixteenth and final draft. 'The purpose of this document is to set out the aims to be achieved on the day of Anglo's anticipated enforcement ("Day One") of its security over the shares of Quinn Group (ROI) Ltd and the proposed actions for achieving these aims,' it read. The scenarios had been worked and reworked. With so many people involved, Wallace marvelled that they had managed to keep a lid on the operation. 'You don't organize something like this in three days. It had been going on for weeks, but word never got back to Cavan,' said a source involved in the operation. 'Quinn still thought he had the upper hand, that they [Anglo and the bondholders] were going to do exactly what he wanted them to do.'

Anglo wasn't taking any chances. A security company, Risk Management International (RMI), would be planning and coordinating all the logistics of the enforcement operation. Headed by Peadar Duffy, a former army officer with an appetite for mountain climbing and parachuting, RMI had started out offering to handle kidnap situations and ended up carving out a niche in corporate investigations. It specialized in securing assets and detecting fraud. Since the recession had taken hold, Duffy was finding his company's services more and more in demand. 'You only really get the truth when people are in trouble,' Duffy liked to say.

As the receivers, bankers and advisers gathered in the pre-dawn, RMI was calling the shots. A fleet of hire cars was waiting, each with a security-trained driver. The cars were small, so as not to arouse suspicion, and they would be dispatched individually to ensure there was no large convoy of vehicles travelling together. 'The security guy gave us our instructions – what to do and what not to do. We were under their control. We could not do anything without their approval; we could not go anywhere without them knowing,' said a person involved in the operation. Another joked that RMI only just stopped short of painting their faces for camouflage. Despite the meticulous planning, on the way out of Dublin Airport there was a minor drama when some of the cars took a wrong turn off a round-about and had to be redirected.

Wallace travelled with Andrew O'Leary, a KPMG colleague, and Rory O'Ferrall, a former Deloitte executive who was to be one of the new board appointees at Quinn Group (ROI). Tom Hunersen, Anglo's head of corporate and institutional recovery, nicknamed the Gunner, was the most senior bank executive to make the trip. The bank's head of security and head of internal audit travelled, too, with a number of bank executives drafted in to do the preparatory work and generally help out. Some bank staff had travelled to Cavan the previous day with staff from RMI and William Fry, the law firm. They had set up an 'operations centre' at the Radisson Blu Farnham Estate, a luxury hotel on the outskirts of Cavan town, and made sure everything was ready to roll.

Despite the significance of the day, Richard Woodhouse and Mike Aynsley did not make the trip. They had their own part to play, back at Connaught House, Anglo's new headquarters. The bank had to serve paperwork on Quinn, but wanted to avoid giving the business-man an opportunity to disrupt events. Anglo's solution was to get Quinn to attend a meeting with Aynsley and Woodhouse at Con-naught House on the morning of 14 April while the enforcement operation was playing out.

On 13 April, bank staff contacted Quinn and asked him to come to Burlington Road for a meeting at 9.30 a.m. the next day. He should bring Kevin Lunney and Dara O'Reilly. Quinn wasn't told the pur-pose of the meeting. It seems highly likely that Quinn and his colleagues, en route to Dublin early that morning, would have passed the low-key Anglo entourage on the road, going in the opposite direction.

Separately, a large group of Quinn supporters were also making their way to Dublin on 14 April. Their purpose: to deliver a petition with more than 90,000 signatures to the Central Bank, asking the Financial Regulator to call off the administrators to Quinn Insurance and restore Sean Quinn at the helm. Little did any of them know what was about to unfold.

The receivership team's trip from Dublin Airport took about 90 minutes, out on to the M50 motorway and then north along the M3 to Cavan town. The motorway had opened less than a year earlier after a contentious planning battle. The new road skirted the Hill of Tara, the historical seat of the High Kings of Ireland, and protestors had campaigned vigorously against the project. The road traced the route Quinn's business had marched, too: past his twelve-storey Q-Building in Blanchardstown, north Dublin; through Navan in Co. Meath, where Quinn Insurance had significant operations; and on to Cavan town, where the insurance company headquarters was based. Further north again was Derrylin, Quinn's hometown and the birthplace and headquarters of the Quinn Group.

The Anglo team arrived at the Radisson on the outskirts of Cavan town. The Radisson was a classic boom-time project – and one with which some of the bankers were more than familiar. The 1,300-acre estate, the seat for hundreds of years of the Lords Farnham, had been bought in 2001 by a local pharmacist, Roy McCabe. Three years later, with the economy booming, he launched a grand plan to develop the eighteenth-century Farnham Estate mansion into a 158-bedroom luxury hotel and 'retreat to nature' resort. There would be a spa and 40,000-square-foot wellness centre, woodland walks, lake fishing, a golf course and high-end housing developments on the site. The project would cost €65 million and Anglo was the banker. The Radisson had opened in May 2006, barely eighteen months before the economy would begin its spectacular slide.

The Anglo receivership team had booked out the Radisson's conference facilities, a self-contained building a short distance from the main hotel building. The cover story was that they were holding a management training course with a company called Realise. The importance of maintaining secrecy had been drilled into everyone involved; they should only talk to people who could show appropriate ID. 'If you need to find the party at the operations centre or are asked who you are with, these details [of the Realise event] should be given,' according to the Day One memo. After arriving at the Radisson, RMI gave a health and safety briefing with recommendations and advice on possible 'situations' the receivership team might face during the day and how to deal with them. It was a sobering start to the day.

Different rooms had been arranged at the Radisson for the different groups involved in the enforcement action, each named after a species of tree. When some Anglo executives realized they had been allocated the Maple Room, they insisted on a change. It was an untimely reminder of 'Project Maple' – Morgan Stanley's code name for the bank's controversial scheme whereby it ultimately lent money to the ten long-standing bank customers to help unwind Quinn's CFD stake in July 2008.

Anglo and KPMG had done considerable work in advance. The enforcement letters, as well as paperwork formally appointing each new director to Quinn Group (ROI) and the other relevant companies, had been prepared and signed. Emails announcing news of the receivership – to Quinn Group staff and the outside world – were prepared and left, in draft form, in Gmail accounts held by O'Neill and Paul O'Brien. More detailed letters were prepared for each employee, explaining the news and what it meant. A video in which O'Neill explained the situation was stored on a memory stick, ready to be uploaded to the Quinn Group website. O'Neill, Murphy and O'Brien were provided with pre-paid mobile phones so they could keep in touch with each other, and with Anglo and the receivers.

Letters had been prepared and signed, too, for Liam McCaffrey, the Quinn Group chief executive, and Sinead Geoghegan, the group's financial controller and company secretary, who was considered to be extremely loyal to Sean Quinn. The letters terminated their employment at Quinn Group. They were the only two people to officially lose their jobs on Day One. Paul O'Brien, who had arrived on the Quinn Group board as a non-executive director less than six months previously, would be the new chief executive.

As they arrived in Burlington Road for their 9.30 a.m. meeting, Sean Quinn, Kevin Lunney and Dara O'Reilly were closely observed by security staff appointed by the bank. The three were shown to the fifth floor, where there were views out across the rooftops to Dublin Bay and the Dublin Mountains. They met in Aynsley's office, with the three Quinn Group men on one side and the three bankers – Aynsley, Woodhouse and Dukes – on the other. The bankers had agreed in advance that Dukes should do the talking. He was the only Irish person on the senior management team at Anglo, and the news might sound better coming from him than from Aynsley, an Australian, or Woodhouse, an Englishman.

Dukes began by telling Quinn that Anglo would be appointing a receiver, Kieran Wallace, over the family's shares in Quinn Group (ROI). Anglo had agreed a deal with the banks and bondholders to take control of the group and all its operations. The bank would have a 75 per cent stake in the Quinn Group, with the remainder to be held by the other lenders. The group would continue trading and no jobs would be lost, but there would be no involvement from Sean Quinn or his family in the future.

Quinn was also told that Anglo was appointing a receiver to Quinn's International Property Group, with its properties in the UK, Russia, Ukraine, India, Poland and Turkey. In the final part of the plan, an announcement was to be made naming Anglo and Liberty as the preferred bidders to take over Quinn Insurance from the administrators, Dukes said.

It must have been difficult for Quinn and his associates to take in everything that was being said, and Richard Woodhouse had the impression that Quinn wasn't listening very carefully. The businessman seemed physically shocked: the bankers were doing the one thing he had always believed they would never, ever do.

'So you want to take everything?' said Quinn finally.

'Yes,' said Woodhouse.

'It's not just insurance and manufacturing, you want to take the international property portfolio as well?' Quinn asked.

'Yes,' said Woodhouse.

'Well,' said Quinn, firmly, defiantly, 'that will be hard fought.

That will be hard fought.' Of all his assets, it seemed the properties assembled for his children were foremost in his mind.

The bankers gave Quinn a proposal document and asked him to take it away and examine it before coming back to the bank to discuss it. It set out a plan to try to reduce his debts. Quinn spoke quietly but bluntly, referring to himself in the third person. He threatened he would seek legal advice on the bank's appointment of the receiver. Yes, he had lost €3 billion, mostly on Anglo shares, but no one else had created as many jobs in the country as Sean Quinn, he said. His manufacturing and property businesses were trading strongly and were profitable, so they should not be touched by the lenders. The international properties were his children's inheritance and he would fight to keep them, he warned. The meeting lasted half an hour before Quinn stormed out.

At 9.30 a.m., just as Sean Quinn was sitting down with the bankers, Wallace, together with the lawyers from William Fry, had issued repayment demands on Quinn Group and the Quinn property companies on behalf of Anglo. The papers could be served on whoever was there to receive them, and were all that was required to launch a share receivership. There were two demand letters for the attention of the Quinn Group directors – one from Anglo in relation to the money it was owed by the group, and one from Barclays and the bondholders. The letters ran to three densely worded A4 pages and were virtually identical. They started by setting out details of the amounts owed under various loan agreements. Then came the revelation that Anglo and the non-Anglo lenders had reached a 'restructuring agreement' for the Quinn Group.

> As you are aware, the company has financial difficulties and has ma-
> terially breached, and continues to be in breach of, certain of its
> obligations to the creditors . . . It is in their interests to enter into the
> restructuring agreement to achieve a consensual restructuring of the
> financial indebtedness of the group. By completing the consensual
> restructuring . . . it is hoped that the financial difficulties of the
> group can be resolved, thereby reducing the risk that administration
> or other insolvency proceedings would be commenced in respect of
> the company.

The 'consensual restructuring' would not be consensual for everyone. The demand letters outlined that the restructuring could not go ahead unless there were certain changes to the boards of directors of the Quinn Group and the relevant subsidiaries. This was designed 'to prevent certain directors of those companies, who are perceived by the creditors as being aligned with the company's existing shareholders, from obstructing a restructuring'.

It was a condition of the deal that Peter Quinn, the brother of Sean Quinn, and Liam McCaffrey, the group chief executive, would leave the board of directors. Sinead Geoghegan, the financial controller and company secretary, also had to go. Their continued involvement was 'unsatisfactory to the creditors', the letters said.

The demands were signed and served at Quinn Insurance headquarters, on the Dublin Road outside Cavan town, and at Quinn Group headquarters in Derrylin. Wallace travelled, too, to the Slieve Russell to serve a demand on Quinn Finance Holding Ltd and Slieve Russell Hotel Ltd, the companies behind the International Property Group. Each time he went somewhere, he was accompanied by a full security detail from RMI. In Dublin, Anglo staff kept a close eye on the door of Aynsley's office and relayed the news back to the operations centre at the Radisson that Sean Quinn was exactly where they wanted him.

At 10.15 a.m., Pat O'Neill, Paddy Murphy and Paul O'Brien left the operations centre at the Radisson bound for Derrylin. They had no idea what kind of reception they could expect at Quinn Group headquarters. They were still en route when, at 10.30 a.m., an hour after the repayment demands had been served, Wallace was formally appointed share receiver to Quinn Group (ROI), Quinn Finance and other related companies. Within ten minutes, moves were under way to remove the existing directors – Sean Quinn, Patricia Quinn, Kevin Lunney, Dara O'Reilly and David Mackey – and install the bank-approved replacements.

Jimmy Menton would be the new chairman of Quinn Group (ROI) with immediate effect, replacing Sean Quinn. His fellow board members were Ray Jackson, Timothy Quin, Frank O'Riordan, Rory O'Ferrall and John Boyd. It was a heavyweight line-up: apart from

Menton and Jackson, the two KPMG men, Quin was a former chairman of Touche Ross, a Northern Ireland accountancy practice; O'Riordan was a former A&L Goodbody partner; O'Ferrall was formerly of Deloitte; and Boyd was former director of global restructuring at Ulster Bank. They were all in Cavan for the day, with the exception of Menton, who had been unable to return from the USA on time.

Robert Dix, the former KPMG partner, was also in Cavan. He would chair the new board at Quinn Finance Holding, which had been run by Sean Quinn, Lunney and O'Reilly. The new board there would include Ray Jackson, Rory O'Ferrall and Aidan O'Hogan, a former managing director of Savills estate agency, and past president of the Irish Auctioneers & Valuers Institute. At the Slieve Russell Hotel company, Lunney and Colette Quinn, Sean Quinn's daughter, were removed from their board positions. Their replacements included: Pat McCann, the veteran hotelier who had run the Jurys group; Paul McGowan, a KPMG tax partner; and Richard George, a consultant with KPMG Ireland who chaired the New York-based International Ethics Standards Board for Accountants.

Pre-prepared letters were emailed to Pat O'Neill, as chairman of the board of Quinn Group in Northern Ireland, the main operating company, detailing the changes. The letter on behalf of the new Quinn Group (ROI) board pointed out that David Mackey's removal from the ROI board automatically rescinded his observer status at the NI board, and suggested that O'Neill should rebalance the NI board away from Sean Quinn. The new directors gave explicit agreement 'to any steps' needed to exclude the former directors from access to 'Quinn Group IT systems, premises, employees and other stakeholders'.

The letters also gave agreement 'to all necessary steps being taken by Quinn Group and its subsidiaries to ensure that the Quinn Group IT systems are secured and backed up'. Having control of the IT and communications systems was central to what was about to unfold. After thirty-eight years in business, Quinn was being effectively locked out – physically and metaphorically – from the group he had founded.

The letter from the new board to O'Neill was all part of the careful choreography Anglo and Wallace had worked through. O'Neill now had the agreement of the new Quinn Group (ROI) board, representing the new shareholders, to remove Peter Quinn and Liam McCaffrey as directors of the operating company. O'Neill was to call the two men with the news and then email them notice of their removal. RMI personnel would follow up by delivering hard-copy letters to Derrylin. A meeting of the new board would follow, with just one item on the agenda: the termination of Liam McCaffrey's appointment and the appointment of Paul O'Brien as the new chief executive.

Those steps were all taken by 11 a.m., just as O'Neill, O'Brien and Paddy Murphy arrived in Derrylin. Once the demands were served, the board meetings out of the way and the new directors appointed, the lenders were officially in control. They were the new owners of all the cement, glass and radiator factories, the wind turbines, hotels and pubs.

It had taken no more than ninety minutes.

With the legal formalities complete, the receivers could now be a bit less discreet. The group that arrived at Derrylin included a heavy security presence. As well as the drivers-cum-bodyguards, there was an RMI security man with the IT team, a security man installed at reception in the Quinn Group HQ and two on the access road to 'ensure any press presence remains outside the head office perimeter'. Two-man security teams would rotate through the day and night, to ensure the buildings were secure and support the IT team as they backed up the Quinn network. A separate roving team would 'conduct security assessments of the key sites to assess relative risks and potential responses', while back-up response teams would 'provide assistance if required'.

RMI also arrived with its own locksmith, on call during the day to provide access to any area. 'The locksmiths will return to site during the evening of Day One to change all external locks to allow the integrity of the building to be maintained,' said the sequencing memo, slipping into military parlance. A security sweep of the key offices in the two head office buildings at Derrylin would be carried out 'to ensure there are no unauthorised devices on site'. At the end of Day One, RMI would assess the security requirements for the days to come.

RMI had also brought an 'infrastructure team', complete with a van full of IT equipment. Its job would be to 'gain control of the business and protect infrastructure', according to the Day One plan. Once the enforcement process was completed and the new boards in place, RMI would 'gain control of key IT infrastructure and [the] email communication distribution network'. As the new directors set about briefing Quinn Group staff on the situation, its tasks were to 'commence back-up of vital data' and 'protect bank accounts from unauthorised transactions'.

The next step was to tell staff what was going on. Pat O'Neill sent the pre-prepared email from his Gmail account to senior management, the directors of the various sub-boards of the group, and members of the Quinn Employee Forum. There would be a meeting and conference call at noon that day and their attendance was required. Shortly afterwards, staff were informed of the news, in a letter from Pat O'Neill emailed to all employees. Foreign-language versions were sent to employees at the Quinn Plastics sites in France, Germany, Belgium, the Czech Republic and Slovakia. Michael McAteer and Paul McCann were also sent a copy, for circulation to the staff at Quinn Insurance. 'Today a major restructuring of the financial, management and corporate structure of the group has been announced ... As part of the corporate restructuring, Sean Quinn ceases to be a director of the Group and of the holding company and will no longer have a role in managing the business,' it said.

The letter acknowledged Sean Quinn's achievements and commitment to creating jobs in the border area. 'Sadly, in more recent years a number of well-publicised events have left the manufacturing group with substantial borrowings which, quite simply, the group could not service. If these debts were not restructured, the businesses could not survive in their present form.' There would be no lay-offs as a result of the restructuring and there were 'no plans whatever' to break up the manufacturing group. 'I know that the past year has been difficult for every individual in the group,' it said. 'Despite that, we have every reason to be proud of our businesses and of the care you continuously take of our customers. Together we must, we can and we will develop and expand our businesses.'

The letter said the restructuring would permanently relieve the manufacturing businesses of more than €500 million of the €1.3 billion debt, but did not go into detail on the new arrangements. There was no mention of share receivers or bondholders. There was no mention of Anglo Irish Bank. A separate document listed twenty-six questions and answers the employees might find useful, particularly in relation to their jobs. 'If this financial restructuring did not happen,' it said, 'then there is no doubt that, within a short space of time, jobs here would be at serious risk.'

The Q&A told workers the removal of Sean Quinn 'was a prerequisite of the restructuring for the lenders, due to loss of confidence . . . In all circumstances the decision to remove Sean Quinn is not reversible.' It reiterated that there had been no Quinn bid for Quinn Insurance. 'Sean Quinn and his family's dealings with Anglo Irish Bank are a matter between them and the bank. What we have to deal with is the fallout from those dealings.'

Among staff, there was shock, disbelief, horror. 'There was no hostility, just shock,' said one person who was involved in the enforcement. 'People had been living with the fear of something like this happening, and now it had.'

'The latest is that Sean Quinn is out of a job from today,' one employee, Richard Maguire, who had three brothers also working for Quinn, told reporters. 'It's an absolute disgrace, they've hounded that man out. It was political, they wanted to make him pay for his mistake, but the business was doing well before it went into receivership.'

The mood was different at Quinn Insurance, where staff had been told that Anglo and Liberty now had preferred-bidder status. Liberty would have a 51 per cent stake in the venture and run the company; Anglo would be a silent 49 per cent partner, acting solely in a debt-recovery capacity. An office in Manchester would shed twenty-four jobs and the offices in Navan would close, though the workers were guaranteed jobs in Cavan, about forty miles north on the M3, or Blanchardstown, about twenty miles south along the motorway. Cavan would remain the head office.

After more than a year of uncertainty, the news was welcomed at the insurance company. In a statement, the Employee Representative Committee of Quinn Insurance said it was 'delighted' a deal had been done. 'We sincerely regret the closure of the Manchester office and the loss of our colleagues' jobs. However, we are happy that the matter has now progressed and we look forward to a successful future with the company,' the employee committee said.

Not everyone shared the upbeat assessment. Caroline Forde, a long-term employee of Quinn Insurance, had run as a pro-Quinn independent candidate for Cavan/Monaghan in the General Election on 25 February. There was speculation that Quinn had funded her campaign, which gave strong support to the Quinn debt-repayment proposal. On campaign literature, Forde described Quinn's plan as 'by far the only viable solution' to the issue. She got 1,912 first-preference votes in the election, about 2.8 per cent of the total, finishing eleventh in the five-seat constituency.

On 14 April, Forde was among the group that travelled to Dublin to hand in the petition to the Financial Regulator. She was in the capital when word came through about the group receivership and the plan to sell Quinn Insurance to Liberty. She was incensed at what she saw as the government's betrayal of Quinn and the border region. She told journalists she was 'devastated' at Anglo's actions: 'If this [Quinn's businesses] is gone, there is nothing else in the area. There is no future for many people.'

Forde's comments were broadcast on the RTÉ one o'clock news bulletin, watched by staff at the Quinn Insurance headquarters in Cavan. There was disapproving booing: Forde did not represent the majority view. At the insurer, at least, opinion had shifted.

Just before 11.30 a.m., the outside world was told what was going on in Derrylin and Cavan. Quinn Group issued a pre-prepared press release through Brian Bell, its long-standing public relations adviser from Wilson Hartnell PR. Bell had been brought in on the loop in advance, and the text of the press release had been prepared ahead of the appointment. Although Bell had worked alongside Sean Quinn for several years, he had always technically been working for the Quinn Group; now he was answering to a new board and a shareholder bank. His press release broke the news of the appointment of Wallace as share receiver and the removal of Sean Quinn from the business. It would set newsrooms around the country buzzing.

There were also press releases from Anglo and KPMG. The Anglo release included a quote from Mike Aynsley. 'Actions over the past number of years by the owners of the group have destabilised the group and put at risk fine businesses and the livelihoods of over 2,760 people,' it said.

The lenders had together achieved what they wanted to achieve – to take ultimate control of Quinn Group. It could not have gone better. It had taken Sean Quinn completely by surprise.

At noon, O'Neill met the senior management, members of the Quinn Employee Forum and the directors of the various subsidiary boards, in the boardroom of the Quinn Group head office building at Derrylin. Many of those present had worked with Quinn for decades. They included Adrian Curry, chief executive of Quinn Glass, and Denis Doogan, chief executive of Quinn Radiators. Tony Lunney, a brother of Kevin Lunney, who was with Sean Quinn at the meeting with Anglo in Dublin, was an operations director in Quinn's building-products division.

O'Neill's address was carefully scripted. The key was to highlight the seriousness of the situation without making a martyr of Quinn. 'I wouldn't have asked you to come here at such short notice if it wasn't particularly important,' he began. 'Today is a very significant day for the Quinn Group and especially for each of your businesses and the people in them. A major restructuring of the financial, management and corporate structure of the group has been announced today. It will give us the financial stability we need to enable our businesses to survive – and that is no exaggeration, far from it. It does have other implications as well – Sean Quinn will no longer be involved in the group either as a shareholder or in any management capacity. It will be a big news item and I want to make sure, as far as we possibly can, that people within the businesses hear it from us first.'

O'Neill had come prepared. There were information packs for the divisional bosses to give to their staff, focusing particularly on how to deal with any employee and customer concerns. 'Go back to your businesses to reassure employees, customers and suppliers. That will be the key activity for each of you today.' O'Neill didn't mince his words when it came to explaining why the restructuring was necessary: Sean Quinn and his family had borrowed €2.8 billion from Anglo and pledged the business as security for that borrowing. The family had also taken 'significant funds from the businesses' to fund the purchase of shares in Anglo, which had been worthless since the bank's nationalization.

The other element was the €1.3 billion owed to the non-Anglo lenders, which 'the businesses could not possibly manage', particularly following the putting of Quinn Insurance into administration. Suppliers had been getting edgy and the group was 'facing the bleak but clear prospect of an uncontrolled insolvency'. The receivership was both 'a sad day for Quinn Group' and 'a day for breathing a huge sigh of relief', said O'Neill.

'Relief that we are dealing with restructuring rather than uncontrolled insolvency, relief that we will not be having any redundancies as a result of the restructuring, relief that our financial position has been stabilized and that we have been given the opportunity to survive and grow.' The speech was a tour de force.

O'Neill had additional notes prepared if staff asked questions, particularly about Sean Quinn. 'Of course I have huge sympathy for Sean and his family,' read the pre-prepared answer in the Day One briefing document. It came complete with block capitals for emphasis.

Like you and people throughout the country, I've admired what he had built up and what he has achieved, and the employment he has given to so many. It makes it all the more difficult to understand how EVERYTHING was gambled on one massive stock market bet. But that is what happened and we now have to deal with the fallout from that to save the businesses from uncontrolled insolvency. A bleak and pretty sobering reality.

Michael Noonan, the Finance Minister, rowed in behind Anglo and the receiver. In a press statement on what the finance department described as 'Quinn Group matters', the minister noted the appointment of the share receiver and the fact that Sean Quinn and his family would no longer have any role in the management, operations or ownership of the Quinn Group. The deal was a good thing, he maintained.

> I welcome the debt restructuring plan which has been agreed in principle between Anglo Irish Bank and the group's lenders. This structure will enable the good and strong businesses to continue to trade and grow. It is particularly important that there will be no impact on employment, on trade creditors or on day-to-day operations of the Quinn Group.

Noonan was limited in what he could say about the Quinn Insurance deal, noting it was a matter for the administrators, who were appointed by the High Court on behalf of the Financial Regulator. There was a new regulatory regime in town and it was important not to tread on toes. The minister's statement read:

> I note that the sale of Quinn Insurance is nearing completion with the joint venture between Liberty Mutual (a large US insurance company) and Anglo identified by the joint administrators as the preferred bidder. This is subject to regulatory approval, and the completion of contract details. I welcome the positives of the proposed agreement in that almost all 1,500 jobs in Quinn Insurance will be retained.

The minister reiterated his jobs message in a round-table briefing with journalists later that day. He seemed uncertain about some of the details, mistakenly saying Matthew Elderfield had put a receiver into Quinn Group in March 2010, rather than administrators into Quinn Insurance. There were also references to the deal preserving Quinn jobs in Cavan and Monaghan, though Sean Quinn had never had any operations in Co. Monaghan. Through it all, though, Noonan stuck firmly to the message that the share receivership at Quinn Group and the sale of Quinn Insurance was 'a good news story for the workers'.

Noonan highlighted other positives. Liberty, a newcomer to Ireland, was putting 'a big chunk of equity' into Quinn Insurance and intended to 'trade in the [Irish] market and expand if possible'. And as the company built its market share, Anglo's 49 per cent stake would surely increase in value, said the minister: 'If the insurance company is trading profitably, it is going to be worth a lot more in the future. And at some point [Anglo] will probably make a decision to sell their equity stake to cancel out some of the debt that they're owed.'

At Quinn Group, there was good news, too, according to the minister. The restructuring agreement included clauses that did not allow assets to be sold for set periods of time or below certain prices. They had been insisted upon by Anglo, the minister said. Quinn Glass, for example, 'has to operate for at least five years before there is any consideration of sale . . . From that point of view, it's a very good story.' The bondholders were agreeing to park a big chunk of their €1.3 billion Quinn Group debt, after taking 'a heavy hit in the negotiations with Anglo' during the restructuring talks, Noonan said.

Noonan also spoke of the Quinn family's personal debts. 'What's fairly sure is that the Quinn family, stripped of their assets, won't have a capacity to pay their personal debts,' he said. 'So whatever the quantum is there, there'll be significant write-offs in that. But that's not really a matter for me – that's a matter for Anglo to work out.'

Separately, in the same briefing, Noonan said, 'There is no suggestion that Anglo want to recover all the money they are owed. But then there was never any suggestion of that.' It was an intriguing observation but it went unquestioned amid the drama of the day.

Anglo and Wallace had anticipated a huge backlash from Quinn, some immediate attempt at a comeback or a legal challenge. The bank and Wallace had explored their options for each eventuality and were ready to respond, depending on what he did. A list of 'key risks and contingency plans' in the Day One document outlined the various scenarios and what action should be taken if they arose. If Quinn himself came out fighting in the media, the bank had pre-prepared statements 'ready to be released to counter SQ [Sean Quinn] PR'.

If he went for an injunction to delay the receivership, Anglo and the bondholders would immediately submit a petition to put the group into administration in Northern Ireland. Arthur Cox and Deloitte had the groundwork done for that process. If the Quinn Group management decided to resign en masse, replacements with experience in manufacturing had been lined up to take their places on an interim basis. If staff held some sort of protest, a script had been prepared for O'Neill to address them. If the businessman himself, Liam McCaffrey, Kevin Lunney, Dara O'Reilly or Sinead Geoghegan appeared, the instruction was to strip them of their mobile phones and laptops 'to limit their effectiveness or ability to promote disruption'. But they were not to be ejected from the site for fear of escalating the situation.

Nothing was being left to chance.

Anglo and Wallace knew the Quinn Group workforce was fiercely loyal to Sean Quinn. They were prepared for disturbances, possibly even a staff revolt. But none of it happened. And there was no response from Quinn himself, not even a statement. By mid-afternoon on 14 April, Wallace was on the road back to Dublin with Andrew O'Leary, the KPMG colleague he had travelled to Cavan and Fermanagh with early that morning. The receiver was back in his home in Dublin by 5 p.m., in time for dinner. He had not even met Sean Quinn or any of his family. From that point on, he would get updates from the new Quinn directors and report to the bank.

Sean Quinn didn't stay quiet for long. The next morning, as the last of the enforcement team returned to Dublin with RMI, Quinn held a meeting with local politicians in Monaghan. The businessman was emotional and 'quite candid' about the mistakes he had made, said people present at the gathering. Quinn raised particular concerns about the security of jobs at the group and whether individual businesses could be sold off. Most of all, he wanted the politicians to relay his concerns back to Noonan. 'Sean was upset and very distressed; it was an emotional meeting. Everything he had worked for was crumbling before his eyes and he knew it,' a person who was at the meeting told the *Impartial Reporter*, a Fermanagh newspaper. 'He was very upset and felt he had been left high and dry.'

Three days later, on Monday 18 April, Quinn gave his first public response to receivership. In a personal statement released to media, the businessman said:

> The decision by Anglo last week to appoint share receivers was the greatest upset for me and my family in my entire business career. My colleagues and I have spent the past year developing a proposal that is economically sustainable and which would allow us to discharge fully all of our family's obligations to the Irish taxpayer.
>
> During this process we consulted with and secured the support of some of the most respected and experienced individuals in Irish and UK business. I am utterly convinced that our proposal could achieve the retention and increase of skilled employment in the Group. The Quinn Group businesses are among the best and most progressive in the world.
>
> I would like to sincerely thank both our customers and staff for their huge contribution to the success of the business and their allegiance to both me and the Group. There is no workforce anywhere that has the talent, commitment, loyalty and determination of the Quinn workforce. They have created and sustained skilled employment in regions where this was not seen as possible before. At this time my concerns are for those who have made such an enormous contribution to the success of the Group.
>
> Our mistake was to place an overreliance on the Irish banking system and the many predictions for continued sustained growth in the Irish economy from some of the country's leading financial services experts. Ireland needs enterprise and entrepreneurs more than ever at this time but mistakes in business should not result in a life sentence. I value the friendship and support of the many people I have worked with during this difficult time and to the many thousands who have voiced their support in so many ways I say 'thank you'.
>
> I would like to acknowledge the support of my family. The Irish family unit is quite unique for support, loyalty and compassion. Despite all that has happened I am fortunate to have the most wonderful family and it has been their steadfast support that has sustained me during a most difficult time.
>
> Understandably there has been extensive media coverage since last

week on many aspects relating to me, my family and the Group. Amid all of the coverage there has been inaccurate and false reporting. This is the only statement I have made in relation to the current issues and I would ask that reporting of matters relating to me and my family be based on fact rather than speculation.

9

'I'll do a deal, but then I'll sue you'

The meetings in the run-up to Day One had left Robert Dix with one question about seizing control of Sean Quinn's sprawling property portfolio, 'On Thursday, when we go in there, who is actually going to be running this?'

The response came back, 'You.'

Dix would go in as executive chairman of Quinn Finance, the company behind the property division. It had about twenty staff and operated relatively independently of Quinn Group. Charged by Kieran Wallace and Anglo with running the property group, Dix would shuttle between his comfortable Dublin city-centre office and a desk in Quinn Group headquarters in Derrylin.

In preparation for the receivership, Dix had spent some time familiarizing himself with the group's property assets. He felt he had a good grasp of where they were located, what companies owned them, and what borrowings they had. But the property group structure was very complex, a myriad of companies spread across several jurisdictions. The ownership of the properties was mixed up between Quinn Group, Quinn Insurance and members of the Quinn family. Properties that had been announced as having been acquired by the Quinn Group sometimes turned out to be owned by family members. It was apparent that Sean Quinn and his family viewed themselves and their companies as one and the same.

There were forty-four properties in total for Dix to get to grips with. Following the share receivership, the ownership of the properties would be apportioned to the various creditors. Anglo had charges over Quinn's Irish hotels and pubs, as well as the Hilton and Ibis hotels in Prague and the Prestige Mall shopping centre in Istanbul, in Turkey. The bank also had an interest in the properties bought for the Quinn family in Russia, Ukraine and India, while Quinn Group had a direct interest in the Leonardo office block in Kiev and a commercial building in Dublin.

As part of the move to separate Quinn Insurance from Quinn Group and allow the sale of the insurance company, almost twenty assets would be retained by the insurer. They were effectively in the control of Grant Thornton, but Dix and his team would have responsibility for managing them. They included: the Crowne Plaza Hotel in Cambridge; the Sheraton Hotel in Krakow; the Hilton Hotel in Sofia; the Iveagh Fitness Centre in Dublin; seven commercial buildings in Ireland and four in the UK; a landfill site; a wind farm; and two apartments in Manchester.

It was a bewildering assortment of assets, but Dix was impressed by their quality. Quinn hadn't bought just anything; whether in Ireland or abroad, he had typically invested in high-spec, upmarket assets. In his single-minded pursuit of profit, he was willing to invest in any type of property in virtually any jurisdiction. 'The [Quinn] approach was "get me a return in the large teens or above on investment in property",' said one source with knowledge of the properties. 'That's not available in Ireland, so it was a case of "go forth and do that somewhere else". There was nothing in terms of strategy, except getting a return. The usual approach to business is you specialize in something – a product or a market – and get used to doing that. That didn't exist.'

Dara O'Reilly and Kevin Lunney looked after the ventures close to home, mainly hotels and pubs across Ireland, the UK and Eastern Europe. Petey Quinn, Sean Quinn's nephew, had responsibility for the Quinn family properties in Russia and Ukraine. There were twelve in total, including the Kutuzoff Tower in Moscow and the Ukraina shopping centre in Kiev. Gary Conway oversaw the Q-City property in HITEC City in Hyderabad, in India.

Dix, a straight-talker, set out his stall to the employees of the property unit: yes, Quinn Group had new owners; yes, Sean Quinn and his family had been ousted. There would be changes at the top but there would be no job losses among the rank-and-file staff in the property division and no reason why the unit could not go on operating as normal. Given the circumstances in which Dix had arrived in their midst, the staff were naturally suspicious. It would take time for him to win their trust.

Although O'Reilly and Lunney had left the board of Quinn Group (NI) a year earlier to support Sean Quinn's efforts to keep control of Quinn Insurance, they and Petey Quinn were still Quinn Group employees. Petey visited Dix in his Dublin office to talk things through. He was accompanied by his brother, another nephew of Sean Quinn. Petey struck Dix as bright but slightly naïve, a bit rough around the edges. He didn't seem to accept the reality that Sean Quinn would lose control of his properties. As far as Dix was concerned, the nephew was considering working with the receivers to ensure the various properties were properly secured. Given the key role he had played in the property group, his assistance would be valuable. Time would show that Petey had other ideas, though he was keeping them to himself. Once Petey made it clear he would not work with the receivers, Dix began to negotiate his exit from the company, as well as the exits of Dara O'Reilly and Kevin Lunney.

Detailed negotiations took place in the days after the enforcement action, and departure terms were agreed around 23–24 April, Easter weekend 2011. The trio were offered significant redundancy packages, based on the same formula that had been used to calculate Liam McCaffrey's package when he was made redundant from Quinn Group on 14 April. O'Reilly and Lunney, who were now actively supporting Sean Quinn's campaign against the receivership, accepted their pay-offs and left. Petey Quinn initially seemed to accept the severance package, but then refused to take the pay-off from the receivers who had seized his uncle's company. He walked away without the money.

At the same time, senior Quinn Group managers were attempting to negotiate some sort of severance deal for Sean Quinn. They approached Paul O'Brien, the new group chief executive, to see what could be done for 'the boss' in the wake of the all-encompassing receivership. O'Brien met Peter Quinn, Sean Quinn's brother, on the subject. There were various outlines for deals, with terms that included ensuring Quinn could stay in his family home and giving immunity to his children from any future legal action that might arise. Talks dragged on for three days. The sticking point was that Quinn refused to waive his right to sue Anglo Irish Bank and Kieran Wallace. 'He could have done a deal, but his first condition was that he retained the right to litigation,' said a source close to the company. 'It was a case of: "I'll do a deal, but then I'll sue you." We couldn't accept that.'

No deal was done.

Dix, meanwhile, needed a new team to run the property group. He had spent a lot of time in Derrylin in the weeks after the receivership but he didn't plan to be there forever. Though he was happy to be chairman of the property company, now renamed Quinn International Property Management, he hoped to drop the 'executive' part of his executive chairman post sooner rather than later. He turned to Paul Morgan, the former finance director of Quinn's hospitality division.

In early 2010, around the time Quinn Insurance was put into administration, Morgan had just finished a job with CDiscount, an Irish online retailer. Then a phone call came out of the blue: it was Colette Quinn, asking if Morgan, who had left Quinn Group four years earlier, would return. A lot had happened in the meantime and Kevin Lunney needed some help keeping a handle on the property business.

Morgan agreed to return. It was a difficult time: the group was under huge pressure from the banks and bondholders, the mood was tense, and there was sometimes conflict between Morgan and Petey Quinn. Sources said that Petey resented Morgan's return and felt he was being sidelined. The shared feeling, though, was that the group would get through its difficulties, that Sean Quinn was too big to fail.

Morgan kept his head down and did his job, managing the property assets and liaising with the Quinn Insurance administrators and Anglo where necessary. On 14 April 2011, he was in Buswells Hotel in Dublin – then still controlled by the Quinns – when he got a call from a family member who worked at Quinn Insurance. The news was unexpected: staff at the insurer had just been told it was being taken over by Liberty Mutual and Anglo.

When Morgan walked out of Buswells on to Molesworth Street, he met hundreds of Quinn workers marching to the gates of the Dáil to deliver a petition to keep the insurer in Quinn hands. Virtually alone among them, Morgan knew it was too late. Richard Wood-house, the Anglo banker, was among the next to call Morgan. He had even bigger news: Quinn Group and its property assets were in receivership; Anglo and the lenders were in control.

Robert Dix knew that Morgan was highly capable and felt that his years away from Quinn Group meant he had more perspective on the situation than other Quinn employees. Dix asked Morgan to take on the role of chief operations officer of the property group, effectively managing all the properties accumulated by Sean Quinn. Morgan would later become chief executive of the unit. Amid the upheaval, one employee left voluntarily – Gary Conway, who had looked after the Quinn property interests in India, and was close to Petey Quinn.

The immediate priority for Dix and Morgan was to ensure the relevant bank accounts were under control and the authority to sign paperwork and accounts had transferred to the new regime. In the system created under Quinn's regime, all the financial transactions for the various assets were reported back to Derrylin, where the accounting and payments systems were centralized. From his office, Dix could see online ledgers for the companies behind the various properties, the rents flowing in and expenditure going out. For the first two weeks or so following the 14 April receivership, everything seemed to be running as normal. Then, slowly but surely, changes to the normal patterns started to emerge.

Communication from certain companies in the property group became less frequent. Their banking relationships changed. Dix and his team in Derrylin started to lose sight of the ledgers of companies behind certain assets. Information was disappearing. The issues seemed to be centred on properties in three countries in particular: Russia, Ukraine and India.

It was starting to look like somebody was trying to move those assets beyond the control of the receivers.

When Kieran Wallace was appointed as share receiver, there was much speculation about how Sean Quinn would react. Would he challenge the appointment? Would he sue? Would he simply give up?

On 16 May, just over a month after the share receiver was appointed, the receiver and the Anglo bankers finally got their answer.

Through their lawyers, the Dublin firm Eversheds O'Donnell Sweeney, the family filed a plenary summons in the High Court, effectively putting the bank and the receiver on notice that a large legal action was on the way. The plenary summons named the plaintiffs as Patricia Quinn and her five children, Colette, Ciara, Sean Junior, Aoife and Brenda. Sean Quinn himself was not part of the action. Despite his dominant role in everything concerning Quinn Group he was not a shareholder in the group. He had no legal entitlement to contest the receivership.

The summons set out the foundations of the family's planned case against Anglo. First, the Quinns said, the charges that Anglo purported to have over shares in Quinn Group were 'invalid, unenforceable and of no legal effect'. The appointment of Wallace as receiver was therefore also invalid and unenforceable and should be declared null and void, according to the family.

Patricia Quinn and her children also claimed that personal guarantees they had given over loans from Anglo to Cypriot companies in 2008, when Sean Quinn's CFD stake was being unwound, were invalid and unenforceable. The plenary summons was the first step in the legal action, a sort of shot across the bows of Anglo and Wallace, and did not explain in detail the basis for the family's claims.

As a result of Anglo's actions in appointing Wallace as share receiver, the family claimed they were entitled to damages for negligence and breach of trust on the part of the bank. They also claimed damages for 'intentional and/or negligent infliction of economic damage'. In simple terms, they wanted Wallace removed, they wanted their companies back and they wanted to be paid damages for the whole episode. Anglo and the receiver were required to respond within eight days of being served with the plenary summons. They did so, entering an appearance in the central office of the Four Courts. The legal battle was on.

Two weeks after the family's plenary summons was filed, with the agreement of the Quinns and Anglo, Mr Justice Peter Kelly transferred the family case against the bank to the Commercial Court. The specialized court had been set up seven years earlier to fast-track business disputes in which amounts exceeding €1 million were at stake. The Quinn case would involve, by some measure, the largest claim in the Commercial Court's history – indeed, the largest claim in Irish legal history.

Aoife Quinn filed a detailed affidavit on behalf of the family. The second-youngest of Sean and Patricia Quinn's children, she had moved to Kerry after her Leaving Certificate, studying science at Tralee Institute of Technology. After Tralee, she moved back to Dublin, studying law at Blackhall Place, the training ground for Irish solicitors, located a few hundred metres from the Four Courts. Rather than practise law, however, she took a job with Quinn Insurance. It was a circuitous route, but she had come back to the family fold.

After the share receiver had been appointed to the Quinn Group, Aoife had taken a role in helping to devise and implement the family's strategy. Her primary focus was on helping to mount an almighty legal battle with Anglo. Her affidavit laid out the family's version of events leading up to the group being put into receivership.

It confirmed publicly, for the first time, that Sean Quinn had spent a staggering €3.1 billion on his CFD bet on Anglo shares. Aoife Quinn said that €750 million from 'Quinn resources' had been invested in buying Anglo CFDs before the end of 2007. From September 2007 on, as the bank's share price fell and Quinn faced margin calls to cover his CFD losses, Anglo provided loans of €2.34 billion. The loans were all to meet the CFD margin calls, but were described 'completely falsely' by Anglo executives at the time as being for developments in Russia and India, according to the Quinn affidavit. (The bank's total exposure to Quinn was in fact €2.8 billion, including €455 million that was not related to the CFD investments and was not disputed by the family.)

It said the bank lent the €2.34 billion 'in the full knowledge' that the money was to be used 'to support CFD positions [in Anglo]'. That meant the loans were 'in support of an illegal objective of market manipulation', an offence under EU market abuse rules. Anglo's lending was therefore 'tainted with illegality or was intended to support an illegal purpose', Aoife Quinn's affidavit said. It also claimed that Anglo 'supported and encouraged' the CFD investment in a bid to boost its share price. The bank paid 'no heed to the requirements of corporate governance or the interests of its shareholders', Quinn claimed, citing the concealing of loans to executives and the back-to-back deposit arrangement with Irish Life & Permanent as examples. The affidavit argued the bank's loans to the family were unlawful, invalid and unenforceable. If the loans were unlawful, so too were the charges the bank had taken over the Quinn Group as security for the loans.

The affidavit also provided details of the Maple Ten transaction, which had remained under wraps for almost three years. It outlined how the family had unwound the CFD position in July 2008, taking a 15 per cent shareholding in the bank, under what Aoife claimed was severe pressure from Anglo management. The ten long-standing Anglo customers took a 10 per cent stake in the CFD unwinding, said Aoife Quinn, in a deal put together by the bank supported with loans from the bank. To finalize the deal, in or around October 2008, loans totalling €385 million were channelled to the five Quinn children through five Cypriot companies and €102 million to a Cypriot firm owned by Patricia Quinn, to buy shares directly in the bank. The Quinns gave guarantees over the debts without being told of the 'precarious' financial position of Anglo, Aoife Quinn said.

The affidavit acknowledged that the Quinns had signed various documents for Anglo but said that they 'did so without any autonomy or appreciation as to the consequences'. According to the affidavit, 'the usual practice was only to receive and sign the signature page'. The Quinns argued now that the bank failed in its duty of care to them because it did not seek to meet them personally or explain the nature of the documents. The Quinns claimed they never knew they could face 'significant personal financial liabilities' from the

CFD affair and the loans they had taken out in tandem with the Maple Ten transaction.

'If they had been made aware of the potentially dire personal circumstances in which they could have found (and do find) themselves as a consequence of executing the documentation, they would not have signed it,' the affidavit said. It said that the Quinn family had 'limited appreciation' of the corporate structures created in their names to bet on shares in Anglo or the billions of euro in borrowings to fund the deals.

The family did not put a figure on the damages sought but said it would run to hundreds of millions of euro. It was an unusual argument: the Quinns were acknowledging they had signed loan agreements with Anglo and given guarantees to the bank, but were claiming they were not liable to repay the money borrowed. Despite owning one of the biggest companies in the country, the Quinns were claiming they did not understand – or even know about – what was going on between their father and Anglo. Somewhat incongruously, though he was the central figure in the entire episode, Sean Quinn himself was not a party to the legal action. His absence from the lawsuit prompted speculation of a split within the family, either genuine or strategic, but such speculation was quickly rubbished by sources close to the Quinns. There was not, and would not be, any difference of opinion between Sean Quinn and his wife and children.

In court on 30 May 2011, Paul Gallagher SC, a former Attorney General who was acting for Anglo, said the bank might seek to join Sean Quinn and other parties to the action, even though the businessman was not a party to the lawsuit filed by his family. Mr Justice Peter Kelly approved a schedule agreed between the two sides that would involve months of document discovery and exchange before a hearing in 2012.

As a consequence of the upheaval at Quinn Group, by spring 2011 the group's 2009 accounts still had yet to be finalized. The completion of the accounts had been delayed first by the Quinn Insurance administration and then by efforts to resolve the €1.3 billion Quinn Group debt. Now, with the future of Quinn Insurance more certain and the lenders on side, the figures could be settled. It fell to a board that had been in place for not much more than a month to sign off on the belated 2009 accounts.

The 2009 figures made for grim reading. In its last full year under the control of Sean Quinn, the Quinn Group had total gross revenues of €1.8 billion, down sharply from revenues of almost €2.3 billion in 2008. The 'very disappointing set of results' showed an operating loss of €888.5 million for the year, a drastic reversal from a €239 million operating profit in 2008. The group had a deficit of €192 million on its balance sheet. With liabilities outweighing assets, Sean Quinn's group was technically worthless.

The figures for Quinn Insurance, compiled using more stringent reserving methodology approved by the administrators, showed revenues of more than €1.1 billion but an operating loss of more than €644 million. The figures for the manufacturing businesses – Sean Quinn's traditional businesses of cement, glass, radiators and plastics – weren't much better. The manufacturing group had revenues of €654.4 million in 2009 but made an operating loss of nearly €244 million. With the businesses and the economy generally in trouble, the board approved the write-off of €163 million from the value of various assets and another €60 million for 'loan provisions'.

Nearly €82 million was written off the value of the MMA plant at Leuna outside Leipzig, one of Quinn's pet projects. It had been 'put on hold temporarily' and negotiations were ongoing about getting funds or a partner to finish the project. If those efforts were unsuccessful, the half-finished project, valued at €130 million in the new accounts, might suffer further write-downs on its value.

Another €41 million was wiped from the value of goodwill in Quinn's core construction businesses, and €34 million from his plastics and packaging operation, because of 'exceptionally difficult market conditions'. The value of Quinn Healthcare, the former Bupa business, was written down by €31 million because of ongoing losses. Various lands and buildings in the group were valued at almost €44 million less than they had been at the end of 2008. Even Quinn's 24 per cent stake in NCB Stockbrokers was revalued downwards because of what the group auditors, PricewaterhouseCoopers, described as 'market conditions surrounding this investment'.

The results laid bare the nature of the financial web connecting the group and the family. Property companies and 'investment and finance companies' described as being 'under the control of close family members of Mr and Mrs Sean Quinn' owed the Quinn Group €951 million. That was money that had been taken out of the group to cover the cost of Sean Quinn's CFD gamble on Anglo shares. That money, now completely gone, was distinct from the €200 million 'capital contribution' paid directly to the Quinns in 2008.

For Richard Woodhouse and his colleagues at Anglo, the grim figures justified the complex restructuring and the drastic enforcement action taken on 14 April. 'The businesses were bust. The accounts for 2009 reflected that position,' said a source at the bank. 'Quinn had reached the end of the road and something needed to be done.'

The Quinns and their supporters, however, saw the equation the other way around: the figures were the result of the action taken first by the Financial Regulator, in seizing Quinn Insurance, and then by the lenders, in seizing Quinn Group. They had 'created' the losses by their actions; if Sean Quinn was still in charge, the businesses would still be profitable.

At the end of the first week in June, information began to filter back to the Quinn Group receivers and the Anglo bankers that something was awry in Sweden. Quinn Investments Sweden sat at the top of the complex property group structure, which consisted of layers of companies set up for tax and legal reasons. Below Quinn Investment Sweden there were Swedish subsidiary companies, which in turn owned Cypriot companies. They, in turn, owned shares in the companies in each jurisdiction that held the actual properties.

When he was building his property portfolio, Quinn had used Quinn Finance to borrow money from the bank and feed it through the Swedish companies. The money would travel down through the structure until it reached the companies that held the properties. Now Robert Dix and Anglo were seeing unusual activity in the Swedish companies.

'It started to emerge that things were happening to companies in Sweden that were very odd,' said one source. 'Things were happening to companies that shouldn't be happening.'

It took some time to figure out what was going on. As part of the 14 April choreography, Kieran Wallace had moved to change the board of Quinn Investments Sweden by removing the Quinn directors and replacing them with a Dix-led team. It now emerged that legal proceedings had been launched by the Quinns in Stockholm in the middle of May, in a bid to prevent Anglo from taking control of the company. The old board of Quinn Investments Sweden – Sean Quinn himself, Petey Quinn, Liam McCaffrey, Kevin Lunney and Dara O'Reilly – had challenged the receiver's move in the Swedish courts, and won.

The Stockholm District Court had ruled that the dismissal of directors of the Swedish company and their replacement with directors installed by Wallace was invalid. The court said the Quinn family showed 'probable grounds' that Anglo represented them at a shareholders' meeting on 18 April, at which the new directors were appointed, 'without the correct documentation of competence'. It found Quinn Investments Sweden had not sent all shareholders notice to attend the meeting, and that not all shareholders approved the dismissal and replacement of the board.

The ruling said the decision to appoint new directors at Quinn Investments Sweden should not be implemented until further notice. After the court ruling, the Quinns' lawyers wrote to Kieran Wallace's lawyers seeking any documents he had in relation to the Swedish firm. They demanded that no further steps be taken on instructions from Dix and that any instructions he had given be countermanded.

It was an early victory for the Quinns and a setback for Anglo, Wallace and Dix. Concerned Irish Citizens, the pro-Quinn lobby group, trumpeted the Swedish court victory, highlighting the Stockholm court's ruling to politicians including Michael Noonan. It had 'taken a foreign jurisdiction to stand up for what is clearly right', the group said.

Richard Woodhouse sat down with Karyn Harty, a partner at McCann FitzGerald who was heading Anglo's defence of the Quinn case, to discuss the bank's response. Harty had studied at Queen's University in Belfast, the same alma mater as Petey Quinn, graduating in 1997 with an honours law degree. Qualified as a solicitor in both Northern Ireland and the Republic, she had specialized in media law for a number of years. She had joined McCann FitzGerald in 2005, and had since become a senior litigation partner, working on a number of complex cases.

Harty and Woodhouse knew they could appeal the Swedish court ruling, but in the meantime the Quinns would still have control of Quinn Investments Sweden – and the lucrative international property portfolio. They decided on a more drastic course of action. Anglo was owed €2.8 billion by Quinn and his companies, and the money was overdue. If it sought repayment of what it was owed and Quinn Investments Sweden was unable to pay, the bank could get a bankruptcy receiver appointed to the company and trump the Quinn family's bid to keep control. The receiver would have the power to liquidate the company and sell its properties. The bank would use Quinn International Property Holdings, the company chaired by Robert Dix, to seek the installation of a bankruptcy receiver.

The case was set for hearing on 14 June. Dix was on holiday in Spain when he got the call: he should pack his suit and fly to Stockholm.

10

Asset-stripping

After months of ignoring Petey's warnings, convinced that Anglo would strike some sort of deal, Sean Quinn came around to his nephew's way of thinking. Just days before the receiver rolled into Derrylin on 14 April, Sean Quinn finally gave the green light to Petey's plan to try to put the foreign properties beyond the reach of the bank.

The signs had been ominous for Quinn for some time. Anglo had snookered Quinn on the takeover of Quinn Insurance, backing down from a proposed joint venture with the family and saddling up instead with Liberty Mutual. Then, Quinn had heard rumours that the London office of Cushman & Wakefield, a commercial property agency, was touting his international properties to prospective buyers in Britain and on the continent.

On 31 March 2011, Mike Aynsley, the Anglo chief executive, had gone on national radio and said the ownership of the Quinn Group was likely to change. Quinn would later reveal in court that the Aynsley interview was the turning point, prompting him to contact Petey and tell him to put the plan into action. Petey did not need to be asked twice. Court filings would later reveal that he immediately booked flights to Russia and arranged face-to-face meetings with his legal advisers in Moscow.

After 14 April, when Anglo carried out its corporate coup d'état, Quinn was forced into a rethink. Was Petey's plan still viable? Was it too late to implement it? Those were decisions he wanted his children to make, Quinn decided. After all, they were the actual owners of the group and the foreign properties. A family meeting was called at Quinn's lakeside mansion outside Ballyconnell. For decades, Sean Quinn had been the dominant figure within the family, making all the major decisions, assigning roles for his children within the business. He was the boss; there was never any doubt about that. Now, though, he was ready to stand back from the front line and pass responsibility to the next generation. He told his children they were the owners of the group, and it was up to them to decide if – and how – they wanted to fight back against Anglo and the receiver. If they chose to implement Petey's plan, he would support them, Quinn said. But it was their decision.

The Quinn children intended to challenge the appointment of the share receiver in the courts, but they knew that such a case could take months, if not years, to be heard. In the meantime, they wanted to stop Anglo getting hold of the properties. They gave the green light to Petey's property plan.

It was a complex strategy, made up of several intricate financial moves. It involved removing the assets from companies that Anglo had security over and placing them into new companies with no obligations to the bank. The first phase would involve transferring control of the main group companies to trusted family members for a nominal fee. This would be facilitated by the Quinn family withdrawing their shareholdings in the existing companies. The next phase would be to transfer the assets to the new companies. Because Anglo had security over shares in the companies rather than the actual bricks-and-mortar assets, this would have the effect of eliminating Anglo's security.

To facilitate the shift between companies, Petey needed to create new creditors, who were owed massive sums of money. Large debts would have to be created and assigned to the new companies. The old companies would then be liquidated, leaving the creditors in control of the assets – in this case, the properties.

Petey knew that representatives of Anglo would be dispatched across Europe within days, charged with taking physical possession of the properties and their rent rolls. This was standard practice in any receivership process. But Petey believed he could stave them off in the three countries central to his plan: Russia, Ukraine and India. He reckoned he could prevent the receivers from gaining entry to the properties in those countries in the short term at least: the security teams at each building were loyal to the family, and he had been given assurances they would not allow Anglo easy access. But unless something more sophisticated were done, he knew, the bank would eventually get the real estate.

It was for this reason that the family decided to go legal. By launching court proceedings against the bank, the family could distract Anglo and force them to pump resources into defending the action. Court cases are typically easy to instigate but difficult to defend. It would frustrate the bank, and allow the family time to put the rest of the plan into action. So the family agreed to tackle Anglo in Stockholm, home of Quinn Investments Sweden, the ultimate holding company. Aoife Quinn, with her training as a solicitor, took the lead. Her husband, Stephen Kelly, meanwhile agreed to help Petey alter the shareholdings of the myriad companies in Russia.

As Aoife organized things in Sweden, Petey went to Moscow. There he liaised with Alexander Khokhlov, a Moscow lawyer he knew and trusted. They met at the Kutuzoff Tower, the nucleus of the Quinn overseas property business. Khokhlov worked through the specifics of the plan with Petey, outlining how the loans would be assigned out of the existing Quinn Group companies to new companies.

Khokhlov gave the example of Finansstroy, the Russian company that owned the Kutuzoff Tower. Finansstroy owed $45 million to Demesne, a Northern Ireland-based company owned by the Quinn group. Demesne acted as a legitimate vehicle to channel funds into the international property interests. Khokhlov explained that transferring the $45 million Demesne loans to a third party would create a new creditor of Finansstroy. The new creditor could then claim to be owed the $45 million and challenge Anglo's claim to the tower. To make it happen, Khokhlov said the family should establish a string of new companies to take control of the debts.

Khokhlov sent Petey to visit the offices of a law firm called Attorneys & Business, a short subway ride from Moscow's main business district. It had carved out a niche providing legal business services to small firms and foreigners. The firm boasted of its expertise in 'complex real-estate transactions' and claimed to be able to manage litigation in foreign countries including Ukraine and Cyprus. The firm also made a big play of its attorney–client privilege, stating in promotional literature that 'observation of professional secrecy shall be the unconditional priority' of its lawyers. 'The term of preservation of the secrecy shall not be limited in time,' it said. A&B advised Petey that time was of the essence.

Shortly after Petey returned home to Derrylin from Moscow, a courier delivered a large parcel from Khokhlov. It contained hundreds of documents. Some were in Russian, some in English. Court records would later show that Quinn sat down with his uncle, Sean Quinn, and the two men started signing pages marked with tabs by the Russian lawyers. With each signature, the Quinns were moving the assets away from the reach of Anglo Irish Bank. After the signing spree, Petey dispatched the papers back to Moscow.

In early May, as Robert Dix was still getting to grips with the Quinn properties, A&B was processing the volumes of freshly inked documents. Petey proceeded with the next phase of the plan. He started with the Kutuzoff Tower and its alluring $22 million in annual rent. The Kutuzoff would become the litmus test for his plan; if it worked on the tower, it would work everywhere. On 12 May, he applied to put Finansstroy, the owner of the tower, into bankruptcy. In Russia, putting a company into bankruptcy is one of the best ways to extract any cash in the business. The asset will be sold and the money will be paid to creditors. There is a golden rule, however – whoever controls the most debt controls the bankruptcy process and the appointment of the bankruptcy administrator.

One of the documents appended to the bankruptcy petition for Finansstroy stated that the largest creditor of the company was Cranaghan Property Management, which was owned by the Quinn family. Cranaghan, named after the townland in Cavan where Sean Quinn lived, claimed to be owed $273 million by Finansstroy, arising from a private arbitral court settlement in Moscow. It was not made clear what the award had been for or how it arose. The bankruptcy petition was adjourned for a month in the Russian courts.

Now Petey needed to transfer the ownership of the shares in Finansstroy. The tower had a deliberately convoluted ownership structure, designed to minimize taxes. All of the shares in Finansstroy were owned by a Cypriot company called Carcer Investments. On 3 June, however, in return for a $1,000 payment, Petey was allocated a 0.0543 per cent share in Finansstroy. The agreement was signed by Stephen Kelly on behalf of Carcer; he signed the resolution citing power of attorney granted by his wife, Aoife Quinn. Shortly afterwards, Aoife Quinn withdrew Carcer's entire shareholding in Finansstroy, leaving Petey, with his freshly granted 0.0543 per cent stake, as the sole shareholder. The move meant Carcer lost any interest in control of the tower. That control now resided with Finansstroy's sole remaining shareholder: Petey Quinn.

Stephen Kelly and Petey repeated the share withdrawal trick with another Russian company, Red Sector – the owner of a chain of DIY stores in Russia. The company was transferred to Kelly in exchange for a second-hand laptop computer. The property was valued at $13 million. With those two transactions alone, the family had sold shares in companies with assets worth almost $200 million to related parties in return for a laptop and about $1,000. Anglo, whose security applied only to the companies rather than to the properties, had been cut out of the equation.

The next step was moving the assets to new companies, through a new mirror structure that would be an exact replica of the existing set-up. That meant establishing new companies; lots of them. In early June, Petey purchased eight new shelf companies in Ukraine from the Companies Registration Office in Kiev. He then installed Larisa Yanez Puga, the Quinn employee who looked after the family's Ukrainian interests, as director general of each. The shareholders of the company were members of the extended Quinn family or individuals close to them, including Petey's sister Claire, Sean Quinn's sister Patricia McMahon and her husband Thomas McMahon, and Karen Woods, Sean Quinn Junior's fiancée.

Shortly afterwards, an application was made to the Companies

Registration Office in Stockholm by a Swedish law firm, MAQS. Instructed by Quinn Investments Sweden and the Quinn family, which was still in control of the Swedish company, MAQS registered new shares in eleven of the existing Swedish subsidiaries. Of those eleven companies, Anglo Irish Bank had share pledges in relation to nine. All of the new shares were allocated to Indian Trust AB, one of the new companies, whose chairman was Petey Quinn. Aoife Quinn handled the purchase of the shares from Ireland. Indian Trust was a key company in the mirror structure, which had been dubbed the Cranaghan Foundation.

Anglo Irish Bank was a corporate ruin. It had been nationalized in dramatic fashion in January 2009. It was the subject of multiple official investigations, and had won international ignominy for being possibly the world's worst bank. The government and the Central Bank were still trying to establish exactly how much it was ultimately going to cost the state, but they had warned it could be as much as €34 billion, a staggering number. Despite all that, Anglo had a wonderful headquarters.

Before the bank's spectacular implosion, Sean FitzPatrick and David Drumm, its chairman and chief executive, had signed a lease with Treasury Holdings, the Irish property developer, for office space at Connaught House on leafy Burlington Road, close to the Grand Canal. The bank's private banking operation took up residence in the modern, glass-fronted building. Treasury itself had its head office in the building, as did Macquarie, the investment bank that would handle the sale of Quinn Insurance. CBRE, the property group, and Gilt Groupe, a luxury brands retailer, were also tenants.

In early 2010, with Mike Aynsley now at the helm, Anglo decided to break the link with its headquarters on St Stephen's Green – a scene of regular public protests – and move the management team to Connaught House. Richard Woodhouse's office was located on the fifth floor, across a spacious lobby from the main reception. Separated from the general open-plan working area by a glass door and semi-frosted windows, the office had access to a neat balcony overlooking a courtyard. Woodhouse kept his domain tidy and functional even though, by the middle of June 2011, it was the hub of Anglo's efforts to recover the Quinn debt.

Woodhouse was in daily contact with Karyn Harty and Robert Dix. The bank was still finalizing the financial restructuring of Quinn Group, but the group's trading position was worsening and Anglo's chance of recouping any money was weakening. The bank would have a 49 per cent stake in Quinn Insurance after the deal with Liberty, but its value was also difficult to determine. The international properties were the bank's best chance of recovering some of the mammoth amount of money it was owed by Sean Quinn and his family.

Even now, though, two months after appointing Kieran Wallace as receiver to Quinn Group and the other Quinn assets, the bank had yet to take possession of any of the properties in Russia, Ukraine or India. Nor had it seen a cent of the €35 million annual rent roll. That was why the bank had taken the bold step of seeking a bankruptcy receiver appointed to Quinn Investments Sweden.

With each passing day, unpleasant new information was landing on Woodhouse's desk. Litigator Karyn Harty, initially retained by the bank to coordinate its defence in response to the Quinn family's High Court challenge to the legality of their share pledges and personal guarantees and the appointment of the share receiver, was now occupied with helping Woodhouse get to the bottom of whatever was going on with the foreign properties. She fed him the details of unusual transactions. Dix reported that his team had been refused access to the Kutuzoff Tower in Moscow.

As a matter of routine and precaution, the bank had retained lawyers in countries including Sweden, Russia and Ukraine. Their job was to monitor the ninety-five companies within the property division, and report back if something was stirring. In the first week of June, lawyers in Sweden got in touch to tell Anglo that new shares had been created in eleven group companies. The name Indian Trust started appearing on share registers of Swedish firms. Within days, another dispatch arrived from Ukraine – new companies had been established in Kiev, with Quinn family members listed as shareholders. The bank believed this was in direct contravention of their share pledges, given by the family as security for their multi-billion-euro borrowings.

In June, as part of an investigation instigated by Robert Dix in Derrylin, a document marked 'Strictly Private and Confidential' was retrieved from a computer that had been accessible only to five executives who worked for Sean Quinn. With new management in place, it was now available to Dix and his team. The document had been created on 30 March by Gary Conway, the Quinn executive who had responsibility for the property interests in India. Conway had worked closely with Petey Quinn and was the only property group employee to leave the organization voluntarily after the receivers took control.

The secret document outlined a new corporate structure based around an entity called the Cranaghan Foundation. In the new structure, there were five top entities called 'Irish Family Branch I–V' which sat above something called the Cranaghan Trust. Below those entities sat four named companies all described as 'Sweden'. Two Irish companies and another company sat under a company called Russian Trust AB.

To Dix, it appeared to be a mirror structure, an exact duplicate of the existing property group. It was created in the names of Quinn's grandchildren and had a special provision for any grandchildren that had yet to be born. Quinn's five children were also listed as shareholders of specific companies within the elaborate new structure. It had been prepared in secret, but the details were now in the hands of Anglo. Dix shared the document with Woodhouse and Harty. Coupled with the information that had been obtained from Sweden and Russia, it seemed clear the Quinns were trying to take control of the foreign properties by transferring them into this mirror structure.

Harty and Dix immediately knew they needed a strong legal response to thwart the Quinn plan. They quickly decided they needed to get a court injunction. Harty advised Woodhouse, however, that they needed more information and more evidence if they were to convince the Irish courts to grant an injunction.

Gathering that evidence would take time.

★

Loyalty and locality were always important to Sean Quinn. He had remained steadfastly loyal to his region and his workers while other wealthy Irishmen moved abroad for tax reasons or shifted manufacturing operations to cheaper labour locations in Eastern Europe or Asia. Quinn was neither a tax exile nor a corporate outsourcer.

Now, with his empire under siege, Quinn was learning that people were willing to be loyal to him also, convinced he was being wronged by the Financial Regulator and Anglo Irish Bank. Even after he lost control of Quinn Insurance to the administrators appointed by the Regulator, copies of management statements and financial reports still found their way to his desk, according to several sources closely involved in the receivership process. His manufacturing group had been seized by Anglo's share receiver, but Quinn was still in the loop on everything that was happening within the organization. In the eyes of many people within the company, Quinn remained the rightful owner, the boss. Those people ensured he still had the inside track.

A startling piece of information now found its way back to Sean Quinn: the bank knew all about the Cranaghan Foundation and the creation of the mirror corporate structure to hold the assets. A source said that Anglo was preparing to go to the High Court in Dublin to argue that the family was attempting to put the property portfolio beyond the reach of the bank and to seek an injunction that would effectively stop the family from interfering with the properties and the companies that owned them. If they breached such a court order, they would be in contempt of court.

The family had expected Anglo to fight back; what they hadn't expected was that it would happen so quickly. Petey's plan would have to be adjusted: if Anglo knew about the Cranaghan Foundation, the family needed a new way to get the assets out of the companies. Petey talked it through with the lawyers at A&B in Moscow. With the clock ticking, they suggested an alternative strategy.

Instead of moving the property assets into the Cranaghan Foundation companies, as planned, they would use secretive companies registered in offshore locations. A&B advised that the family should be distanced from these companies. Instead, new shareholders should be found to hold the assets on the family's behalf. It was a common tactic in Russia and Ukraine, known as 'corporate raiding'. A&B would find a collection of individuals who would nominally control the offshore companies. The individuals would receive a modest fee and ensure that the historic owners – the Quinn family – continued to receive the rental income.

A&B told the Quinns it would require a $1 million retainer to help source the individuals and implement the plan. It was a large sum, but given the value of the assets they were attempting to hide, the Quinns decided to stump up. Petey contacted Larisa Yanez Puga in Kiev, telling her to wire the money through Univermag, the company behind the family's Ukraina shopping centre.

In Stockholm, meanwhile, the bank's bankruptcy case against Quinn Investments Sweden was being heard. Arguing against Anglo's efforts to have a bankruptcy receiver appointed to Quinn Investments Sweden, the Quinn lawyers had said the Swedish company owed Anglo just €129 million – the amount of money they claimed had been loaned by the bank specifically to the Swedish company. The family forecast they could raise €344 million from selling properties, a process that could be completed within three months. In that scenario, the Swedish company could not be considered bankrupt, they said.

Not so, said Richard Woodhouse. In evidence, he argued the Swedish company was liable for loans of €1.8 billion owed by the Quinns. Any asset disposals would take a 'considerable time' to complete, given the complexity of doing business in Russia, Ukraine and India. The company was 'hopelessly insolvent', said Woodhouse. 'In my view, liquidation of satisfactory value would take eighteen months to three years. It is possible to sell at an accelerated basis but at a lower value.'

Dara O'Reilly, the former Quinn Group finance director, ran into difficulty on the stand in Stockholm. In evidence, O'Reilly outlined for the first time in open court how massive loans had been channelled from Anglo to cover Sean Quinn's losses on his CFD investments. Quinn Group began in 2007 to borrow money from

Anglo to cover Sean Quinn's obligations, he said, once the available resources of the family and the group had been exhausted. O'Reilly told the court that he would contact a manager at Anglo with a 'rough calculation' of how much was required to cover the margin call. Documents were then drawn up stating the loans were for 'property development', and O'Reilly would get the necessary signatures to finalize the transfer of the funds. 'When I rang the bank on a very frequent basis in 2008, it was very clear it was for margin calls,' he told the Swedish court.

O'Reilly was effectively arguing the family's main case against Anglo, that the loans were issued under a 'false guise' and could not be enforced. But the judge in the Swedish court was not impressed and warned O'Reilly against going any further. The issues being discussed were at the core of the family's claim against the bank and were likely to feature in other proceedings. O'Reilly should think carefully and beware he did not incriminate himself, the judge said.

It was a salutary warning of the seriousness of what was at stake.

The Quinn lawyers reckoned Anglo would ultimately succeed in its efforts to have a bankruptcy receiver installed over Quinn Investments Sweden. That meant Petey needed a new legal frontier in the battle against Anglo. He was now coordinating three key elements of his plan: the recruitment of new shareholders to do the family bidding, the creation of a string of offshore companies to take ownership of the properties, and the launching of a new legal action against the bank.

On 20 June, Petey touched down in Dubai for a meeting with Michael Waechter, principal of Senat Legal, part of the Senat Group. Senat Legal was something of a jack of all trades, claiming to offer international expertise in legal affairs, accounting services and business consulting. It had sister offices in Austria and Liechtenstein. In its promotional literature, the firm gave a grandiose summary of its services: 'We at Senat understand ourselves like one of these masterpieces of mechanical watchmaking that you find in Switzerland: dozens of little elements work seamlessly together to provide the customer with exact precision and reliable work.'

Waechter agreed to come on board to coordinate the family's legal actions against Anglo, and to secure the offshore companies to facilitate the asset transfers. Unlike the Cranaghan Foundation, these companies would be acquired in far-flung destinations; they would be companies with impenetrable and secretive corporate structures. To deal with this mammoth dispute between an Irish family and a nationalized Irish bank, a Dubai lawyer was looking to Central America and to Belize and Panama.

Waechter contacted the Belize office of a law firm called Aleman, Cordero, Galindo & Lee, which also had offices in the British Virgin Islands, Panama, the Bahamas and Luxembourg. Its clients included large, reputable businesses such as Citibank and HSBC, tobacco giant Philip Morris, telecoms firm Cable & Wireless, and several large pharmaceutical multinationals. Two days after Waechter was in touch, the lawyers at Aleman purchased a number of shell companies for Senat, including one by the name of Galfis. They were shelf companies with no assets, no liabilities and no directors.

On the same day that Petey met Waechter in Dubai, the family launched their next legal missile. Aoife Quinn had been knuckling down with lawyers, devising a tactic to take on Anglo in another court. With her training as a solicitor, Aoife was taking a hands-on role, receiving advice from a string of law firms, including Evgeny Ustin in Moscow, Eversheds O'Donnell Sweeney in Dublin, and MAQS in Sweden. The family had also engaged two commercial law firms in Cyprus: Andreas M Sofocleous & Co and Soteris Pittas & Co. It was in Cyprus that the family decided to strike next.

If Sweden was the head of Quinn's International Property Group, Cyprus was its heart, with a number of Cypriot companies holding pivotal positions within the group. Each of the Quinn properties was indirectly owned by a Cypriot company; whoever controlled those companies could control the properties. On 20 June, the Quinns went to the District Court of Nicosia, seeking an injunction preventing Anglo from 'interfering' in their property companies in Cyprus and Russia. It was an ex parte application, meaning that only one side was represented. Anglo had not been told the action was coming.

The family outlined its position to the court, again claiming that

the money advanced by Anglo to the family was for the illegal purpose of supporting the bank's share price. As such, they claimed the
bank had no entitlement to their assets. Three days later, the Cypriot
court granted the injunction, preventing Anglo from interfering
with the ownership of three companies – Carcer Investments,
Krostein Investments and Samonaca Holdings. It was a temporary
injunction, granted until all the issues could be heard in a courtroom.
It was not a ruling on the merits of the main allegations made by the
Quinns, but it bought the family the time it needed.

Carcer was the shareholder in the Russian company that owned
the Kutuzoff Tower, while Krostein and Samonaca owned the
Russian DIY store group and a fifty-acre Russian site respectively.
Due to a peculiarity in Cypriot law, the injunction would only come
into effect when the family paid a €500,000 bond. Once it was paid,
the injunction would prevent Anglo or its agents from taking any
steps in relation to the three firms. Still Anglo knew nothing about
it – and the Quinns were not minded to tell them.

Back in Dublin, interesting documents had arrived on Richard
Woodhouse's desk in Connaught House. Unfortunately, no one
could read them – they were in Ukrainian legalese. When they were
translated, it eventually became clear that they were challenges to the
validity of Anglo's mortgage charges in that country.

Documents had also arrived from Russia, showing how Petey had
shovelled €4.5 million out of Finansstroy, the Russian company
linked to the Kutuzoff Tower, just days before seeking to put the
company into bankruptcy. All Anglo's attempts to take control of
the tower had failed and the bank had no access to its bank accounts.
Now, €4.5 million had been withdrawn from an account set up to
channel loan repayments to the bank. It seemed Petey had appointed
himself general director of Finansstroy, giving him full power over
the company. Then he presented a new signature card to Finansstroy's Russian bank on 2 June, making him the sole signatory on the
company account until 2016. The next day, he instructed the bank to
transfer the €4.5 million, withdrawing almost all of the funds in the
account.

Woodhouse drafted a strongly worded affidavit, outlining his firm belief that the Quinn family was 'trying to wrest control of the various companies so as to put those assets beyond the bank's reach'. Robert Dix prepared his own legal statement, which set out the nuances of the Swedish share transfers to a new entity, Indian Trust. He said this was aimed at 'circumventing Anglo's attempt to appoint a receiver to Quinn Investments Sweden'.

With the paperwork signed, the bank was ready to act. On 27 June, Anglo launched a multi-jurisdictional onslaught, sending its lawyers into courts in Sweden, Russia and Ireland. In Stockholm, it lodged formal proceedings, alleging that new shares in seven Swedish companies had been created with the intention of moving the assets into the Cranaghan Foundation. In Moscow, it sought to block further changes to Quinn companies incorporated there, pointing to the €4.5 million transfer of cash out of Finansstroy.

The bank simultaneously moved in the Four Courts in Dublin, making an ex parte application for an injunction to prevent the family from interfering with the ownership structures of the companies behind the assets. Paul Gallagher SC was retained by Anglo for the action against Sean Quinn, his five children, his nephew Petey and two sons-in-law (Aoife's husband, Stephen Kelly, and Ciara's husband, Niall McPartland). Two companies in Sweden, Indian Trust and Quinn Investments Sweden, were also named in the fresh action.

The High Court heard the injunction was urgently sought, as there had been attempts to interfere in contractual arrangements between the Quinn companies and the bank. Those actions would undermine the security on Anglo's loans, the bank said. Anglo claimed the transfers were being made for the benefit of the Quinn family, in particular the grandchildren of Sean Quinn. Attempts to transfer assets into this new structure were 'severely hampering' the bank's ability to deal with the properties and it was concerned that the assets might 'simply disappear'. The bank told the court that it intended to serve a full writ against members of the family, claiming they were involved in a 'conspiracy' designed to strip assets from the bank.

Mr Justice Frank Clarke granted the bank a temporary injunction:

17. (*left*) Matthew Elderfield, the Financial Regulator, who appointed administrators to Quinn Insurance in March 2010 (*Feargal Ward / Sunday Business Post*)

18. (*above*) Michael McAteer of Grant Thornton, appointed joint administrator to Quinn Insurance by the Financial Regulator (*Maura Hickey / Sunday Business Post*)

19. (*left*) Murdoch McKillop, who was appointed to the board of Quinn Group to represent the interests of its creditors and spearhead a debt restructuring (*Talbot Hughes McKillop*)

20. Mike Aynsley, chief
executive of Anglo Irish
Bank, later Irish Bank
Resolution Corporation
(*Fergal Phillips /
Sunday Times*)

21. Richard Woodhouse,
head of specialized asset
management at Anglo/
IBRC; he spearheaded the
bank's efforts to lay claim
to Sean Quinn's assets
(*Fergal Phillips /
Sunday Times*)

22. (*left*) Kieran Wallace, head of restructuring at KPMG, who was appointed share receiver to Quinn Group by Anglo Irish Bank on 14 April 2011 (*Maura Hickey / Sunday Business Post*)

23. (*left*) Robert Dix, the former KPMG partner appointed to manage the former Quinn property group following the share receivership (*Bryan Meade / Sunday Times*)

24. (*below*) Paul O'Brien, appointed chief executive of Quinn Group following the share receivership (*Fergal Phillips / Sunday Times*)

25. (*right*) The Kutuzoff Tower in Moscow, the Quinns' primary property asset in Russia and the headquarters of its operations there; the Quinns went to great lengths to keep it out of the hands of Anglo/IBRC

26. (*below*) The Ukraina centre in Kiev, another major asset the Quinns kept out of reach of the bank

27. Quinn buildings at the HITEC City in Hyderabad, India, another major asset that the bank could not get at

28. (*above left*) Peter Darragh Quinn outside the Four Courts in Dublin, followed by his uncle Sean Quinn and cousin Sean Quinn Junior, during their trial for contempt of court in early 2012 (*Courtpix*)

29. (*above right*) Sean Quinn Junior and his wife, Karen Woods, outside the High Court in Dublin (*Courtpix*)

30. Sean Quinn's four daughters – Brenda, Ciara, Colette and Aoife – outside the Four Courts in Dublin, October 2012 (*Courtpix*)

31. A sign in the heart of Quinn country advertises a rally in support of the Quinn family in Ballyconnell, 14 October 2012 (*Catherine Daly*)

32. Sean and Patricia Quinn lead the rally of support through the streets of Ballyconnell, 14 October 2012 (*Lorraine Teevan*)

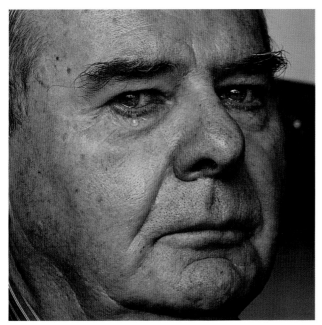

33. (*above left*) Sean Quinn becomes emotional during a support rally held for him in Ballyconnell, 14 October 2012 (*Mark Condren / Irish Independent*)

34. (*above right*) Quinn supporters found inventive ways of making their feelings known (*Lorraine Teevan*)

35. (*below*) A sign of support for Sean Quinn in a shop window in Ballyconnell (*Catherine Daly*)

36. Patricia Quinn with her daughters Aoife and Ciara during the rally of support in Ballyconnell, 14 October 2012 (*Mark Condren / Irish Independent*)

37. Sean Quinn Junior, flanked by former Quinn Group executives Liam McCaffrey and Kevin Lunney, at a meeting in Ballyconnell in December 2012 to air concerns about job losses at the Quinn Group (*Lorraine Teevan*)

it would prevent the family from transferring assets out of Quinn companies in Sweden, though only for one day. The judge wanted to hear both sides of the story. Hours after Clarke's ruling, €500,000 was transferred from Ukraine to Cyprus and lodged with the District Court in Nicosia. The Quinn family's Cyprus injunction immediately came into effect. Anglo didn't know it, but the bank's small advantage had already been lost. The tables had been turned.

The following day, 28 June, the Quinns' lawyers went to the High Court in Dublin to enter an appearance on behalf of the family. During the hearing, the lawyers revealed that the family had secured the ex parte injunction in Cyprus. Justice Clarke put back the matter until the middle of July. The temporary Irish injunction would remain in place in the meantime. For the next three weeks, any interference by the Quinns with the property assets would be a breach of the court injunction and constitute contempt of court.

Woodhouse was shocked by the Cyprus injunction. He later learned that someone had tipped off the Quinns about Anglo's plan. 'They got wind that we were moving to injunct through somebody who was loose with their words,' said a bank source. 'Their injunction trumped us in Cyprus by a couple of days, and that did certainly cause us headaches for a while.'

Now there were legal battles raging on four different fronts – Sweden, Russia, Ireland and Cyprus – and a bizarre stand-off had been reached. The injunction in Nicosia stopped Anglo from interfering with the family's companies in Cyprus or Russia, but Anglo's injunction in Dublin immobilized the corporate structure worldwide as it covered Quinn Investment Sweden, the property group's ultimate parent company, and the various family members.

There were other matters occupying the minds of Woodhouse and his fellow Anglo bankers. From 1 July, Anglo Irish Bank would cease to exist. The government had decided to merge Anglo with Irish Nationwide Building Society, a small-time mortgage provider that had ballooned into a reckless commercial lender during the property bubble, now bust beyond rescue and effectively nationalized.

Anglo and the rump of Irish Nationwide were to be merged to

become the Irish Bank Resolution Corporation (IBRC). Mike Aynsley was to run the enlarged bank while Woodhouse, his right-hand man, remained responsible for pursuing Sean Quinn.

On 5 July, the Swedish court ruled in favour of Anglo, and Quinn Investments Sweden was declared bankrupt. Anglo – now IBRC – had won. The Swedish company would be taken over by a bankruptcy receiver empowered to liquidate its assets in order to compensate creditors. Leif Baecklund, a senior lawyer with Setterwalls, a Stockholm law firm, would be formally installed the following day, once the bank had reconfigured the board. A total of thirty-one subsidiaries to the Swedish company would be bankrupted, preventing the Quinns from extracting value at that level.

In the days that followed, the bank got further information that confirmed its belief the Quinns were actively involved in asset-stripping. It came from a most unlikely source – documents sent by the Swedish law firm MAQS, which had worked for the Quinn family. The paperwork, addressed to Quinn Holdings, had ended up in the hands of Paul Morgan, the senior executive at the property unit in Derrylin. He brought it to Robert Dix. MAQS had dispatched an invoice for work 'in advising the Quinn family on the establishment of the Cranaghan Foundation'. There was also a reference to the 'McPartland subsidiaries'. The work was carried out for the Quinns and the invoice mistakenly sent to the group they no longer controlled.

Within days, Woodhouse also learned of Petey's eight new Ukrainian companies. As far as the banker was concerned, they were designed to be the Ukrainian arm of the Cranaghan Foundation. Woodhouse was convinced that he now had enough ammunition to go back to the High Court and ensure that the temporary injunction already in place became permanent. Both Woodhouse and Dix drafted further legal depositions detailing the new information. This, Woodhouse believed, would bring a halt to the Quinn plan, and also demonstrate to the world what the family was attempting to do in relation to the property assets.

Aoife Quinn signed the responding affidavit on behalf of the family. The affidavit denied there was 'activity calculated to interfere with contractual arrangements with the bank'. When the Quinns returned to the High Court on 20 July, however, they consented to the injunction, though their lawyers were quick to point out that it was not an acknowledgement of any wrongdoing.

The family lawyers also argued the Irish courts were not the appropriate jurisdiction for the case, on the grounds that the legal proceedings already instituted in Cyprus took precedence. Justice Clarke granted the bank an injunction, in force until early September, which barred the family from interfering with companies connected with the property portfolio. In the meantime, the judge would consider the appropriate jurisdiction for the legal battle.

Finally, Richard Woodhouse felt he was getting somewhere. The Quinns were constrained by a court injunction and the property assets might at last be within reach. Nonetheless, he told Karyn Harty to maintain her watching brief on corporate activity by Quinn companies in Sweden, Russia, Cyprus, India and Ukraine. Given what was at stake, the bank could not be too careful.

The Quinn family vehemently denied the existence of any asset-stripping scheme. The denials were made in courts in Stockholm, Dublin and Nicosia. They were made in public statements and they were made in notarized affidavits, lodged with multiple courts. Petey, in one affidavit, said that Woodhouse's allegations were 'without any foundation or factual basis'.

In a written submission to the courts in Cyprus, signed on 8 July, Aoife Quinn said the bank was offering 'mere speculation without fact or evidence' about the scheme, adding that her family had 'no case to meet'. In her submission, she said the Cranaghan Foundation 'has not acquired any assets in Russia, India, Ukraine or Turkey'. Technically, Aoife Quinn was right. By the time she signed her name to that affidavit, the family had little intention of moving the assets into the Cranaghan Foundation. The bank had uncovered the Cranaghan paper trail, so the plan had changed. The assets were being transferred instead to the offshore companies in Belize and Panama.

Petey was leading this process, aided by Senat Legal in Dubai and A&B in Moscow. The Kutuzoff Tower, the most valuable of the properties, was the first priority. The application to put Finansstroy, the company behind the tower, into bankruptcy was due back in court on 22 July. Petey needed everything in place by then.

A&B had been busy justifying its $1 million retainer. The law firm had sourced a collection of individuals willing to act as the nominal owners of the new offshore companies. They would be paid a small fee for their involvement. It was decided that Yaroslav Gurnyak would be the new owner of the Kutuzoff. Gurnyak, a Ukrainian national, was a part-time railway worker. He was working on a Moscow railway site in early July 2011 when he was approached by his cousin, a lawyer with A&B. The lawyer offered Gurnyak money in exchange for signing a few legal documents. Gurnyak, who had been struggling to hold down a long-term job, agreed. Within the stroke of a pen, he became the owner of Galfis, the offshore company incorporated in Belize, and the beneficial owner of the $188 million Kutuzoff Tower in Moscow.

Petey and Sean Quinn signed for twenty-nine separate transactions, transferring loans worth $130 million from Demesne, the Quinn company in Northern Ireland, to Galfis and Gurnyak. In return, Demesne received just $2,900 − $100 for each of the transactions. Galfis was now a large creditor of Finansstroy, the Russian company that sat in the middle of the ownership structure for the Kutuzoff Tower. However, Petey was still worried that the new company might not be the largest creditor and IBRC might still outrank it, which would leave the bank in a position of strength. He needed the Galfis debts to be larger than just $130 million.

As director general of Finansstroy, he signed two further agreements to boost the standing of Galfis, this new so-called 'friendly creditor'. He more than doubled the interest rate on the freshly assigned loans to 30 per cent and backdated the new rate to April 2007. Then Petey signed a surety agreement that made Finansstroy guarantor on the debts of a string of other Quinn Russian property companies, including the money they owed to Demesne. The moves had the effect of grossly inflating the value of the debt to $419 million. Galfis would be by far the biggest creditor of Finansstroy, giving it the power to bankrupt the company and take control of the Kutuzoff Tower.

There was one problem, however: the injunction. The deal with Galfis was clearly in breach of the Irish court order preventing the family from interfering with any of the assets. Petey knew that better than anyone. To get around it, he backdated all the documents to 4 April, long before the injunction had come into effect and ten days before the Quinn Group had been put into receivership. It was a bold move: Galfis, the offshore shell, had only been acquired in July, but Petey was now claiming it had struck a $419 million deal three months before that. Sean Quinn signed the backdated documents on behalf of Demesne, even though he had resigned from that company some months before. Petey signed on behalf of Finansstroy, while Gurnyak, the railway worker, registered his name on behalf of Galfis.

When the Finansstroy bankruptcy case came to the Russian courts on 22 July, the paperwork no longer referred to Cranaghan Property Management as its main creditor. A&B, on behalf of Finansstroy, said the creditor was now Galfis, a mysterious entity IBRC knew nothing about. The bank protested, but the court went ahead a month later and put Finansstroy into bankruptcy. Galfis was admitted as a creditor; IBRC was not. The bank appealed the decision, resolving to unwind the debt assignments to Galfis and follow the paper trail. Woodhouse, Dix and Harty also resolved to find out just who owned this secret Belize company that had snatched the valuable Moscow asset from under their noses.

Petey repeated the scheme for other property assets in Russia, including the DIY stores, business parks and development sites. As the bank focused its attentions on Galfis and the Kutuzoff Tower, the smaller properties were moved into other offshore companies with different owners.

The Quinn family now turned their attention to extracting cash from the property group. Implementing the property scheme and fighting in the courts was an expensive business and the family members no longer had their jobs in the family business. They needed cash flow to cover their overheads. Petey and Sean Junior set about creating employment contracts for various family members. They would be given unspecified jobs in Russian companies, and paid handsomely for it. Under the new contracts, Petey was to be paid a €221,000 salary from Finansstroy, Sean Quinn Junior was to be paid €147,000 a year from another firm, while Colette, Ciara and Aoife Quinn were to get €295,000 a year from Russian companies. Karen Woods, Sean Junior's fiancée, was to get €295,000 a year as well. To facilitate the payments, the family members opened bank accounts at Ocean Bank in Moscow.

There was another clause inserted into all the contracts, providing for massive severance payments in the event that the contracts were terminated. Sean Junior was to get up to €15 million, while his wife was to get €36 million from a number of companies if her employment ended. The same applied to Colette, Ciara and Aoife, as well as to Ciara's husband, Niall McPartland. Petey was to receive €26 million if he lost his job.

Russia was the main priority; it was where the majority of the assets were. But the family had not forgotten about the properties in India or Ukraine. The primary asset in India was Q-City in HITEC City in Hyderabad, valued at about €60 million. The property was originally controlled by Quinn Investments Sweden through a string of subsidiary companies, one of which was an entity called Mack Soft. In June 2011, an extraordinary general meeting of Mack Soft was held in Cavan which authorized the creation of 300,000 new equity shares in the company.

Shortly afterwards, Petey helped transfer the newly minted shares in Mack Soft to a Dubai-registered company called Mecon FZE. As a result of the transfer, Mecon was able to stake a claim to the Indian asset. Mack Soft, meanwhile, saw its ownership of the building diminish from 99 per cent to just 2.5 per cent of the shares. Mecon, an unknown entity, was firmly in control.

The most valuable asset in Ukraine was the Ukraina shopping centre, bought by the Quinn Group in 2006 for $59 million and now valued at $78 million. Petey opted to use an offshore shelf company called Lyndhurst Trading to take control of the centre. Lyndhurst had been bought at the same time as Galfis, but it was registered in the British Virgin Islands. Demesne, the family's financing vehicle, was owed $42 million by Univermag, the company that owned the shopping centre. The plan this time was to transfer that debt to another Quinn-controlled company, Innishmore, before eventually moving it to Lyndhurst. In September, the first act was implemented, with Innishmore taking over the Demesne debt. The debt was later moved to Lyndhurst, through a document signed by Petey bearing the Innishmore company seal.

By the end of September, the Quinn family plan had broadly been implemented. The Kutuzoff Tower was under the control of Galfis. The Indian property had been moved to Mecon, while eight smaller Russian assets had been eased into offshore companies. The Ukrainian asset transfer was in train, though Lyndhurst had not yet staked its claim in the Ukrainian courts. The family had lost the legal battle in Stockholm but was still fighting in Cyprus.

More than five months after seizing Quinn Group and its associated property companies, IBRC had yet to secure any of the assets or their rents.

As the plan progressed, the Quinns moved their battle to another front: publicity. Notoriously media-shy, the family felt they were losing a battle against Anglo that was being fought in the national media.

James Morrissey, a public relations adviser and former journalist, arranged off-the-record briefings between family members and a small number of journalists. Sean Quinn Junior and Ciara Quinn, the second-eldest of the five children, met the journalists at offices linked to Fleishman Hillard, the Dublin PR company with which Morrissey was associated. It was the first time the family had come directly to the media, opening up a new front in the struggle against Anglo, the insurance company administrators and the group receivers.

Sean Junior did most of the talking, openly acknowledging that the trouble had started with his father's CFD investments. It was totally wrong and should never have happened, Sean Junior said. But at the time of the investments, nobody could envisage that the banks and the country would go bankrupt. Nobody could foresee that Anglo would be nationalized and the Quinn family debts would become debts owed to the taxpayer. Sean Quinn had never asked for that.

Then Sean Junior launched into a detailed rebuttal of the Financial

Regulator's motivations in putting Quinn Insurance into administration. The cross-company guarantees on the insurance company assets were contingent and would never be called upon; there was no threat to the insurer's solvency or customer policies. PWC had audited the accounts and did not raise any issues; the Moore Stephens report commissioned by the family backed up that position. The family had made a mistake in not challenging the appointment of the administrators, Sean Junior said. By the time they realized their error, it was too late.

He produced pages of detailed figures, pointing out the reasons why the Regulator was wrong and the family was right. Their father and the family felt extremely hard done by, he said. People were saying the business was badly run, that there was a financial hole in Quinn Insurance that needed to be filled from the Insurance Compensation Fund, and that was not true.

Ciara Quinn chipped in occasionally. Their world had changed on 14 April, she said; only then did they realize there would be no deal with Anglo, that everything was lost. The family didn't owe Anglo €2.8 billion, she said vehemently. Their court case would prove that.

The family had a twin-track strategy. The main court case against Anglo and Kieran Wallace would go ahead in time, and they were advised they had a strong case, said Sean Quinn Junior. Dealing with the property assets was a more immediate concern, and the family approach was simple: if Anglo had security over the asset, then it had the asset. But where the security on the assets was weak, or non-existent, the bank could expect a fight.

Even after IBRC had secured its injunction in the High Court in Dublin, the reports kept flowing in to Richard Woodhouse. Finansstroy and two other Russian subsidiaries had applied for bankruptcy, and Galfis was claiming to own the debt, though neither Woodhouse nor Robert Dix had ever heard of the company. In Derrylin, Dix trawled through the monthly management accounts and financial records of Demesne. There was nothing to indicate that there had been any transfer to a third party like Galfis before the group receivership, as was now being claimed. It simply did not stack up. Information was also emerging about unsecured assets in Russia being transferred to third parties and then shifted on to offshore entities.

In September, Woodhouse instructed the bank's lawyers to write to the Quinn family, telling them to desist from any action that might be considered in breach of the High Court injunction. Later that month, he returned to court seeking further injunctions, explaining that he believed the family was in breach of the earlier court orders. Woodhouse also upped the rhetoric. He had read every article about this rumbling saga, but he felt the significance of what the family was attempting to do was not fully understood by the public. The audacity of the scheme was getting lost amid the incredibly complex detail. Woodhouse decided it needed to be explained in a clear, precise manner, and not the usual legalese.

In his next court appearance, he claimed that there was a 'sinister conspiracy' by the Quinns to put assets beyond the reach of IBRC, a state-owned bank. The Quinn family were in breach of a High Court injunction and engaging in a 'covert' scheme to avoid paying their debts, he said. IBRC's lawyers outlined how new information was coming to light 'on almost a daily basis' regarding the asset-stripping scheme.

The Quinn family continued to claim that the Irish court had no authority and the matter should be dealt with in Cyprus. Mr Justice Frank Clarke referred the issue of jurisdiction to the European Court of Justice, but said his initial injunction stood. The injunction remained in place, extended beyond the initial September deadline. For the first time, Woodhouse felt the Irish public had some appreciation of exactly what was going on.

A few weeks later, Woodhouse lodged an affidavit in Cyprus, outlining a string of unorthodox Quinn transactions the bank had uncovered. They included the family's swapping of the laptop computer for the DIY properties in Russia. The family fought to keep Woodhouse's affidavit confidential, but lost. When the details emerged, they made headlines in every major Irish newspaper.

'Valuable Moscow building sold for $1,000' was how the *Irish Times* summed it up.

The *Irish Mirror* reported: 'Quinn sold £127 million assets for a laptop and £870.'

The *Irish Daily Mail* said: 'Quinn family swaps $200 million for a laptop: Trade was designed to put assets out of Anglo's reach, Cyprus court is told.'

On 3 November 2011, *Prime Time*, the RTÉ current affairs programme, broadcast a fifteen-minute report on the asset-stripping, the first in-depth media explanation of what the bank believed was taking place. The report outlined how the valuable assets were being moved through various companies and territories.

The Quinns, who had declined to contribute to the programme, were furious. They claimed the programme was defamatory and that there was no asset-stripping scheme in existence. James Morrissey, the family's PR man, contacted the reporter, Ian Kehoe, threatening action. Ciara Quinn, on behalf of the family, later lodged a detailed complaint with the Broadcasting Authority of Ireland, saying *Prime Time* had tried to 'unfairly portray the Quinn family in a negative light'. The Quinns claimed the broadcast accused them of espionage, 'inferring criminal activity', and favoured IBRC over the family. *Prime Time* stood by the programme. (The authority subsequently ruled in favour of *Prime Time*, dismissing all the claims.)

Richard Woodhouse felt he had achieved one thing, at least – people were now appreciating the seriousness of what was going on. In his mind, the Quinn family was doing everything it possibly could to keep control of half a billion euro in property assets, despite owing billions to a taxpayer-owned bank. He decided to up the ante. As the family fought the bank on every front, it was time to go after the patriarch himself.

Sean Quinn had given Anglo personal guarantees over borrowings of more than €2.1 billion. The loans had been called in as part of the receivership process, but had not been repaid. Woodhouse and Aynsley decided it was time to seek a High Court judgment against Quinn for the money.

11

War of attrition

The call came around 11 p.m. on 8 August 2011. It was a Monday night and Paul O'Brien, the new Quinn Group chief executive, was at the end of the first week of a family holiday in Portugal. It was almost four months since the dawn raid by Anglo Irish Bank had installed him as the new Quinn chief, and the break was welcome. The call from a neighbour back in Ireland changed all that. O'Brien's car alarm and the alarm on his home in Ratoath, Co. Meath, were both going off. The neighbours were concerned.

It struck O'Brien as unusual that both alarms were going off at the same time. He soon found out why. His BMW 4 x 4, parked in the driveway outside his home, was on fire. The gutters and window fittings on his home had started to melt. The fire crews later told O'Brien that the car had exploded. The house – home to O'Brien, his wife and three children – was just minutes from going up in flames when they got the blaze under control.

The Gardaí and firemen confirmed what O'Brien feared: it was arson. An 'accelerant' had been poured on the BMW and set alight. It was a deliberate attack – and, to all appearances, an escalation of a campaign of sabotage and intimidation against the Quinn Group and its new management.

Paul O'Brien had not been daunted by the prospect of running Quinn Group. A native of Dromiskin, a village near Dundalk, O'Brien knew the border region and he knew Sean Quinn's standing in it. Like everyone in business in Ireland, he knew the stories of the rise and rise of Quinn's companies – the competition battles, the ambitious investments, the sheer success of it all. Like everyone, he had watched as the wheels started to come off the enterprise when Quinn Insurance was put into administration in March 2010. When he was approached by Paddy Murphy, a non-executive director of Quinn Group, seven months later about joining the board as a non-executive, he had welcomed the chance to see the business from the inside.

O'Brien had liked Sean Quinn on the occasions he had met him, but the personal rancour between the Quinns and Anglo didn't concern him. What concerned him as a director was that Quinn Group had taken on debt from banks and bondholders that it couldn't repay. The responsibilities of O'Brien and the other directors were no longer to the shareholders in the group – Sean Quinn's five children – but to its creditors, the banks and bondholders.

A burly former Gaelic footballer and Dundalk RFC rugby player in his mid forties, O'Brien had seen sticky situations in business before. He had cut his teeth as an accountant with Glen Dimplex, the Irish manufacturing group, and gone on to work for Digital, the technology multinational. O'Brien progressed from junior trainee to group financial controller at Compaq, which had acquired Digital in a $9.6 billion deal in 1998. Amid dotcom fever, he quit Compaq in the hope of making his fortune with a start-up company. When the dotcom bubble burst, the start-up got burned. O'Brien had to find alternative employment.

In mid 2002, he was hired by IWP, the publicly quoted group run by Joe Moran whose product range included household names such as Parazone and Jeyes Fluid. IWP was struggling with a heavy debt load. Two weeks after O'Brien joined, the company sold a majority stake in its Jeyes business, which accounted for more than half of annual sales. The business he had joined was suddenly much smaller, still heavily indebted, and had an uncertain future. It was the start of a rollercoaster ride for the company and its management. O'Brien's immediate boss, Bernard Byrne, later a senior executive with ESB and AIB, launched a management buyout bid for the business, but failed. Within eighteen months, O'Brien, by now finance director of

IWP, launched his own proposal to buy the company. It never progressed, but O'Brien stayed on to oversee a financial overhaul of the business, which led to its 90 per cent takeover first by its banks and bondholders and then by private equity. He stayed four years, gaining valuable experience in taking a business apart and rebuilding it again.

In December 2006, he left IWP for the finance director job at UTV, the Belfast-based media group. There he was involved in the purchase of FM104, the Dublin radio station, for €52 million and a major fund-raising commitment, completed just before the credit crunch kicked in. After UTV, he went into business for himself as a restructuring consultant. He worked on the refinancing of the Beacon Hospital, a €183 million private hospital built in Dublin with the benefit of tax breaks and big bank borrowings. As the economy dipped, it reworked its debt load and brought in an American group as majority shareholder. One of the banks involved in the Beacon liked O'Brien's style and hired him to run Four Leaf Investment, the operator of a chain of hotels in Belgium and France. It was a familiar scenario: the group was over-borrowed and there was a restructuring job to be done.

O'Brien was still running Four Leaf when Paddy Murphy approached him to join Quinn Group. When matters came to a head six months later, culminating in the events of 14 April, he was seen by the board as the natural choice to replace Liam McCaffrey as group chief executive. By accident rather than design, Paul O'Brien had become a restructuring expert.

As he settled into the wood-panelled corner office Sean Quinn had previously occupied at Quinn Group headquarters, he knew there were major challenges ahead. The bones of a deal had been worked out with Anglo, the banks and bondholders, but the flesh of the financial restructuring still had to be agreed. The manufacturing companies were under pressure from the poor economic environment, and workers were worried and concerned about their jobs. On top of that, O'Brien knew, there were many people who simply didn't want him there.

The first attack had happened within days of the change of control at Quinn Group. On the morning of 18 April, the first Monday after Kieran Wallace was appointed share receiver, a huge dumper truck was driven into bollards at the entrance to the group HQ in Derrylin. There were reports of threats against staff and evidence of deliberate sabotage. When a fibre-optic cable between the headquarters and the nearby cement plant was cut, the staff member who repaired it was called a 'traitor' by an unidentified caller and told to mind his personal security.

There were attempts by unidentified parties to sow doubt and confusion. The *Irish Times* reported that a man claiming to be from KPMG had contacted managers at the group's hotels in Cambridge and Nottingham saying that they should cease trading immediately. Another person claiming to be a KPMG employee contacted the general manager of the group's glass plant in Elton in Cheshire, calling for a meeting to discuss the restructuring and sale of the business.

As time went on, the sabotage became more severe. More than €300,000 worth of damage was done to a cement factory and several vehicles were burned out at the Quinn tarmac plant, a secluded site close to the group headquarters. A month before O'Brien's car was set on fire, three electricity poles carrying power to the manufacturing business were cut down. It was the fourteenth time that power lines had been damaged in the space of three months.

Attacks on factories were one thing; targeting the home of the chief executive was another. After the arson attack in Ratoath, Quinn Group issued a strongly worded statement describing it as 'a terrorist attack' and those responsible as 'thugs and vandals'. The group 'will not be intimidated', it said. Anglo described the incident as 'a sinister and potentially fatal turn in the campaign of sabotage waged against the Quinn Group of companies since the share receiver was appointed'.

O'Brien, who seriously considered resigning after the attack, put it bluntly. 'It is escalating to a very dangerous level where somebody has the potential to be killed,' he told RTÉ. The chief executive revealed that Sean Quinn had been asked to make a public appeal calling for an end to the attacks. The people carrying out the attacks were clearly Quinn supporters. If the businessman made a public appeal for them to stop, it might have some effect. Quinn had refused the request, O'Brien said. 'What he's [Quinn] failed to recognize is the significance of the impact of what he could say to make things stop. Either he fails to recognize it or he's choosing not to,' said O'Brien.

The comments infuriated Quinn. He responded angrily, saying O'Brien had 'by inference and innuendo' suggested that Quinn was associated with the attacks. 'I wish to state in the most categoric terms that I have no knowledge whatsoever of any unlawful acts in relation to individuals or property associated with the Quinn Group other than what I have read in the media,' Quinn said in a statement after the arson incident at O'Brien's house. 'Several weeks ago I spoke with a Chief Inspector of the PSNI [Police Service of Northern Ireland] in relation to the reported acts of sabotage surrounding the Quinn Group. I stated, in clear and unequivocal terms, that persons carrying out such acts were not acting in my name and requested them to cease.' Despite his appeal, however, the attacks continued.

The task O'Brien faced inside the office was scarcely less daunting. During his time as a non-executive director, he had got to know the structure of the group. It was really four distinct manufacturing businesses: construction industry supplies such as cement, gravel, concrete blocks and insulation products; glass bottles; plastics and packaging; and radiators, both domestic and commercial.

Each of them was a sizeable business in its own right. The cement factory in Ballyconnell could produce 4,000 bags of cement an hour, though demand had collapsed since the economic downturn started in 2008. The glass business had state-of-the art factories in Derrylin and in Elton, in Cheshire, the results of up to €500 million in investment. There were solid, valuable contracts with Diageo, Irish Distillers, Britvic and others. The Elton plant could make 2.5 billion bottles a year, and included five filling lines where drinks companies could put their products directly into the bottles. Those investments had helped Quinn win 28.5 per cent share of the UK glass bottle market. Plastics and packaging, the business that started with the acquisition of Barlo in 2004, was a big employer in Europe, with strong sales in France, Belgium and Holland. The group's radiator factory, in Newport in South Wales, was less than five years old, the newest – and biggest – in Europe. It was a million square feet, one and a half times the area taken up by the Croke Park stadium in Dublin, and could make four million radiators a year.

Each of the four core businesses would need attention and nurturing. Then there was the half-built chemical factory at Leuna, near Leipzig. Mothballed since January 2009, it had already swallowed almost €200 million and would need another €200 million to be completed. O'Brien and the group board would have to consider what to do with that.

O'Brien admired how Quinn had built his businesses, but he could see there wasn't much of a focus on return on capital – the difference between the rate of interest a company was paying on its borrowings and its rate of return on its investments. Quinn had borrowed heavily and sunk the money into his massive factories. No expense had been spared in building and kitting out his manufacturing plants, in line with his belief that efficient businesses making the highest-quality products would eventually see off all competitors. If that meant enduring losses from a particular factory or business unit for a number of years – suffering a negative return on capital – then so be it.

At one board meeting early in O'Brien's tenure as a non-executive director of the group, someone had queried the return on capital from various assets. The question was dismissed by existing management, then led by Liam McCaffrey. Taking their lead from Quinn, the executives focused on cash flow, profits and losses; return on capital was not seen as a key indicator. With the income from Quinn Insurance boosting its balance sheet, Quinn Group had been able to report bumper profits. But now, with Quinn Insurance out of the picture, and three years into the economic collapse, return on capital from the manufacturing business was a huge issue. The group had borrowed €1.3 billion from the banks and bondholders – a vast amount of money – and it wasn't making enough money to repay the debt.

As part of the receivership move, the banks and bondholders had agreed to the proposal from Murdoch McKillop to split the debt load, lightening the burden of borrowings on the manufacturing companies. The plan involved boxing off about €550 million of debt into a holding company. It would own 'non-core' Quinn assets, including Quinn Healthcare, which remained outside the administration process, the half-built chemical plant in Germany, three Quinn hotels in Central Europe and the group's private jet and helicopter. The manufacturing group would have no responsibility for that debt. The plan would leave €720 million of debt with the manufacturing businesses, considered a manageable number based on the group's financial projections at the time.

As they settled into their new roles, the new board and management considered the business plan that was already in place. O'Brien and the other directors, including McKillop, decided to approach the existing forecasts with caution. 'In some of the previous attempts to do business plans, there was an edict coming from on high about where things should end up in terms of numbers,' said one source close to the situation. If there was to be a clean break with the past, they needed their own forecasts. They had to be able to stand over the numbers.

The new management did extensive due diligence, digging deep into the various business units. They drew up weekly short-term cash flow reports, detailed monthly management accounts and robust financial forecasts. The exercise revealed that the existing forecasts were too optimistic.

The new forecasts suggested that the group's earnings for the next twelve months would be one-third lower than forecast by previous management. Instead of €120 million in operating profit, the manufacturing group was likely to make €80 million. That meant the reduced €720 million debt burden was still too high. The debt split had been designed to save the group and show the outside world that, with the proper funding structure, it was a viable business. But if the debt load was too high, it would be only a matter of time before the business defaulted and Quinn Group was back at crisis point again.

McKillop and O'Brien had to go back to Anglo and the other lenders, the banks and bondholders, and break the news. If the group was to survive, it needed to offload even more of the debt into the non-recourse holding company. There was a mixed reaction. Because of the turmoil surrounding the business, the bondholder debt had been changing hands at a heavy discount in the bond market. The recent buyers of debt at knockdown prices were comfortable with the idea of removing more debt from the group. Many of the original lenders, however, felt they had taken enough pain as it was. Doing a deal with the constantly changing bondholder group would be a protracted and painful process.

In the midst of the negotiations, Liam McCaffrey approached the board with a proposal. He was part of a consortium that wanted to buy parts of the business. The buyout group was offering about €200 million for the assets, focused on Quinn's cement and radiator divisions. It was reported to have the backing of Kohlberg Kravis Roberts (KKR), the legendary New York private equity house. The buyout group, advised by NCB Corporate Finance, comprised seven people formerly involved in Quinn's businesses, including Denis Doogan, the former chief executive of the radiator business, who had resigned in July, three months after the Quinn Group receivership. The group rejected the offer, which it described in a statement as an 'exploratory approach'. It was 'made clear by the Quinn Group board that, in line with the commitments already made, the businesses are not for sale'.

As the Quinn Group refinancing talks progressed, some bondholders pushed for IBRC to give up its veto on the sale of international businesses within the group. The change would effectively mean there was nothing to stop the sale of the radiator plant in Wales or the bottle factory in Elton, Cheshire. Sean Quinn's group could be headed for break-up.

At IBRC, meanwhile, Richard Woodhouse was feeling frustrated. No matter what he did in relation to the Quinn international property assets, the British banker felt he was always one step behind. Woodhouse told friends it was like playing a 'three-dimensional chess game', only his opponents didn't have to follow the rules. As the official agent of a state-owned bank, he was bound to the strict letter of the law. Yet, as far as he was concerned, the Quinn family had gone to great lengths to cheat IBRC out of what it was rightfully due.

When he thwarted the family's efforts in Sweden, they had simply moved on to Cyprus. He had sought injunctions in Dublin, but the family had fought back in Russia and Ukraine. Along with Robert Dix, the accountant installed to manage the property portfolio, Woodhouse had uncovered details of the Cranaghan Foundation. Now, the assets had been reassigned to companies in Belize and the British Virgin Islands. Woodhouse was convinced that the Quinn family was behind both Galfis and Lyndhurst, the mysterious offshore companies that had staked a claim to the Russian and Ukrainian assets. But, as of yet, he had no evidence to prove it.

On his desk, Woodhouse kept a document titled 'Irish Bank Resolution Corporation Limited IPG Summary'. Stamped 'FOR INTERNAL USE ONLY', the document listed all of the assets within the original Quinn International Property Group. They were divided into two categories. One showed the name and valuation of the assets the bank had control over, including the Irish pubs, a hotel in the Czech Republic and a retail investment in Turkey. The other listed all the Russian, Ukrainian and Indian properties that remained outside of the bank's control. There was a special appendage for the Q-City property in India; it had rocketed in value after its occupancy rates had risen from 30 per cent to 90 per cent. The value of the properties outside the bank's control was close to €500 million. The annual rent roll was €35 million. The money was going somewhere, and Woodhouse knew that it was not going to his side.

Events in Russia were making headlines, but Ukraine was actually proving to be even more troublesome. Robert Dix was forced to hire burly bodyguards when he went to Kiev; there had been threats and intimidation against his team. Menacing locals had taken an unwelcome interest in the Ukraina shopping centre, preventing the bank's representatives from setting foot in the mall. Physically and figuratively, IBRC had been locked out.

Corporate raiding was not unusual in Ukraine. Local interests would claim possession of a building or business through a fabricated ownership document. In 2011, Martin Raiser, head of the World

Bank in Ukraine, warned that raiding was so prevalent in the country that it was undermining its economy and hampering investment. On this occasion, however, Woodhouse and Dix believed that it was an Irish family doing the raiding, with the support of locals on the ground.

The Ukrainian legal system was not helping. In Ukraine, judges are allocated to cases on a random basis, a measure designed to stymie attempts at corrupting the judiciary. Yet the same judge was selected for several cases between IBRC and the Quinns. The Ukrainian courts were continually rejecting applications by the bank aimed at getting control of the Ukraina centre. At the same time, the courts were quick to grant rights to Lyndhurst in relation to the asset.

Confused and increasingly concerned, the bank had appealed to its ultimate shareholder, the Irish government. Brian Hayes, the junior minister in the Department of Finance, had raised the issue with Ukraine's Finance Minister, Yuriy Kolobov, at a meeting in Kiev in early June. Hayes said his department was 'fighting' to ensure full ownership reverted to the IBRC. 'These assets in the Ukraine and elsewhere are assets of the Irish people, because they are now under the ownership of the IBRC,' he said. The following month, Enda Kenny, the Taoiseach, had brought the bank's worries to the attention of Viktor Yanukovych, the Ukrainian President, at an EU conference in Warsaw.

Robert Dix also wrote an open letter to Ukraine's Prime Minister, Mykola Azarov, which was published in several local newspapers. The letter cited 'a series of unlawful activities . . . which make it impossible for us, the owners of almost 93 per cent of the shares of the Ukraina shopping mall, to exercise our lawful rights' to take control of the centre. Dix's open letter concluded by appealing to the Prime Minister to 'take this matter under your personal control'. Dix subsequently wrote another letter, this one addressed to 'representatives of the foreign business community and Ukrainian media', which spoke of 'a real threat' that the Ukraina mall 'will be seized from us in Ukraine through a raiding takeover'.

Within days of the second Dix letter being published, the Kiev Commercial Court ruled that Lyndhurst had a rightful claim to the

Ukraina, and threw out yet another application by IBRC. Wood-house, normally suave, was seething. When the verdict came in, he told local reporters in Ukraine that the country's judicial system 'acts as a tool of legalized robbery'.

Woodhouse filed formal complaints against officials within the Ukrainian judiciary, though he knew nothing would come of it. Fighting a legal battle in Ukraine was looking more and more like a waste of both time and money.

On 6 October, the High Court approved the sale of Quinn Insurance to the new joint venture company formed by Liberty Mutual and IBRC. Liberty would have a 51 per cent stake and full day-to-day responsibility, while the bank would have a silent 49 per cent stake. The ruling gave the green light for €738 million to be paid out of the Insurance Compensation Fund to the company to shore up its reserves to the level recommended by IBRC.

The fund, set up in the 1960s to protect policyholders if an insurer fell insolvent, had been used after the collapse of PMPA and the Insurance Corporation of Ireland in the 1980s. The government had recently introduced a new 2 per cent levy on all insurance premiums, projected to raise about €65 million a year, in order to cover the cost of the Quinn Insurance bailout. At that rate, it would take more than eleven years to cover the €738 million approved by the High Court for Sean Quinn's insurance company.

By late October, the Quinn Group management were making headway with the debt restructuring. It was decided to execute the change through a so-called Company Voluntary Arrangement. The approach gave the group protection from the risk of some of the creditors rejecting the restructuring. With the CVA approved on 31 October, the lenders voted in favour of the new debt load – instead of €720 million, the manufacturing group would have debt of €475 million, not due to be repaid until 2016. The amount of borrowings to be boxed off into the holding company rose to €811 million, to be paid down by the sale of the non-core assets. The deal cut the group's annual interest bill from €60 million to €40 million, giving it some leeway for investment. The banks agreed on a €130 million capital expenditure programme and the guarantees over Quinn Insurance assets were released.

Under the restructuring announced on 14 April, Anglo Irish Bank was to have a 75 per cent equity stake in Quinn Group, with the banks and bondholders holding the remainder. Under the new agreement, with the non-Anglo lenders facing the prospect of recouping far less of what they were owed, the shareholdings flipped – IBRC, the Anglo successor, would have a stake of just 25 per cent. The banks and bondholders would have effective control of Quinn Group; the debt-for-equity swap with the lenders, resisted so vehemently by Sean Quinn, was a reality.

After eighteen months of work on the Quinn situation, the bank had a 49 per cent stake in an insurance company, a one-quarter stake in the manufacturing group and multiple legal actions to show for its efforts.

On 10 November 2011, Sean Quinn travelled to Belfast. It was a trip he had planned for some time, though he hoped he would never have to make it. In the Belfast courts, using his birth name of John Ignatius Quinn and the address of the Quinn Group in Derrylin, he filed a petition for bankruptcy. The personal insolvency regime in the United Kingdom was more lenient than in the Republic, allowing a person to exit bankruptcy in one year; in the Republic, it was twelve years.

In a statement of affairs with his petition, Quinn listed modest assets: €11,169 in three bank accounts, a 2004-registered Mercedes S600 worth €4,670 and an interest in some forestry in Co. Fermanagh valued at £35,000. Quinn declared two pension funds, one valued at €160,000 and another at almost €40,000.

The luxury family home at Greaghrahan, outside Ballyconnell, was not listed among his assets – it was owned by his children. In his petition, Quinn said he had sold a site at the same address to his children a month earlier for €100,000. Quinn estimated his monthly outgoings at £2,380 – £850 on housekeeping, £1,200 on utility bills, £100 on clothing, £80 a month on travel and £150 for miscellaneous expenses. He had no income, he said, as a result of an ongoing dispute with IBRC.

A question on the form asked whether the petitioner had incurred any gambling debts in the previous two years.

No, answered Quinn.

The following morning, the Belfast High Court's Master in Bankruptcy, Fiona Kelly, heard the petition. Quinn was represented by solicitor John Gordon, an insolvency specialist and managing partner of Napier and Sons, a Belfast law firm. Quinn's petition noted he was not resident in Northern Ireland, but said his 'centre of main interest' was in Derrylin, where the Quinn Group was headquartered. 'I am domiciled for taxation purposes in Northern Ireland and my tax affairs are conducted within the United Kingdom under UK National Insurance and Tax References,' he said. Kelly accepted Quinn's petition and granted a bankruptcy order.

Barely four years after being ranked Ireland's richest man with a €6 billion fortune, and without any warning to IBRC, Sean Quinn was bankrupt. Shortly after 11 a.m. on Friday 11 November 2011, Quinn issued a personal statement through James Morrissey. It was both deflated and defiant.

> It is with great sadness and regret that I have applied for voluntary bankruptcy in the High Court in Belfast today. I was born, reared and worked all my life in County Fermanagh. It is for this reason that my bankruptcy application was made today in Northern Ireland.
>
> I have done everything in my power to avoid taking this drastic decision. The vast majority of debt that Anglo maintains is owed is strenuously disputed. However, I cannot now pay those loans which are due, following Anglo taking control of the Quinn Group of companies, which I and a loyal team spent a lifetime building. I find myself left with no other choice.
>
> I worked tirelessly to find a solution to the problems, which arose from the ill-fated investments in Anglo. Anglo, and more recently the Irish government, are intent on making scapegoats of my family and I. Anglo has consistently ignored its own wrongdoing in affairs. Anglo has sought every means to avoid acknowledging the lack of corporate responsibility, the self-interest, the illegal lending practices and lack of regulation that prevailed at the time, all of which are now the subject of High Court proceedings.

I am certainly not without blame. I am not in the business of pointing fingers or making excuses. However, recent history has shown that I, like thousands of others in Ireland, incorrectly relied upon the persons who guided Anglo and who wrongfully sought to portray a 'blue chip' Irish banking stock. [...]

The Quinn companies did not fail, notwithstanding the untruths, creative accounting and spin now being generated. Anglo is now tirelessly working with its PR advisers to tell a different story of how I supposedly brought down the Quinn Group. This is wrong. Anglo's actions, in taking control of the businesses, have led to the present situation.

The Quinn Group, prior to Anglo's takeover, was a very profitable business, which was paying all the interest on 100 per cent of its debts, as well as having sufficient surpluses to develop further. Anglo's chairman, board and management have failed to have the foresight to work jointly with me, my family and the team which established and grew the Quinn Group. Instead, Anglo has supported and promoted an ill-conceived and highly damaging receivership programme, which I believe, if it continues on its current road, is destined for certain and catastrophic failure. This will have wide-reaching effects on the local community in which I grew up and where I still live. [...]

Today, in this time of enormous personal sadness, I want to publicly express my gratitude and thanks to my family, friends, customers, former colleagues and staff, and to the wider local communities for the continued support, loyalty and prayers. I know and am grateful for the fact that these people will continue to be supportive. With this in mind, I must look to the future with hope for the opportunities which lie ahead of me.

The bankruptcy caught IBRC by surprise. In a short statement, the bank said it noted Quinn's bankruptcy and was examining its validity 'in the light of Mr Quinn's residency and extensive business interests and liabilities within the state'. Its mandate, the statement said, was to recover as much of the debt as possible on behalf of the Irish taxpayer. 'Mr Quinn and his family, who live in Co. Cavan, owe the Irish state, through IBRC, almost €2.9 billion,' it said.

The bank had set its legal actions seeking summary judgment

against Quinn in motion in the High Court in Dublin on 2 November. They were returned for hearing on 14 November. Quinn's Northern Ireland bankruptcy came between the two dates. Despite the development, the bank pushed ahead with the proceedings. Mr Justice Peter Kelly agreed to transfer the cases to the Commercial Court, the fast-track court for multimillion-euro corporate disputes.

On 17 November, IBRC filed an application to have Quinn's Northern Ireland bankruptcy annulled, backed up with an affidavit from Richard Woodhouse. The bank argued that Quinn was not entitled to apply for Northern Ireland bankruptcy. His bankruptcy adjudication had been obtained 'through misrepresentation and/or non-disclosure', IBRC said. The matter came before Mr Justice Donnell Deeny in the Belfast High Court a week later. Deeny was an accomplished and well-regarded judge, educated in Dublin and Belfast and called to the Bar in Northern Ireland, the Republic and England. A former Alliance Party councillor and chairman of the Arts Council of Northern Ireland, he had been knighted just months after being appointed a High Court judge in September 2004.

Deeny was familiar with the relationship between Quinn and the bank. In a judgment delivered in April 2011, in a dispute between Anglo and a borrower unrelated to the Quinns, the judge had said the bank's Maple Ten transaction appeared to be 'improper and unlawful'. It was an opinion rather than a ruling, but it had given the Quinns hope. Deeny's views on Anglo and the Maple Ten deal did not mean Quinn could expect favourable treatment, however. The judge said he would decide the issue of jurisdiction based on European insolvency regulations. The rules said insolvency proceedings could only be taken in the jurisdiction where a person had their centre of main interest – and that place had to be known or easily ascertainable by third parties, especially creditors.

As the Belfast proceedings got under way, IBRC stepped up its legal actions against Quinn in Dublin. With no dispute from Quinn, the Commercial Court granted the bank's judgments against the businessman. The ruling meant the bank was entitled to recoup massive sums of money – €1.74 billion in one judgment and €416 million in another.

The bank was also seeking a repayment order for a €3 million 'home improvement' loan advanced to Patricia Quinn in 2006, which meant the former billionaire's wife, who had always kept a low public profile, was pushed into the limelight. On the stand in the High Court, she argued against the bank's description of her as 'business lady'. Despite the fact she had been a director of more than ninety Quinn companies, including the main group company, she had been a 'homemaker' for thirty-six years, looking after her husband and children from the time she married, aged twenty-one.

She claimed she was under the 'undue influence' of her husband and regularly signed legal and financial documents he put in front of her without reading them. She claimed she did not realize she had signed up for the €3 million loan, had not received legal advice before signing, and had never received the benefit of the money. Though it was described as a loan to complete the interior decoration of the Ballyconnell mansion, the money had been paid on to Quinn Manufacturing, a group company. 'This is embarrassing to admit but it is the truth,' she said in an affidavit, claiming she was not liable to repay the money.

Justice Peter Kelly, the head of the Commercial Court, was not impressed. Patricia Quinn, he said in his ruling, was advancing the proposition she was 'a cat's paw' for her husband and 'clueless' about being a director of many companies, he said. Her claim was 'startling' and 'astonishing'; she was saying she had no will of her own. If the law presumed she was under the undue influence of her husband, then 'the law is an ass', the judge said, quoting Mr Bumble from Dickens' *Oliver Twist*. She was liable for the loan.

The next day, 16 December, IBRC issued a bankruptcy summons for Sean Quinn – or at least, it tried to. Several attempts to serve the summons on Quinn failed. He simply refused to open the locked gates to his luxury home at Ballyconnell. The summons server saw a man he thought was Quinn walking around his car outside the house, waiting for the server to leave. Eventually, the man had simply driven past. Quinn's solicitors on both sides of the border had also declined to accept the summons on his behalf. Stonewalled by Quinn, the bank decided to hold off until the Belfast bankruptcy proceedings were settled. Confident of success, they could afford to wait.

In the meantime, a number of other pieces of the jigsaw had fallen into place. On 2 December, the last of the legal work on the financial restructuring of Quinn Group was completed. A deal was finalized, too, to sell Quinn Healthcare to the management team of the business, led by Donal Clancy and backed up by a subsidiary of Swiss Re. The health insurer, the former Bupa business bought by Quinn in 2007, was run separately from Quinn Insurance, and at a geographic remove, in Cork; it had never gone into administration. But Liberty Mutual had no interest in buying it, so a separate sale process had run through 2010 and 2011.

It was hoped the sale of Quinn Healthcare could raise up to €100 million, money that would go to repay the banks and bondholders. Irish Life, the life assurance unit of Irish Life & Permanent, had expressed interest, but eventually dropped out. Clancy, who had made his interest in the business known from the start, cranked up his efforts to take control. In December, a deal was struck, though not for €100 million – or anything like it. It would later emerge it was a 'non-cash' transaction, involving a complex mix of deferred payments and debt write-downs. There would be no immediate windfall for the Quinn Group lenders.

After the deal closed, Clancy received a letter from Sean Quinn, wishing him well with the healthcare business. In the midst of an acrimonious bankruptcy process, Quinn took time to write to the very people taking over one of his businesses. Clancy was impressed with that.

The challenge to Quinn's Northern Ireland bankruptcy was heard on 19 and 20 December in Belfast. Quinn and his lawyer, John Gordon, had filed affidavits, while Woodhouse had sworn a supplemental affidavit to his original document. The banker was cross-examined by Quinn's lawyers. The bank didn't put Quinn on the stand, though he did respond to some queries it posed.

It was a bitter affair. Quinn's legal team argued that IBRC was being vindictive – it wanted to annul the Northern Ireland bankruptcy simply so it could bankrupt the businessman under the Republic's harsh twelve-year regime. It was an 'attempt to oppress'

Quinn and make sure he would never again be in business, they said. The bank responded that it merely wanted to avoid the extra layer of costs that would be involved if the bankruptcy was in a jurisdiction other than the Republic, where Quinn and the bank were already involved in extensive legal proceedings.

Judge Deeny filleted Quinn's bankruptcy petition. The business-man had claimed Derrylin was his centre of main interest, yet he lived in the Republic and had resigned from the Derrylin-based Quinn Group in April 2010, more than eighteen months earlier. He had then claimed to be working from an office in Derrylin Enterprise Park from May 2011, shortly after the Quinn Group went into receiv-ership. Quinn said he 'worked from there most days'. He was busy dealing with the family's legal action and had 'a number of embry-onic business ideas' he was considering.

But the £50-a-month lease for the Derrylin premises was a 'some-what curious document', the judge said; just a slip of paper, signed only by Quinn and Michael Brady, the owner of the property, and not witnessed by a solicitor. There was no way either of verifying an invoice for new letterheads and business cards, dated July 2011. There was no evidence Quinn had sent any letters from Derrylin Enterprise Park or received any replies. And if he was using that address, why had he not used it – rather than the address of the Quinn Group headquarters – on his bankruptcy petition?

IBRC hammered away at the details. Quinn had not declared the Derrylin lease on his bankruptcy petition; he claimed to be working on new business ventures yet declared himself unemployed on the petition; he had not given any details of an accountant or solicitor. Quinn was arguing the bank didn't know about the Derrylin office because he wanted privacy, yet he said it was 'common knowledge' in the area that he was working from there. He couldn't have it both ways.

It was Deeny's view that the lease had been prepared at a much later date than claimed, solely to 'bolster' the bankruptcy applica-tion. 'He may have recently taken possession of this office at Unit 1 in the Derrylin Enterprise Park but not, on the balance of probabili-ties, before 10 November, and he certainly has not used it on a regular basis.' The judge was saying Quinn's petition was a sham.

There had been media reports that Quinn was planning to set up a new insurance company or other venture based in Belturbet in Co. Cavan, close to his home. A company hired by the bank to serve legal documents on Quinn had seen the businessman visit the Belturbet premises, a converted tyre factory where office space had been fitted out, on a number of occasions. 'I consider it more likely that that is where Mr Quinn is discussing any new business proposition,' Deeny said.

The judge also noted that all of Quinn's dealings with Anglo were via the bank's main office in Dublin. His loans from the bank were in euro, yen and dollars – never in sterling. 'This is an Irish bank pursuing him in the High Court in Dublin,' Deeny said. Quinn did not even have lawyers in the North, apart from John Gordon, who had been recruited for the bankruptcy case. There was 'a very considerable and compelling weight of evidence' that the Republic was Quinn's centre of main interest, Deeny said. He had lived south of the border for thirty-two years. He had an Irish passport and voted in the Republic. He no longer had business interests in Northern Ireland.

'I find that Mr Quinn's main interests in recent months were the litigation in which he and his family are embroiled and the salvaging of what he can from the situation in which he finds himself,' the judge said. 'I find the centre of Mr Quinn's main interests is in the Republic of Ireland. I find that prior to 10 November 2011 he was not conducting the administration of his interests on a regular basis in Northern Ireland. I find that the probability is that the administration of his interests was shared between his home, Belturbet and Dublin where he continues to have professional advisers.'

Summing up, the judge said Quinn had failed to disclose he had an Irish passport and no United Kingdom passport; he had not disclosed he voted in the Republic; and he had claimed to be a UK taxpayer while 20 per cent of his taxes were paid south of the border. The Northern Ireland bankruptcy order 'should not have been made', Deeny said. He annulled the bankruptcy, and ordered Quinn to pay the legal costs of both IBRC and an official receiver involved in the case.

Outside the court, Quinn denied he had tried to mislead the court. 'I never done a day's work from Southern Ireland in my life. I never done a day's work in my home. I never had any computers, I never had any IT system. Everything was always done from Derrylin. There was never any question of me deceiving the court and there was never any need for me to deceive the court.' It was in stark contrast to his appeal for customers in the Republic when he was building his cement factory in Ballyconnell, Co. Cavan, in the late 1980s.

Quinn again claimed he was being made a scapegoat for the collapse of Anglo Irish Bank. 'The bankruptcy is just a deflection of what's going on here,' he said. 'What Anglo Irish has done to the Quinn Group is like somebody taking a sledgehammer to a child's toy – they've destroyed it.'

Deeny's ruling left the way clear for IBRC to bankrupt Quinn on its own terms. In the High Court in Dublin three days before Christmas 2011, Mr Justice Michael Peart said the bank could serve the summons on Quinn by hand-delivering it into the letter box of his home. It should also be delivered to Quinn's Dublin lawyers, the judge said. There was no way for Quinn to avoid it.

On 16 January 2012, Sean Quinn was declared bankrupt in the Dublin High Court. The man once worth billions had no income and would need permission to borrow more than €650. He would be seventy-six years old by the time he emerged from bankruptcy.

Quinn did not oppose the bankruptcy application but said afterwards that IBRC was pursuing a 'personal vendetta' against him and his family. 'Today Anglo achieved their goal of ensuring that I will never create another job . . . The position of the Irish taxpayer could have improved significantly, by a more reasonable approach to the issues involved,' he said in a statement.

He expanded on his comments in an interview with the *Impartial Reporter*, the Fermanagh newspaper, published three days later. 'I am now heading into retirement penniless, and I'm very sad that it has come to this,' he said. He reiterated his claim that IBRC's pursuit of him was motivated by a 'personal vendetta' rather than commercial rationale. Quinn Group, he said, was 'dead and gone', and losing €40 million a week. 'I said two years ago that bringing in

the administrator to Quinn Insurance was one of the worst decisions in the history of the state. People laughed at that but I think
they are laughing less at that today, and they will laugh even less in
a year's time.'

To Mike Aynsley and Richard Woodhouse, it was typical Quinn blus-
ter. And it was all academic, anyway. Quinn Group had been refinanced,
the bank had its judgments against Quinn and the patriarch was bankrupt. Now they would shift their focus fully to the legal actions
involving the €500 million international property portfolio. Making
little progress in the Russian and Ukrainian legal systems, Woodhouse
and his legal advisers at McCann FitzGerald had decided it was time for
a fresh approach to seizing control of Quinn's properties.

Sean Quinn Junior had given hints he might be willing to cooperate with the bank. At a meeting with the bank's investigators,
Risk Management International (RMI), in January, he had talked
about cutting a deal. He was vague on detail, but RMI had believed
he was genuine. The bank scheduled a second meeting with Sean
Junior to try to flesh out the details. At the next meeting, however,
everything changed; his eldest sister, Colette, had turned up
with him and did most of the talking. There would be no deal, she
had stated defiantly, while her brother sat silently for most of the
meeting.

Richard Woodhouse decided to increase the stakes. If he could
prove the Quinn family were in breach of the High Court orders
restraining them from interfering with the assets, members of the
family could face imprisonment. The threat of a custodial sentence
might convince Sean Quinn and certain members of his family to start
cooperating. But Woodhouse needed to prove beyond a reasonable
doubt that the family had disobeyed the court order. To do this, he had
to get to the bottom of the ownership structure of Galfis and Lyndhurst. These two offshore companies were claiming to be owners of
the most valuable assets in the Quinn portfolio, the Kutuzoff Tower in
Moscow and the Ukraina centre in Kiev. If IBRC could link them to
the Quinn family, the bank would be able to argue that the family had
secretly sought to move the properties beyond the reach of the bank.

The Quinn family was maintaining in a number of jurisdictions that the assignments of the debt from the properties to Galfis and Lyndhurst were made before the bank's appointment of Kieran Wallace as share receiver to the Quinn Group. In their correspondence with the bank as part of the legal battle, the Quinns had provided documents apparently showing that the loans had been transferred in early April, before the bank had seized control of the group and the property assets.

Woodhouse refused to believe this, however. The British banker was convinced that there was no way that the loans had been assigned to these companies in the days before the appointment of the receivers. He had been there on 14 April 2011 when Sean Quinn was summoned to Dublin and told that his empire was being taken from him. Quinn had been genuinely shocked at the move, utterly taken aback. Woodhouse did not believe the businessman had seen the receivership coming and sanctioned a plan to transfer the assets before April 2011.

The Quinn story was simply not plausible, Woodhouse told Mike Aynsley. Instead, he was utterly convinced that the moves had been made much later, with some of the transactions coming after the initial injunction in the Irish courts in June 2011. Now, he had to prove it. To do this, he needed all the background documentation on Galfis and Lyndhurst. 'These companies are the key to the whole thing,' Woodhouse told Aynsley. 'If we can unlock these, we can unlock the whole thing.'

The bank's new plan centred on a seldom-used court order known as a 'Norwich Pharmacal Order', typically used when legal proceedings for alleged wrongdoing cannot be brought because the identity of the wrongdoer is not known. The name comes from a 1974 UK case, Norwich Pharmacal Co. v Customs and Excise Commissioners, which dealt with the alleged violation of a patent on a chemical by unknown importers. The order forces the disclosure of documents or information. IBRC believed that such an order might force the release of paperwork for Galfis and Lyndhurst. In addition to seeking the Norwich Pharmacal Order, the bank also decided to get broader injunctions in a number of other jurisdictions connected to the properties. It was a dual strategy – injunct the firms, and then seek out information about them.

On 21 December, the bank's lawyers had sought injunctions in the High Court in Belfast against Galfis, the Belize company that was claiming control of the Kutuzoff Tower. The case was taken in Northern Ireland because the tower debt had been transferred to Galfis by Demesne, a Northern Ireland-based company owned by the Quinn family. As part of its application for the injunctions, the bank argued that the loan assignment to Galfis from Demesne was designed to 'defraud' the bank and other creditors.

The Belfast High Court granted the injunctions, preventing Galfis from selling or transferring its interest in the disputed property. The next day, the bank gained a similar order in Belize, again restraining the activities of Galfis. The bank also secured the Norwich Pharmacal Order forcing Galfis to reveal details of its ownership structure and origin. This order needed to be obtained in Belize as the company was located and incorporated there. If the bank wanted to know who was behind Galfis, it needed the green light from the Belize courts.

On 23 December, the bank returned to the Belfast High Court, seeking an injunction against Lyndhurst, which had been assigned the debt on the Ukrainian asset by Innishmore, another Northern Ireland company controlled by the Quinns. The same day, lawyers went to the courts in the British Virgin Islands, where Lyndhurst was registered, seeking another injunction and a Norwich order forcing it to reveal its ownership.

As soon as IBRC secured its Belize injunction against Galfis, Yaroslav Gurnyak, the Ukrainian railway worker plucked from obscurity by the lawyers at A&B to be owner of the Kutuzoff Tower, challenged the move in the Belize courts. He claimed that he was the beneficial owner of Galfis and should be allowed to contest the bank's claim over the company.

Gurnyak did not travel to Belize for the case, which commenced in early February 2012. He claimed his leg was aching, and said he had a number of business meetings to attend in Russia. He did file a number of affidavits, however, one of which said he had spent the past twenty years working in corporate restructuring. He also agreed to provide oral evidence by way of video link from Moscow, using an interpreter. For IBRC, it was the first occasion to quiz this mysterious Russian about how he came to acquire the tower.

Gurnyak quickly veered off course. He told the court he finished secondary school in Ukraine in 1983. He studied in the 'university for oil', he said, but did not get a degree, and then joined the Soviet army in 1987. He had left the army in 1989, after which he got a job on the railways in Ukraine. He had left this job in 2011 to work as a businessman, he said through his interpreter. Gurnyak was not able to name the companies he claimed to have restructured. Asked where he had trained in restructuring, he said through his interpreter, 'He was not trained in any special place. It was by his own. He trained by his own.' Asked what he meant by restructuring companies, Gurnyak said he was a bit nervous and could not remember.

IBRC's lawyer, Eamon Courtney, who was in the Belize court, complained that Arthur Zafarov of A&B, the Russian law firm, was 'constantly shaking his head and telling [Gurnyak] whether to say yes or no'. When the presiding judge asked Zafarov to leave the room, the video feed from Russia was terminated. Efforts to restore the video connection were unsuccessful. An arrangement was made to resume the interview the next day, but Gurnyak did not turn up. The Belize court was subsequently told Gurnyak had been threatened by an unidentified lawyer. In his absence, the judge ruled that Gurnyak was 'evasive and uncooperative' and the challenge to the IBRC injunction was dismissed.

As the courtroom farce unfolded, Richard Woodhouse finally obtained the company records of Galfis and Lyndhurst through the Norwich Pharmacal Order. It was the breakthrough he had been seeking. The documents did not explicitly show that the companies were under the control of the Quinn family. But they did show that the companies could not possibly have bought the loan assignments in early April 2011: until 6 July that year, they were dormant shelf companies and had no shareholders. That meant the companies did not exist when the Quinn Group and properties were put into receivership; they did not even exist in June 2011 when the bank got its injunction against the Quinns. The loan assignments to Galfis and Lyndhurst had clearly been backdated.

Woodhouse now believed he had enough evidence to pursue Sean Quinn and Petey Quinn for contempt of court. The bank had also uncovered evidence that the employment contract of Larisa Yanez Puga, who managed the family's Ukrainian assets, had been altered to ensure that she was paid $500,000. Sean Quinn Junior and Petey had been party to that deal. Again, Woodhouse was convinced the contract had been altered after the Irish court order.

The bank decided to pull the trigger. On 13 February 2012, IBRC issued contempt of court proceedings against Sean Quinn, his son and his nephew. During its initial application a few days later, IBRC focused on the three specific actions: the assignment of the $130 million debt from the Kutuzoff Tower to Galfis; the transfer to Lyndhurst of the $42 million debt from the Univermag Ukraina shopping centre; and the $500,000 payment to Puga.

James Morrissey, the Quinn family spokesman, said the family rejected the allegations being made against them. They would defend their position 'vigorously'. The Quinns would not have to wait long: the High Court decided to fast-track the case, giving it a start date of 21 March.

12

Contempt

The contempt of court case, heard over fifteen days in March and May 2012, was tetchy and ill tempered. IBRC had zeroed in on the controversial transactions involving the Kutuzoff Tower in Moscow and the Ukraina shopping centre in Kiev, and also alleged Quinn involvement in the $500,000 payment to Larisa Yanez Puga. The bank was pursuing Sean Quinn and Petey Quinn on all three alleged breaches, while the allegations against Sean Junior were confined to the Puga payment.

The bank alleged that Petey Quinn and Sean Quinn Junior had travelled to Kiev in August 2011 to meet Puga. During the meeting, IBRC claimed, the pair falsified and backdated Puga's employment contract. Puga had a salary of $7,000, but the altered contract ensured she would be paid $500,000 in the event of her contract being terminated. Her contract was subsequently terminated and Puga received the money. The bank claimed that the Puga payment, and the Kutuzoff and Ukraina debt transfer, breached the High Court injunction granted in June 2011 by Mr Justice Frank Clarke, as they involved money being moved out of the International Property Group.

Paul Gallagher SC, a combative lawyer with a stern face and bristly white beard, represented the bank. Three years earlier, Gallagher had been Attorney General to the Fianna Fáil/Green Party coalition government that had nationalized Anglo Irish Bank. During his time in the witness box, Sean Quinn Senior had been quick to repeatedly point this out.

Before their appearances in the box, various members of the Quinn family had strenuously denied the existence of any asset-stripping scheme. During previous court actions in Cyprus, and in public statements, they said it simply did not exist. Now, in court, Sean Quinn Senior acknowledged that there was a plan to put assets beyond the reach of the bank, and that he, as the head of the Quinn family, had sanctioned it. In spite of an intense verbal assault from Gallagher, however, Quinn maintained that the plan had been halted as soon as the bank had secured its High Court injunction on 27 June 2011.

In the witness box, Quinn seized on every opportunity to turn his answers into anti-Anglo diatribes. He said the family's movement of assets was 'Mickey Mouse stuff' when compared with the 'destruction of the Quinn Group' by Anglo. 'And, by the way, if you're talking about destruction you can go back and talk about the nationalization of the banks which the Attorney General was involved in. That is real destruction,' he said. Clearly emotional, he accused the bank of putting Quinn Group into receivership 'to cover up a bigger issue' about its loans to cover Quinn's CFD losses. 'They did not want me or anybody to tell the truth,' he said. 'Anglo . . . does not want the main case to be heard. So I think it is wrong and think society is entitled to know the truth. Anglo is trying to cover up the truth and that is why we are here today and that is why all these court cases are being run . . . I think the cover-up should be opened up.'

The evidence given by Sean Junior, by contrast, was short and sharp. Like his father, he confessed to the existence of the scheme to hide assets, acknowledging that he had a role within it. Like his father, he was also adamant that they had halted the plan as soon as the High Court stamped its injunction the previous June. During intense questioning, he stuck to that line.

Petey, the mastermind of the asset-stripping scheme, took a battering. He was clearly uncomfortable on the stand. 'I am just an employee,' he had said. 'I am not willing to get involved in something that keeps getting me accused of various different things which affect me personally, affect my family, affect my mother. It's not nice for them to be reading allegations about me in the paper.' Compared with the composed and confrontational approaches of his cousin and uncle, Petey seemed almost contrite.

The IBRC legal team could not understand it. Given that he was not the owner of the properties and therefore did not stand to gain as much from the asset-stripping as the other family members, had Petey decided to put his own interests first? Had he, along with the other family members, adopted a deliberate strategy of admitting to some elements of the plan, but denying others? No one was sure.

Petey's testimony provided the IBRC bankers and their lawyers with a wealth of new information. He talked at length about his discussions with his uncle and cousin, and the rationale for the asset-stripping machinations. He explained how the family sought to focus Anglo's attention on large assets like the Kutuzoff Tower, while moving smaller unsecured Russian assets into shelf companies in Panama and Belize. It was, he said, 'all a smokescreen'. Petey explained how the plan had been conceived, designed, structured and implemented. Despite all of his admissions, however, he maintained that all activities had stopped once the court injunction had been granted to the bank. He remained steadfast on this point: there had been no activity after the injunction came into effect.

It was on this point that the entire case hinged. Woodhouse did not believe that the asset transfers took place before the 27 June injunction, let alone before the Quinn Group receivership. What he and the bank had to prove was that the transfers continued after the bank secured its court injunction telling the Quinn family to desist from any further interference with the property assets. The final word on this would rest with Ms Justice Elizabeth Dunne.

The hearings in the contempt case had adjourned for a day, Friday 11 May, so that Sean Junior could marry his fiancée, Karen Woods.

Petey was best man at the ceremony in the picturesque St Mochta's Church in Porterstown in west Dublin. Father Gerry Comiskey, the parish priest in the Quinns' home parish of Drumlane, officiated at the wedding Mass and Colette Quinn read a Communion reflection. The reception took place at the opulent Ritz-Carlton Powerscourt

Hotel in Enniskerry, Co. Wicklow, one of the country's most expensive hotels.

The 200-bedroom five-star property had been built at the height of the economic boom by Treasury Holdings, owned by buccaneering developers Johnny Ronan and Richard Barrett. Complete with a Gordon Ramsay restaurant and 30,000-square-foot spa, the €200 million Ritz had opened its doors in October 2007, just as the first cracks appeared in the Celtic Tiger economy. By the time the Quinns' 150 wedding guests were sitting down to their Irish beef fillet and roasted monkfish, washed down by Veuve Clicquot Rosé Vintage 2004, the property was drowning in debt.

Judgment day in the contempt case came just over six weeks later, on 26 June 2012. Sean Junior slalomed his way across the back of the congested courtroom, swerving past gowned lawyers and pinstriped bankers. His father was already nestled in the back corner of Court 5 in the Four Courts, fidgeting with a half-empty bottle of water. Petey was there, too, restlessly shifting his weight from one foot to the other.

It was less than ten metres from the door of the courtroom to where Sean Junior's father and cousin, his two co-defendants, were waiting, but it took him several minutes to reach them. Dozens of friends from home packed the benches of the courtroom in a show of solidarity, and the 33-year-old earnestly shook their hands, thanking them for their continued support. Finally, he took his place beside his cousin and father, standing pensively, with his shoulders back and his head held high.

From his position at the back of the courtroom, Sean Junior could easily pick out his adversaries. Richard Woodhouse and Mike Aynsley were huddled at the other side of the court, surrounded by a personal security detail. IBRC's security experts had advised the two bankers not to attend court on safety grounds, but they went anyway. As a compromise, they were escorted by well-dressed, well-built men with earpieces. Nothing was being left to chance. Sean Junior tapped his father on the shoulder and pointed out the bodyguards. His father merely shrugged.

The media were out in force, too. All the major newspapers and broadcasters were represented, journalists tapping away on laptops and smartphones. In mid May, just days after Sean Junior's wedding, BBC Northern Ireland had broadcast a Spotlight Special, *Sean Quinn's Missing Millions*, on the hunt for the Quinn properties. Jim Fitzpatrick, the economics and business editor for BBC Northern Ireland, had followed the paper trail from Ireland to Sweden, Russia, Ukraine and, eventually, a post office box in Belize. It was compelling viewing, though it raised as many questions as it answered.

Today, some of those questions might be answered. Today would be a landmark day. The Quinns knew it. And the bankers knew it, too. It was the reason why Aynsley and Woodhouse had defied their security advisers, and the reason why so many of the Quinn family's supporters had made the journey to Dublin.

At 10.32 a.m., Justice Dunne, a middle-aged lady with thin framed glasses and a sharp turn of phrase, took her seat at the head of the packed courtroom. In a matter-of-fact tone, she delivered the highlights of her 56-page judgment. The judge found that the three Quinns had participated in a 'blatant, dishonest and deceitful' scheme to put valuable international property assets beyond the reach of the bank, and that they had carried on with this in defiance of a High Court injunction. All three were in contempt of the court, she said. Dunne found in favour of IBRC on all three substantive arguments: the Kutuzoff Tower issue, the Ukraina centre transfer and the $500,000 payment to Puga.

Sean Quinn Junior remained impassive in the back corner of the courtroom, taking it all in. His father continued to juggle his water bottle. Petey wore a nervous smile.

The fresh information revealed in Petey's evidence clearly had not impressed Justice Dunne. She simply did not believe his testimony that there had been no activity in relation to the properties after IBRC secured the June injunction. The judge said that Petey had been 'evasive, less than forthright, obstructive, uncooperative and at times untruthful' in his evidence. He had 'conveyed the impression of someone reluctant to be in court [who was determined] to say as little as possible and of someone who simply did not tell the whole truth'. The judge concluded Petey 'would have said and done any-thing to aid the plan he conceived to put assets beyond the reach of Anglo'. Sean Quinn Junior was simply 'not telling the truth', Justice Dunne said, highlighting in particular his role in the $500,000 payment to Puga.

His father, Sean Quinn Senior, according to the judge, had been 'evasive and uncooperative'. Dunne noted that 'on a number of occasions during the hearing, rather than answer questions put to him, he embarked on lengthy criticisms of Anglo'. She said she found it impossible to accept the evidence of Sean Quinn Senior that 'he had no hand, act or part in the matter after April 2011'. Instead, she was 'satisfied that not only did he give Peter Quinn his imprimatur to implement the plan described in evidence, but also that he took whatever steps were required of him by signing documents'. She added, 'It may be that he did not have every detail required to implement the plan but I am satisfied beyond doubt that he was fully supportive of it and actively involved in doing what was required.'

It was a damning verdict that went from bad to worse for the Quinns. 'In the course of his evidence, Sean Quinn Senior spoke of the Quinn Group and its importance as an employer of some seven thousand people,' the judge said. 'One can appreciate the ability that led to the creation of such a business empire. Sean Quinn Senior also spoke of the honourable, respectable way in which the businesses comprised in the Quinn Group were run. I wish I could say the same about the manner in which the respondents have dealt with the adverse circumstances in which they now find themselves having regard to the collapse of the Quinn business empire.'

The judge acknowledged the bitter dispute between the family and the bank over the CFD borrowings and the seizure of Quinn Group. But, she said, 'What has never been in dispute is the fact that a sum of €455 million approximately is due to Anglo,' she said. Whereas the Quinns were challenging the legitimacy of the €2.3 billion they owed the bank in respect of loans linked to Sean Quinn's CFD investments, this other considerable debt was uncontested.

Justice Dunne continued, 'Instead of trying to repay the admitted debt due, the Quinn family and, in particular, the respondents have taken every step possible to make it as difficult as can be to recover any amount due. They have engaged in a complex, complicated and, no doubt, costly, series of steps designed to put the assets of the IPG [International Property Group] beyond the reach of Anglo, in a blatant, dishonest and deceitful manner. They have consciously misled courts here and elsewhere. They have sought to deprive Anglo of the assets which would go some way to discharging an admitted indebtedness. The behaviour of the respondents outlined in evidence before me is as far removed from the concept of honour and respectability as it is possible to be.'

It was a phrase that would dominate media coverage of the case: 'as far removed from the concept of honour and respectability as it is possible to be'. Sean Quinn's reputation, built up over almost four decades in business and arguably his most prized possession, had been torn to shreds by a High Court judge. 'A folk hero's fall from grace' said the *Financial Times* the next day. 'Blatant, dishonest and deceitful' said the *Irish Times*, describing the asset-stripping as 'a ploy that ranks high in the league of Irish scandals'.

As soon as the judge finished, adjourning the case for three days, Mike Aynsley turned and shook hands with Richard Woodhouse. Karyn Harty continued making notes on McCann FitzGerald headed notepaper but allowed herself a small smile. Based on the details that had emerged during the trial, they had been confident of success. Indeed, in the weeks between the culmination of the evidence and Justice Dunne's delivery of her judgment, IBRC had actually returned to court, armed with fresh allegations of shady assets deals. In a separate application, the bank had secured a worldwide freezing order against the assets of the wider Quinn family. It was in the process of appointing a receiver to the family's bank accounts, including a number of accounts in Moscow and Dubai. It had been a bold move, given they were still awaiting the judgment from the contempt case. But they had now been vindicated.

Found guilty of contempt of court, the Quinns could purge their contempt only by reversing the property transactions. They would be forced to recover the assets for the bank or face jail. For the first time in a long while, the IBRC bankers felt the assets were within their grasp.

The three Quinns remained in the courtroom for a few minutes after Justice Dunne had returned to her chamber, holding a brief discussion with their lawyers from Eversheds. Then they left the courtroom and made their way past the media scrum to a waiting BMW X5 Jeep. The media pursued them, eager to hear what the bankrupt industrialist had to say.

Pushed for comment, he described the judgment as 'interesting, very interesting'. As he sat in the back seat of the jeep, he added one statement: 'I am not dishonest.'

On 1 July, the *Irish Mail on Sunday* published details of a secretly filmed video. It showed a meeting in a Kiev restaurant between Petey, Sean Junior, Larisa Yanez Puga and unidentified Russian-speaking individuals, discussing a major cash deal. The newspaper said it was filmed on 21 January, nearly seven months after IBRC injuncted the Quinns from interfering with the property assets. The video showed the unidentified parties offering the Quinns $100,000; but Sean Junior was unhappy they weren't receiving the $5 million they had expected.

'We're not happy with the $100,000 but we'll take it,' he said on the video, published on the newspaper's website. Later, he told the Russians, 'Youse need to think and discuss what youse can do to resolve our issues.'

The fifteen-minute video also showed Petey saying he was in breach of the Irish court injunction. To stay out of jail, he said, he had to deny he had signed the contract assigning the debt for the Ukraina shopping centre to Lyndhurst in the British Virgin Islands. Petey had been ordered by the High Court in Northern Ireland to swear evidence in the Ukrainian courts that his signature was forged on a document relating to the debt transfer to Lyndhurst.

'I'd have to lie to the court,' he said on video, sitting back and shrugging. 'That wouldn't overly worry me.' In a separate exchange, Petey said the Quinns and the Russian individuals didn't 'have to stay together' any more. 'The only reason we would stay together is if we get our money. If we don't get our money we won't stay together,' he said.

The video footage was explosive, appearing to make a mockery of the Quinn claims that they had no involvement with the overseas properties after April 2011. On the weekend the video appeared, the Quinns gathered at the family's mansion outside Ballyconnell. They had been back in Justice Dunne's courtroom on 29 June, three days after the judgment had been delivered, and the judge had given them three weeks to undo the asset-stripping scheme and purge their contempt. Away from their lawyers and advisers, the family sat down and discussed how they would respond.

It was decided that Sean Junior would travel to Moscow and Dubai to explain the situation to the lawyers there and see what could be done. Petey had resigned from the management companies in the International Property Group a number of months before, and Sean Junior had taken a more active role with regard to the property interests. Quinn's only son had held the most senior role of any of his siblings in the old Quinn Group, and as far as the family was concerned it made sense for him to replace Petey at this point. It was agreed that Stephen Kelly, Aoife Quinn's husband and Sean Junior's brother-in-law, would join Sean Junior for the trip. The flights were booked on Monday 2 July, and Kelly and Sean Junior boarded a plane for Moscow two days later. The details of what happened over the following five days would be hotly disputed.

According to an affidavit filed by Sean Junior after his return to Ireland, the purpose of the trip was to explain the family's predicament to A&B, the Russian law firm that had been so instrumental in moving the assets beyond the reach of the bank. With the threat of jail looming for three family members, the Quinns reckoned that it was time for Yaroslav Gurnyak, the mysterious Ukrainian railway worker, to return ownership of the Kutuzoff Tower to the family.

Before the two men left Ireland, Kelly had tried to contact Dmitry Sctukaturov, a lawyer at A&B. Kelly had established a relationship with Sctukaturov a year before, when the asset-stripping plan was taking shape, and the two men had stayed in relatively frequent contact since then. This time, however, Kelly struggled to contact

Sctukaturov. He eventually got the lawyer on the phone directly on 4 July, the day of their departure from Ireland, and the Russian arranged a meeting between Sean Junior, Kelly and the law firm's representative, Arthur Zafarov.

The next day, 5 July, Kelly and Sean Junior made their way to A&B's headquarters on Moscow's Pyatnitskaya Street. 'We explained to him that it was essential that all transactions completed in 2011, in respect of any IPG assets through or involving A&B, including the loan assignments and the transfer of unsecured assets/companies, must be set aside,' said Sean Junior in his affidavit. 'We also emphasized the need to end all ongoing Russian litigation on behalf of the various Russian entities which had previously been within the IPG. We told him that A&B must do everything within their power to assist us in complying with these orders.'

According to Sean Junior's affidavit, Zafarov's response was 'calm but forceful'. The Russian lawyer said that his firm had never acted for the Quinn family. Instead, his firm merely acted for the companies and the assets that the Quinns had so willingly handed over. A&B was now acting for most of the new owners of the properties, he said. Furthermore, Zafarov claimed the new owners had all paid full market value for the properties. Sean Quinn Junior said in his affidavit that he was stunned to hear this, and felt the family had been double-crossed.

According to the affidavit, Zafarov 'told us that A&B and their clients had spent considerable time, effort and expense acquiring and protecting the assets in question and there would be no reversals. He stated that the transfer of the unsecured assets had been completed at fair value and fully complied with Russian legislation. We explained that it was our understanding that we would be able to come to some agreement with the buyers at a future date, to either sell us back the assets at a reasonable price to provide us with some future benefit from the assets. We explained we were following through on our agreement and we wanted our assets back. He disputed that there was any such agreement and concluded by saying that it was not possible and that if we wanted to pursue the matter further we would have to engage our own lawyers in Russia as his firm would not assist.'

According to the Quinn affidavit, Zafarov said that as a courtesy he would ask the new owners if they would return the properties. Zafarov also agreed to hand over documents and accounts in relation to a Russian company called Red Sector, on the grounds that Stephen Kelly remained the general director of that company. Kelly had acquired Red Sector, the company behind a DIY chain, when he was awarded shares in the properties in return for a $380 second-hand laptop. Aside from that, said Sean Junior, Zafarov was adamant that he was not in a position to help.

The next day, according to the Quinn affidavit, a similar meeting was played out: Quinn and Kelly repeated their requests for help from the Russian lawyers, and again Zafarov said he was not in a position to help. That afternoon, they went to the Kutuzoff Tower for a meeting with one of their accountants, Alla Satdarova. Court papers filed by the Quinns would later state that they asked for all documents relating to the Russian assets. After keeping Quinn and Kelly waiting in the boardroom for half an hour, Satdarova returned. The only assistance she could give, she said, was to release documents relating to Red Sector, as the family had no interest, control or equity in the other assets.

Frustrated in Russia, the two men went to the Gulf, and the Dubai offices of Senat Legal. Senat had been central to the international property scheme, buying the offshore companies in Belize and the British Virgin Islands, and coordinating the family's international legal efforts. In Dubai, Sean Junior and Kelly asked Michael Waechter, the Senat lawyer, to reverse a share transfer at the company that owned the €60 million Indian property in a high-tech park in Hyderabad. Waechter, however, said he was not in a position to do it, stating that he did not control the company that benefited from the deal.

As with A&B, the Quinn family would later claim, Senat was preventing the return of assets. The family were left merely as helpless bystanders in a scheme they had admitted to masterminding. A day later, it was back to Russia, and another forceful exchange on Pyatnitskaya Street with Arthur Zafarov. The lawyer had contacted his clients. As expected, the owners of the unsecured assets had decided not to hand them back – some of the properties had even been auctioned off, including a business park, Zafarov said.

Sean Junior and Kelly did not even bother going to Ukraine, where IBRC was still trying to secure the Ukraina shopping centre. Sean Junior had been there before and had heard the stories of corporate raiding. He was afraid to go back, having been threatened by some of the individuals they engaged to hold the assets in the first instance. He believed Puga had teamed up with some unsavoury locals to retain control of the shopping centre. He had been warned about going there again.

In the Quinn version of events, they had been duped out of Russian, Ukrainian and Indian properties worth hundreds of millions of euro. Their companies had been raided, their assets hijacked and their rents commandeered. The family was claiming that, in an attempt to hide the properties from the bank, they had mislaid them entirely. Now, even with the threat of jail time looming, they could not secure their return.

That, at least, was the tale relayed to IBRC and the courts when Sean Junior and Kelly returned home empty-handed. Richard Woodhouse read Sean Junior's affidavit, and read it a second time in sheer disbelief. There were two possibilities. The first was that the Quinns, in their frantic attempts to retain control of the assets, had been outplayed and outmanoeuvred by unscrupulous characters and had actually lost possession of the assets. Given the sums of money at stake, this was not altogether implausible: other companies, including well-regarded international businesses, had fallen victim to similar ruses in the past.

However, for Woodhouse to believe this, he also had to believe that the members of the Quinn family transferred €500 million of assets to anonymous characters without any legal mechanism in place to get them back – a sort of gentleman's agreement with gentlemen they had never met. He simply could not buy it. Sean Quinn had lost his billions and the business he had built from the ground up, and Woodhouse could not believe that he would so readily hand over €500 million of assets without any recourse. The banker could not comprehend how an intricate and costly international enterprise involving lawyers in ten jurisdictions ultimately came down to taking a Russian rail worker at his word, believing a vague verbal statement that he would simply hand back a Moscow skyscraper on request. Instead, Woodhouse concluded that the Quinns were willing to do and say whatever was necessary to keep the assets – even if that meant serving some time in prison.

Sitting in the offices of Eversheds in the early hours of Friday 20 July, Petey Quinn was edgy, downing cup after cup of coffee as he finalized his affidavit. Within hours, Petey was due to return to the High Court to appear again in front of Justice Dunne with his uncle and cousin. Given the scale of the problem and the tone of Justice Dunne's judgment, it was possible, even probable, all three could be sent to jail.

The High Court contempt case had centred on three alleged breaches of court orders. Petey was at the centre of all three of them. He had helped assign $130 million in debt to Galfis, the Belize entity, with the intention of securing ownership of the Kutuzoff Tower. He had executed a similar manoeuvre to retain the Ukraina centre in Kiev, moving $42 million in debt to a company in the British Virgin Islands. And finally, he had helped falsify the employment contract of Larisa Yanez Puga, enabling her to get a $500,000 payment when she was sacked. Petey's fingerprints were everywhere.

After Justice Dunne had delivered her scathing judgment on 26 June, Petey had sought to cut a deal with IBRC. On 3 July, as Sean Junior and Stephen Kelly prepared to jet off to Moscow, Petey told his lawyers to write to the bank's legal team saying he would do everything in his power to purge his contempt. He offered to meet the bank's representatives directly, in the presence of a stenographer, to answer any questions they might have about the asset-stripping scheme, and to offer his advice on how best to retrieve the assets.

The bank was unsure of what to make of it all. Was Petey cutting his ties with the Quinn family and going solo? He had maintained in the witness box that he was a mere employee, while his cousins were the owners of the properties. The bankers felt there had been a shift in the dynamic between Petey and the rest of the family.

On 5 July, Petey's lawyers dispatched another letter, saying he was willing to travel to Moscow to transfer his shareholdings in Finansstroy, the company behind the Kutuzoff Tower, and in Red Sector, the Russian company behind the DIY properties, to the bank. The bank's response was curt: given the scale of the contempt, they felt that merely transferring his shareholding in two companies was not enough and would not help them recover the actual assets.

Other issues were starting to emerge, issues that further undermined any potential entente between IBRC and Petey. A new name had appeared on the share register of the Russian companies, a Mr Volkow. The bank wanted Petey to make sure that Volkow also surrendered any claim to the companies. The trouble was that Petey claimed never to have heard of Volkow. In an affidavit, Quinn acknowledged he did not expect the bank to believe him, but protested at some length that it was the truth.

In that affidavit, Petey described a meeting in Kiev earlier in the year at which, he claimed, mysterious characters associated with Larisa Yanez Puga intimidated him into signing forged documents. He outlined how he had dispatched seventy-five separate letters to lawyers and company directors in an effort to undo the asset-stripping scheme. He even suggested he might be willing to give IBRC power of attorney for him over certain Russian and Ukrainian companies. But the bank was rebuffing his advances.

As the deadline set by Justice Dunne for the Quinns to purge their contempt drew close, trust between the IBRC and the Quinns had reached a new low. The bank had rejected Petey's offer of a 'tell all' meeting. According to evidence lodged in court, Petey had developed an 'accurate realization of his position'. It was too late: the bankers simply did not believe Petey would tell the truth or aid their recovery efforts. They felt it was a mere token gesture to stave off a likely period of imprisonment.

Petey signed his affidavit in the early hours of Friday 20 July in the offices of Eversheds, across from the National Concert Hall in Dublin city centre, and just a few hundred metres from the old St Stephen's Green headquarters of Anglo Irish Bank. Once it was sworn, he left the office, got into his car, and drove home to Co. Fermanagh.

When the name of Peter Darragh Quinn was called in court later that morning, there was confusion. Petey was not present. He had left a message to say he was sick, the court was told. His lawyers said they had no idea where he was; they were as shocked as anybody that he had failed to turn up for the hearing. They tried, unsuccessfully, to track Petey down through other members of his family. His two co-defendants, Sean Senior and Sean Junior, claimed to be in the dark, too. They had been with him in Eversheds' offices hours earlier, but hadn't seen him since.

In his absence that morning, the High Court sentenced Petey to three months in prison for contempt of court and issued a bench warrant for his arrest. Ms Justice Elizabeth Dunne then turned to Sean Quinn Junior and handed down the same sentence – three months for contempt of court. His father clutched a handkerchief and bowed his head as Dunne delivered the sentence.

IBRC had decided it would not seek to jail Sean Quinn Senior only because it wanted him available to take steps to unwind the asset-stripping measures. Brian O'Moore, senior counsel for Quinn, said it was wrong to lock up one member of the family in the hope of forcing another to act. 'This almost medieval approach of holding the son to see what the chieftain father will do in terms of freeing the son's liberty is wholly inadequate,' he argued.

Justice Dunne was unmoved. Far from 'medieval', she considered keeping Sean Quinn Senior out of prison 'a practical way' of procuring compliance. However, the patriarch was warned that he, too, faced jail if he did not cooperate and secure the safe return of the assets.

'You cannot put smoke in the bottle,' Quinn told reporters that day, claiming it was impossible to undo what had been done. The bank and the court, however, believed the sight of his only son being locked up and the threat of jail time for himself might help compel Sean Quinn to figure out a method of getting the smoke into the bottle.

Within minutes of the sentence being handed down, Sean Quinn Junior was escorted to a prison van and transported to Mountjoy Prison to be processed for his three-month sentence. He would serve his time in the prison's Training Unit, a low-security jail with a workshop and educational facilities. Prisoners in the Training Unit can mingle and move about without being accompanied by a prison guard. There are no steel bars on the windows and the inmates have keys to their own rooms. Compared with the hard edge of the main prison, Sean Junior, once the heir to an empire, would be incarcerated in relative comfort.

Petey's whereabouts were a mystery. In the immediate aftermath of his sentencing, there was speculation he might have gone overseas to avoid his sentence, or that there was a split in the family. 'I have not spoken to Peter and do not know where he is,' Ciara Quinn, sister of Sean Junior, told the *Sunday Independent* on 22 July. 'However, when you are ordered by a court to do something which physically cannot be done, it leaves you in a very difficult and frightening place.'

As it turned out, Petey had decided he was better off at his home near Derrylin, just across the border in Northern Ireland. Because he had been found guilty of civil contempt of court rather than a criminal offence, Petey could not be pursued across the border or extradited to the Republic to serve his sentence. Within days, he was photographed in the crowd at a Teemore Shamrocks match. In an interview on local radio days after the sentence, his father, Peter, the former GAA president and former Quinn Group director, claimed his son could not get justice in the Republic.

In his family home a few miles north of the border, Petey was out of reach of the Irish courts and the Irish authorities. He was untouchable.

Within days, IBRC scored another court victory. Justice Peter Kelly granted a temporary injunction preventing Karen Woods, Sean Junior's wife, from moving any assets. The appointment of a receiver was also approved to several companies connected to Sean Quinn, his children and their spouses, and the judge extended an order freezing their assets. Only their family homes and certain personal bank accounts were now outside the all-encompassing battle with the bank.

Judge Kelly was scathing about the Quinns' behaviour. 'All evidence before the courts points in one direction,' said Kelly. The family had operated a scheme 'of mesmeric complexity' on a 'deliberate and premeditated basis' in order to put assets out of the reach of IBRC. In eight years as head of the Commercial Court, Kelly said, he had seen 'fraud on a national and international level, sharp practice, dishonesty and chicanery'. However, he added, 'Never before have I seen such conduct on the scale demonstrated here nor with the deviousness with which this scheme has been operated.'

Across the Quinn heartland of Cavan and Fermanagh, the jailing of Sean Quinn Junior went down badly. Throughout the legal action – indeed, since the administrators had been installed at Quinn Insurance more than two years previously – local support for Sean Quinn and his family had been unwavering. Now that support moved up a notch. Prayers were said for the jailed Quinn at a number of local Masses. Fermanagh District Council voted unanimously to dispatch a letter of support to the family. Signs of solidarity started to appear on the streets of Derrylin and in Ballyconnell.

Four days after Sean Junior was jailed, Sean FitzPatrick, the former Anglo Irish Bank chairman and chief executive, appeared before the Dublin District Court. At a short hearing, the 64-year-old was charged with sixteen offences relating to the Maple Ten transaction. The charge sheet alleged FitzPatrick had given 'unlawful financial assistance' to its ten long-standing clients, the five Quinn children and Patricia Quinn to buy shares in the bank, in breach of Section 60 of the Companies Act.

On 29 July, thousands of people gathered on the streets of Ballyconnell for a rally of support for the Quinns. The event was organized by the pro-Quinn lobby group, Concerned Irish Citizens. The group had invited a number of household names, including high-profile figures from the GAA, to the Ballyconnell rally. Sean Quinn Senior, flanked by his wife and other members of his family, walked through the main street of the town to cheers and applause. A flatbed trailer had been set up as a temporary stage.

Joe Kernan, who had managed Armagh to the county's first ever senior All-Ireland football title in 2002, sat on a plastic chair on the back of the lorry. Beside him was Colm O'Rourke, an All-Ireland-winning footballer from Meath who was now a columnist with the

Sunday Independent and football analyst on RTÉ. Mickey Harte, the respected manager of the Tyrone football team, was there. So, too, was Father Brian D'Arcy, a Passionist priest in Enniskillen who also worked as a journalist, presenting a radio show on BBC and writing newspaper columns. D'Arcy's relatively liberal views had brought him into conflict with the Vatican's Congregation of the Doctrine of the Faith and led to a censure from the Vatican.

Standing beneath a banner demanding 'natural justice' for the Quinn family, D'Arcy addressed the crowd, declaring that Sean Quinn had 'brought prosperity and jobs to the area from stony rocks. In doing so, he brought peace to the country by creating thousands of jobs and this removed the oxygen for violence.' D'Arcy stated that it should be the regulators, auditors and banks before the courts, not the Quinn family. 'The main reason I'm here is because as Christians and good neighbours we have a right and a duty to stand by our families and neighbours,' he said. 'They built an industry the like of which has never been seen in this country. When Northern governments and Southern governments wouldn't give us a penny, when not a single one of them provided a job, it was Sean Quinn and his family who took up the battle.'

Joe Kernan called for justice, and for official Ireland to 'let Sean Quinn build another empire'. There was thunderous applause when it was announced that Michael O'Leary, the chief executive of Ryanair and one of Quinn's inspirations in business, had expressed support for the Quinns. Across the crowd, the speakers could see home-made banners that read: 'Trial of Injustice by Media', 'Let the Quinn Case Go to Brussels', 'No Justice in Ireland'.

Sean Boylan, a legendary manager of the Meath football team, also addressed the crowd. There was never any love lost between Cavan and Meath, but he had come out to support the Quinns. 'The Quinn family are not thieves, not vagabonds, they're not people who don't care,' said Boylan. 'They are Irish people who have the guts and ingenuity to create a better life for thousands of people in this country and we owe them a massive favour of thanks and gratitude.'

The biggest cheer was reserved for Sean Quinn himself. 'It might be a bit emotional for me this evening speaking in my home town,' he said, wiping back tears from his eyes with a handkerchief. He continued, 'Since March 2010, when Quinn [Insurance] was put into administration, the support has been outstanding. A propaganda war has been waged against Quinn for the past twenty-eight months. A story has been told that is not a true story. We hope that the intelligent people will understand the difference.' Quinn referred to his fugitive nephew, claiming Petey's reputation had been damaged. 'I'd like to thank especially young Peter who's getting a bad reputation. Peter has been a huge support to his family. And the Quinns will continue to be the Quinns and we will stand by each other.'

Quinn and many of the other speakers referred to the bankers in Dublin, the regulators in Dublin and the Dublin media. The battle between bank and borrower was being painted as a clash of two Irelands: the close-knit, rural Ireland that Quinn seemed to embody, and the urban plutocracy represented by the bankers and regulators. One Quinn supporter at the rally told the *Irish Times* that if Quinn was from 'D4' rather than Teemore, the bankrupt businessman would be treated differently by the authorities now pursuing him.

Deliberately or otherwise, Quinn and his supporters were tapping into a broader sense of rural disempowerment. In the weeks before the rally, the government had announced it would be closing a number of small Garda stations. AIB and Bank of Ireland had announced the closure of dozens of rural branches. Rural post offices had been closing for months, and more were slated to pull down the shutters. There was a new tax on septic tanks. Even the government had a distinctly urban feel to it: of the fifteen government ministers, nine represented constituencies in Dublin. Only Enda Kenny, the Mayo-born Taoiseach, came from a constituency north of Dublin.

Given these dynamics, it was unsurprising that many people saw Sean Quinn as a local hero fighting a bank that helped bankrupt the country. No banker had gone to jail, but Sean Quinn's son was in prison. A leaflet distributed by Concerned Irish Citizens illustrated the point. It showed Sean Junior in his wedding suit with the words: 'Anglo have put this man in jail because he wouldn't agree to their illegal theft of his companies.' It listed email addresses and phone numbers for senior IBRC executives, including Alan Dukes, Mike

Aynsley and Richard Woodhouse, as well as contact details for Paul Gallagher and Karyn Harty, the bank's lawyers. Quinn supporters were urged to contact the bankers, the Taoiseach and the Minister for Finance.

To the supporters who turned out in Ballyconnell, it had always been, and always would be, Quinn country. Quinn had provided pay cheques. At its peak, his wider group had employed 7,000 people directly, and helped support tens of thousands of other jobs. It was a Quinn economy and, as far as his supporters could see, it had been unjustly taken from him.

Two days after the Ballyconnell rally, on 31 July, the administrators to Quinn Insurance told the High Court they would need still more money – significantly more – from the Insurance Compensation Fund. The trading business of Quinn Insurance had been sold to Liberty and IBRC, but the back book of old claims remained in administration, and the costs were mounting.

As they continued investigating the reserving practices and on-going claims at Quinn Insurance, the administrators' estimate of the bailout needed from the Insurance Compensation Fund had risen steadily. Based on their latest estimates, they now believed they would need between €1 billion and €1.3 billion from the fund. In a worst-case scenario, the drawdown could be as much as €1.65 billion. The 2 per cent 'Quinn levy' on insurance premiums would be in place for as many as twenty-five years.

The president of the High Court, Mr Justice Nicholas Kearns, was the first to hear the new figure. It was 'truly shocking', he said, and he wanted the 'clearest of explanations' from Michael McAteer and Paul McCann, the Grant Thornton administrators. Lawyers for the administrators said a number of factors had led to the increase in the sum being sought from the fund, including a more pessimistic provision for claims, the euro weakening against sterling and the reduced value of Quinn Insurance investments in assets, including property assets.

The new figures were spectacularly bad, and had the effect of formally wiping out the insurer's profits from 2007 onwards. Reacting to the scale of the losses, the Central Bank informed the government that the huge cost of bailing out the insurer arose from 'poor underwriting and management' during Sean Quinn's time in charge. When the company was controlled by the Quinn family, Quinn Insurance had total provision for future claims of €1.13 billion. Based on the same book, the company was now forced to increase that to €2.3 billion, a hike of more than 100 per cent. New accounts for 2010 showed Quinn Insurance made a loss of €1.04 billion for the year, on top of revised losses of €714 million for 2009. At the end of 2010, the company had a negative balance sheet of €1.03 billion, according to accounts signed off by Deloitte, which had replaced PricewaterhouseCoopers (PWC) as auditors to the insurer.

Underlining the seriousness of the situation, the administrators initiated legal proceedings against PWC. The case was taken on foot of the firm's failure to highlight the €488 million of cross-company guarantees on the insurer's assets, which had forced the administration process. In correspondence with the Department of Finance, the administrators also revealed that they were considering taking legal action against Milliman, the actuaries to the insurance firm, for professional negligence. The administrators said they had sought legal advice to see if there was a case against Milliman for its alleged failure to flag the under-provisioning on the company's insurance book while it was being managed by Sean Quinn.

In an interview with the *Sunday Business Post* on 4 November 2012, Michael McAteer said the under-provisioning was probably a result of Quinn's lack of understanding of the insurance industry. An insurer could take in €100 million and reserve €70 million for future claims, giving the appearance of a €30 million profit on the business. But there was no way of knowing that the claims on those policies would only total €70 million.

'It may take years, and you may pay more,' said McAteer. It would be more prudent to reserve at a higher level and take the profit in later years if the claims ultimately came in lower than the reserve. 'By marking it down at €70 million, the actuaries then think you have made a profit on this particular piece of business. Therefore, they price that business, thinking it is profitable. It is a vicious cycle. You are cheaper, and so you get more business. But unfortunately, it is loss-making because you are under-reserving for claims. Ultimately, you are attracting the wrong business. That was a fundamental flaw.'

It emerged, too, that disciplinary action had been taken against several senior staff at Quinn Insurance who, it was alleged, deliberately suppressed the potential pay-out for large insurance claims in order to boost the company's balance sheet. The move came after the administrators noticed 'unusual and significant reserve movements' at the company. The administrators had also been forced to provide an amnesty to claims handlers at the company, in an effort to get them to come clean about the true state of the firm's insurance book.

The finger was pointed squarely at Sean Quinn himself.

Under his regime, claims handlers were financially incentivized to settle claims at or below reserve levels – the reserve being the money put aside to cover the claim. According to the administrators, this resulted in a general reluctance within the group to 'adequately reserve for large cases'. This was an important point for the administrators. Under-reserving on large claims made the company look more profitable than it was: the company was saying that less money would be paid out in claims, leaving more money to be classified as profits.

Michael Noonan, the Minister for Finance, wrote to the administrators, seeking an explanation for the rising reliance on the Insurance Compensation Fund. It was 'remarkable', the minister said, that losses continued to climb substantially, even 'following examinations by teams of actuaries and accountants'. The Department of Finance, in a letter to the administrators that was lodged with the High Court, expressed concern at these figures, suggesting it had been misled on the scale of the bailout that the company would need.

As of late August 2012, Sean Quinn Junior was in jail. Peter Darragh Quinn was out of the jurisdiction. Sean Quinn Senior was down but not quite out. And Quinn properties valued at more than €300 million still remained outside the control of IBRC.

The bank had managed to seize the Kutuzoff Tower, having finally overcome the Russian legal quagmire to appoint its own administrator

to the bankruptcy process. It was the only property IBRC had succeeded in securing. Elsewhere, the bank was being hindered at every
turn in foreign courts by shadowy companies with clandestine shareholders. With each passing month, Richard Woodhouse knew that the
assets would become harder to reclaim.

There was also the significant matter of the rents paid by the tenants of the properties since 14 April 2011, the day the properties
should have transferred into the hands of the old Anglo Irish Bank.
That money was missing. Woodhouse suspected that the Quinns
were taking the rental payments on properties they claimed not to
control, and using at least some of the proceeds to defend legal
actions, buying time and putting the properties even further from
the bank's control.

An affidavit had come in from Russia, outlining new evidence that
the Quinn family was moving rental proceeds to offshore bank
accounts. Acting on behalf of the bank, Kroll, the international
investigators, had dispatched agents to the South Pacific, following
the route taken by Sean Quinn Junior and Karen Woods on their
honeymoon just weeks before Sean Junior was found in contempt of
court. For some reason, the newlyweds had stopped on the island of
Vanuatu. Hardly a typical honeymoon destination, Vanuatu had cul-
tivated a reputation as a venue for hiding cash in impenetrable
company structures. The bank wanted to know why he went there.

Investigators also spent time in Australia and New Zealand, following what they believed to be a money trail. Reports were later
filed back from Singapore, outlining new corporations linked to
Quinn family members. Investigations into this trail revealed that
millions of euro had been channelled through Irish bank accounts
held in the names of Sean Quinn's grandchildren to overseas
accounts in Singapore and Australia.

The transfers were made over a two-year period, and were processed
through Ulster Bank accounts held by two Quinn grandchildren in
Dublin and Cavan. Both grandchildren were under the age of two at the
time of the transfers, according to the dispatch on Woodhouse's desk.
Another report highlighted significant transfers of money from Irish
accounts held by family members to accounts in Australia, Britain,

Russia and the Far East, including transfers of $1.74 million to Senat Legal in Dubai. IBRC had information that the law firm was being paid to shield the money for the family.

The global freezing order on the family's assets, granted by Justice Peter Kelly, was still in place, but the family was challenging the independence of the receiver appointed by the court over the assets. They alleged that Declan Taite, an insolvency specialist with RSM Farrell Grant Sparks, and the lawyers working with the receiver, Arthur Cox, were too close to IBRC and had a conflict of interest. Taite and other accountants from RSM Farrell Grant Sparks had been appointed as receivers to a number of companies by IBRC and its predecessor, Anglo Irish Bank. The Quinns claimed Taite was acting on the direction of IBRC to obtain information that might help the bank defend the family's claim against the bank.

Niall McPartland, Quinn's son-in-law, told the High Court that some of the partners in Arthur Cox were involved in the restructuring of the Quinn Group. He claimed the firm had been involved over years with IBRC and Anglo Irish Bank. The allegations were denied by the receiver and the lawyers, but the challenge to Taite and Arthur Cox delayed the bank's receivership application by several weeks.

Frustrated at the lack of progress and constant delays, Richard Woodhouse considered an alternative approach to the asset recovery. A number of Russian banks and companies had emerged over the previous months offering to help IBRC regain control of the former Quinn properties. It would be risky to get involved with the Russians, and any partner would want a cut of the proceeds, but Woodhouse felt it might just work.

A breakthrough came courtesy of a Russian called Aleksandr Sherykhanov. Sherykhanov had been installed as bankruptcy receiver over Finansstroy, the company behind the Kutuzoff Tower, in July, and IBRC trusted him. Following his appointment, Sherykhanov found that files had been removed and that the building's computer server had been seriously damaged. He hired a technology expert to try to repair it. It was the best money he ever spent – amazingly, more than 26,000 emails were recovered from the carcass of the computer server.

A number of the emails pointed to the continued involvement of the Quinn family in the international properties long after they claimed to have lost control of them. It was just the sort of information Richard Woodhouse required. In an initial trawl of the data, the bank found forty-three emails to and from Peter Darragh Quinn, which appeared to show how he exercised day-to-day control over companies in the International Property Group on behalf of the Quinn family until the end of February 2012. In one email, Petey stated that any transfers from Finansstroy above $5,000 were to be authorized by him alone. Other emails showed him approving the cost of company business cards, or seeking information about Christmas presents for clients.

The bank discovered a further thirty-three emails showing how Sean Quinn Junior took charge in February 2012 when his cousin bowed out. The emails, the bank believed, showed that Sean Junior was actually making decisions in relation to the properties while the contempt of court action was active in the High Court in Dublin. The emails also showed that relations with A&B and Arthur Zafarov, the A&B lawyer, were not as frosty as Sean Junior indicated in his affidavit. In fact, they showed a regular stream of communications between the two sides after Sean Junior's visit to Moscow in July.

Something else struck Woodhouse: foreign travel. Lots and lots of foreign travel. Aoife Quinn, for example, travelled to Moscow eight times between July 2011 and July 2012. She also travelled to Abu Dhabi once, to Dubai on seven occasions, to Ukraine twice, to London, to Cyprus and to Zurich. All the costs were paid by Finansstroy and another company, Red Sector. Sean Quinn Junior travelled to Moscow between sixteen and twenty times, to Kiev twelve times, and to Dubai twice. Colette Quinn, Ciara Quinn and Niall McPartland travelled to Moscow at the end of July 2011 to set up bank accounts with Ocean Bank in order to receive salaries paid to them by international property companies.

Crucially, however, it was the foreign companies that were picking up the tab – companies that the family claimed no longer to control. There was also travel recorded to Geneva. The Swiss trips caught Woodhouse's attention. During his evidence, Petey had talked about a Swiss trust. Its existence had subsequently been denied, but his investigators had continued to pursue the lead.

And there was more. Much more. Material retrieved from the smashed server revealed to IBRC the steps the family had taken to provide for massive payments in the event their employment was terminated: almost €36 million each for Aoife, Ciara and Colette Quinn, €26 million for Peter Darragh Quinn, and almost €15 million for Sean Junior.

Under other contracts dated 15 June 2011, Sean Junior's then fiancée Karen Woods was to receive termination payments of more than €36 million and an annual salary of about €560,000. Some of the contracts were backdated to make it appear they were signed before IBRC had secured its injunction against the family moving assets on 27 June 2011. None of the termination payments had been paid out, but it was further ammunition for IBRC's case.

Woodhouse was armed, but he was cautious. Proving that the Quinn family retained the assets was one thing, forcing their return another.

After Sean Quinn Junior's imprisonment on 20 July, the Quinn family, normally media-shy, launched a media blitz. Sean Quinn Senior was interviewed by the *Irish Mail on Sunday* (the same paper that had published the secret video from Kiev), by the *Financial Times* and by Vincent Browne, the veteran journalist, for his current affairs programme on TV3. On Browne's show, a combative Quinn admitted he had made mistakes but claimed the Financial Regulator had acted illegally in appointing administrators to Quinn Insurance. Again, he denied the asset-stripping of the foreign properties took place after the High Court injunction. IBRC 'were taking everything from us, putting our children on the dole', he said.

On 16 August, Aoife Quinn and her husband, Stephen Kelly, appeared on the same show, with journalist Sam Smyth standing in for Browne. Quinn said she feared her father would go to jail because he could not purge his contempt of court. 'You cannot give what you do not have. We do not have these assets so we can't give them back,' she said. 'There is no way I would leave, that any member of our family would leave, our brother sitting in Mountjoy Prison for the sake of not purging contempt, for the sake of sitting on our hands.'

During the interview, Quinn and Kelly revealed they didn't know how much their own wedding had cost and said they did not know if it had been paid for by the Quinn Group. 'All of our personal and company dealings were dealt with from Derrylin, from [the Quinn Group] head office in Derrylin. That went for everything – from wills advice, from tax advice, from personal expenses,' Aoife Quinn said. 'We owned the companies. The companies looked after all our tax affairs. Everything was dealt with appropriately in Derrylin.'

Just weeks later, the *Sunday Independent* reported that the cake at Ciara Quinn's wedding to Niall McPartland in 2007 had cost €100,000. She was furious at the revelation, and made it clear to journalists she believed it had been leaked by IBRC in order to damage the family in the eyes of the public. She claimed the cake had cost less than half that amount but could not provide an exact figure – because all the paperwork for her wedding, like her sister's, was in Quinn Group headquarters, now under the control of the bank and other lenders.

Ciara's remarks effectively confirmed that the cake – which dated from the same year Sean Quinn made his speech about his 'simple life' – had cost a vast amount of money, and also suggested that Quinn Group had paid for the wedding. The cake became a news item in itself, alongside stories about the family mansion, the expensive clothes and accessories that Karen Woods wore, and the Mercedes, BMW and Audi cars the family drove despite their claims to be broke.

The population of Ballyconnell, Co. Cavan, according to the 2011 census, is 1,061 people. On the evening of Sunday 14 October 2012, an estimated 5,000 people crowded Ballyconnell Main Street in another show of solidarity for Sean Quinn and his family. This time, Sean Junior was due to be released from Mountjoy in five days. Sean Quinn Senior did not speak; the bankrupt businessman merely sat on the flatbed truck stage alongside his wife, Patricia, listening to speakers passionately defend his reputation.

From the back of the lorry, his daughters rolled out the rhetoric.

Ciara, who had worked as a mid-ranking claims reviewer within Quinn Insurance, told the rally her family had built over two hundred companies and employed tens of thousands of people over four decades.

'My name is Ciara Quinn and I, alongside my brother Sean and my three sisters, Colette, Aoife and Brenda, are the true and rightful owners of the Quinn group of companies. In 2007 and 2008, Anglo Irish Bank pumped €2.3 billion into our companies without asking us, without telling us and without ever even meeting us – this was illegal.'

There were loud cheers from the crowd.

She insisted her family could not be held responsible for Anglo's activities in the past. 'A new Anglo management cannot rewrite history. I and my siblings were innocent parties to this and we will not be Anglo's scapegoats,' she thundered.

Colette, who once held a senior role in the hospitality division, was next to the podium. 'It is important for us that the people from this area, who have worked with us all our lives, understand us and understand why we are fighting so hard in this issue. As Ciara said, we want to contribute to this area again, we want to bring prosperity to this area once again and we look forward to the day we can do that,' she proclaimed.

Mickey Harte, the Tyrone manager, had informed the rally's organizers that he could not make it, but he turned up at the last minute. The attendance of so many GAA luminaries at the first rally had made the association's hierarchy in Croke Park uncomfortable. Sean Kelly, a former GAA president who had built a second life as a Fine Gael politician, initially had some sympathy for the family, but had quickly rowed back. The association's president, Liam O'Neill, had distanced the organization from the rally, saying that any issues relating to Quinn or the former Anglo Irish bank were 'none of our business' and had nothing to do with the GAA's role as a sports body.

'I came here from a couple of reasons,' Harte said. 'The first one is to prove that I am not delusional. I have come here of my own free will because I believe the Quinn family deserve our support. They've been so supportive to people over the years. I have come here because

I want to, and I think it's been made very clear here tonight that we have had a very selective view of what's going on.'

But it was the speech of Peter Quinn, Sean Senior's brother and Petey's father, which set the tone for the evening. It was a lengthy diatribe that ranged from criticism of the administration of Quinn Insurance to comment on the similarities between Anglo Irish Bank and the SAS. 'Where I come from, we know how the SAS operate,' said the former GAA president, drawing parallels with the bank's cloak-and-dagger actions on the day the share receiver was appointed to Quinn Group. He then turned his attention to the press, saying, 'The bastards are not prepared to investigate what really goes on in this country.'

Quinn, who had served on the board of the Parades Commission in the North, went through a list of people he felt had wronged the family: the Financial Regulator, Matthew Elderfield; IBRC's chairman, Alan Dukes; Taoiseach Enda Kenny; and Kenny's Finance Minister, Michael Noonan. 'Neither Anglo nor the media will break the Quinn resolve,' he declared. 'Neither Elderfield or Dukes, nor Kenny or Noonan or any of the other bastards in Dáil Éireann, will ever break the Quinns' spirit.'

When the speakers name-checked Anglo, the crowd jeered. When they mentioned the Quinns, the crowd cheered. Several pre-prepared placards read: 'Anglo Irish Bank, IBRC and their receivers are the new Oliver Cromwell of Ireland.' Others bore a large picture of Sean Quinn with the caption: 'Quinn for Taoiseach.'

Although the public tone of the Quinns and their supporters was combative, behind the scenes, in his Ballyconnell home in the days that followed, Sean Quinn Senior signed any document the bank put before him. And, as Petey had frantically done back in July, the patriarch wrote dozens of letters to international firms and lawyers asking them to help him purge the contempt. In a letter to IBRC, written in a personal capacity in his own handwriting, he said that if he could undo the scheme, he would have done it before his only son was sent to Mountjoy.

Eversheds, meanwhile, had stopped representing the family. With their assets frozen, the Quinns declared they could no longer afford the high-powered firm. Eversheds had its own reasons for parting company with the Quinns. It could not prove it, but the firm was afraid it had been paid by the Quinn family from the rental proceeds of the disputed properties. If this was the case, and the law firm was found to know about it, it would be in trouble for helping flush the money through the system. Instead, Eversheds decided to hold all payments from the family in a special account pending the outcome of the Quinn litigation.

There were reports of a fund being raised to finance the Quinns' legal costs. Large sums of money were being pledged by anonymous sources. A new law firm was eventually found – Kevin R. Winters, a Belfast practice that described themselves as 'human rights lawyers'. Winters had worked on high-profile cases, representing Sean Hoey, who was acquitted of charges of committing the Omagh bombing in August 1998. The firm also assisted the Scottish lawyers of Abdelbaset Ali Mohmed Al Megrahi, the Libyan convicted for involvement in the Lockerbie bombing, and advised the lawyers of the family of Madeleine McCann, the missing English schoolgirl. Now the firm would represent Sean Quinn, the bankrupt former billionaire, with Eugene Grant QC as their main barrister.

A Supreme Court challenge to get Sean Junior out of jail had failed, though one judge, Adrian Hardiman, dissented from the judgment on the grounds that the case against Sean Junior was 'entirely circumstantial'. Hardiman said the contempt of court case had been treated as a 'summary criminal trial' by Justice Elizabeth Dunne. The other four judges, however, including the Chief Justice Susan Denham, backed up Justice Dunne's ruling. The four-to-one majority ruling said there was 'ample evidence' in the High Court case to make the finding beyond reasonable doubt that Sean Junior was party to the $500,000 payment to Larisa Yanez Puga. The court said the sentence of three months was 'amply justified'.

Sean Quinn Junior was released from prison on 19 October, having served his three-month sentence. He had filled his days in the Mountjoy Training Unit working in the kitchen, playing football and learning first aid. None of the property assets had been returned to IBRC during his incarceration, however, and he, his father and his fugitive cousin were still in contempt of court.

On the same day that Sean Junior was released from Mountjoy, the two sides were back in the High Court to update the judge on the developments in the contempt battle. Acting for IBRC, Paul Gallagher SC unleashed a string of revelations that undermined testimony previously given by members of the family, much of which it had gleaned from the computer server in the Kutuzoff. Gallagher told the High Court that Sean Quinn Senior, despite all his paperwork-signing and letter-writing, had accomplished nothing to purge his own contempt. IBRC remained worried, he said; with each passing day, the assets were becoming further entangled in a legal web, and 'their ultimate recovery more difficult'. The case was adjourned to allow Quinn's new legal teams to familiarize themselves with the complicated narrative.

On 25 October, a low-profile meeting was arranged between the family and the bank. Alan Dukes, Mike Aynsley and Richard Woodhouse were in attendance for IBRC, as was Karyn Harty of McCann FitzGerald. Quinn was accompanied by his son and two other unidentified family members. The bank had been reluctant to take the meeting, but had been placed under tremendous pressure by politicians from the border region, who lobbied incessantly on the family's behalf.

During the short meeting, Quinn said that the matter could be dealt with by mediation, not played out in court. Too much money and time had been spent, he argued. However, he maintained they were no longer in control of the property assets, holding firmly to the story about the family having been double-crossed in Russia and Ukraine.

Sources close to the Quinns say that the bank said it would not call in the sums of money personally guaranteed by the Quinn children as part of the Maple Ten deal. In return it wanted the family to come clean on all their assets and hand over everything above a value of €100,000. It also wanted the right to take the Quinn family home, the lakeside mansion near Ballyconnell, in five years' time. The sources claim that Alan Dukes said the family had to 'put everything back the way it was'. With Quinn insisting the properties were gone from the family's control, that would not be possible.

In the end, there was no resolution, no compromise, no deal. IBRC told the court that the meeting was unproductive and unsatisfactory, declining to confirm anything that was even discussed.

Karyn Harty and Richard Woodhouse were meeting on a daily basis now; sometimes several times a day. They joked that they were like an old married couple, they were spending so much time together. All told, the broader Quinn battle consisted of twenty-four court actions in ten jurisdictions. In a five-day period at the end of October alone, there were five hearings in Russia, one in Belize and a procedural application in Ukraine. The previous week, there had been three days of hearings in Russia in relation to the bankruptcy of Finansstroy and Logistica, two Russian companies.

In mid October, the bank's one victory was snatched from it. Aleksandr Sherykhanov, the Russian whose efforts to fix the Kutuzoff Tower computer server yielded over 26,000 emails, had been removed as bankruptcy receiver over Finansstroy, the Kutuzoff company. He was ousted after a Moscow appeal court allowed a number of companies to regain entry to the list of creditors of Finansstroy. This changed the game – whoever controlled the most debt controlled the administrator. With the new companies added to the creditor list – one of which IBRC maintained was secretly controlled by the Quinn family – they, rather than IBRC, controlled the process. Plus, these new companies were voting in unison in an effort to get their own receiver appointed. So Sherykhanov was sacked, and Andrey Demitrov installed.

Woodhouse now believed that Demitrov was preparing to undo much of his predecessor's good work. He could even potentially sell the tower on the cheap before the bank had a chance to bring an appeal. Gaining control of the Kutuzoff Tower had been a big win – the first of the disputed assets that had been recovered by the bank. Losing control was a big loss.

It was a similar tale in relation to the Indian property. Mecon FZE, the company established by Senat Legal in Dubai to take ownership of Q-City in Hyderabad, was now trying to wangle its way free of an Irish court action. Woodhouse was convinced that Mecon was secretly controlled by members of the Quinn family. Pressed by the bank's lawyers to identify the owners of Mecon, the company's Indian directors merely told the High Court that it was not a Quinn company. They declined to elaborate further.

In Ukraine, a court overturned a freezing order on the $500,000 payment by a Quinn-controlled company to Larisa Yanez Puga. Again, no one seemed to know who was behind the court action. 'In Russia and Ukraine, it seems these things just happen,' Woodhouse told colleagues. The banker was perplexed and increasingly frustrated. On his desk was yet another affidavit from a member of the Quinn family, claiming that Puga had teamed up with Ukrainians to take control of the Ukraina shopping centre. Puga, according to the family, had cut them out of the equation and was no longer returning calls or emails. Yet, the Russian computer server had thrown up a constant stream of communications between Puga and the family. Woodhouse was convinced that she still controlled the assets on behalf of the family. 'None of it makes sense,' he briefed his work colleagues. 'None of it.'

Woodhouse had hired some of the best investigators in the world. He had dispatched bankers to Switzerland, lawyers to Belize and sleuths to the South Pacific. Literally and metaphorically, he had pursued the wider Quinn family to the ends of the earth. Yet, by Woodhouse's own admission, IBRC had been outmanoeuvred throughout the process. It was continually playing catch-up. The bank was playing by the rule book, guided by the limit of the law. In contrast, the banker and his employers believed the Quinn family was defying the law in order to move ownership of valuable assets in Russia, India and Ukraine.

In late October, Woodhouse briefed Aynsley and Dukes on the state of play. The Kutuzoff had been won, but then promptly lost. The Ukraina shopping centre was slipping further away. Eight properties, where the bank had only share pledges rather than direct mortgage security, were 'at varying stages of distress', he said. Woodhouse explained how the shareholdings had been transferred on behalf of Quinn family members in recent weeks to more companies in Belize and Panama. There was, he said, evidence that the entities were controlled by the Quinn family. 'We have had to go to extraordinary lengths to obtain this information; and we could not even get it for all of the entities,' he said.

In other cases, receivers were being appointed to offshore companies before the bank even knew they existed. Furthermore, he explained how the Russian courts had little time or appetite for 'extraneous evidence or affidavit evidence', which were the cornerstones of commercial litigation in Ireland. Woodhouse had exhausted all options, bar one. With nothing else left to lose, he decided he needed to call in external assistance. It was not a decision he had wanted to make, but with the assets slipping further and further away, he felt he had no other option.

Over the previous months, a number of banks and financial institutions had approached him about IBRC's interest in the Quinn properties. Several had tabled offers to purchase the loans held by the bank, albeit at a significant haircut. Others sought to purchase the bank's security over the loans. A number of institutions had offered to create joint ventures with IBRC in an effort to reclaim the properties.

Woodhouse looked at the list of companies seeking to do a deal, and contacted A1 Group, an asset recovery specialist ultimately owned by wealthy Russian oligarchs. 'A Russian problem needs a Russian solution,' he told colleagues. He had done his research. A1 had extensive experience of recovering assets in Russia and Ukraine, working with other foreign companies to retrieve properties and investments that had been the subject of such corporate raids. In its corporate biography, the company said it focused 'on special situations investments in Russia and the CIS'. Woodhouse remarked to associates that this was 'a very special situation'.

A1 was the primary investment arm of the Alfa Group, one of Russia's largest conglomerates, with interests spread across natural resources, telecoms, retail, finance and leisure. It owned stakes in oil wells, gas fields and banks. Its balance sheet was impressive – total assets of \$59.9 billion, \$21.7 billion in equity and a 2010 profit of \$2.8 billion.

The company was owned by some of Russia's richest men: Mikhail

Fridman, German Khan and Aleksey Kuzmichev. Certainly, it was not afraid to protect its financial interests, having been accused in the past of using 'raiding' tactics similar to those IBRC believed the Quinn family was using. The accusations stemmed from Alfa's association with Telenor, the Norwegian telecoms group. Alfa and Telenor were both major shareholders in Vimpelcom, a Russian telco with shares traded on the New York Stock Exchange. Telenor had accused Alfa of trying to steal its shares through illegal means. Anonymous companies, including one in the British Virgin Islands, were central to the claim.

In 2009, a court in New York held four Alfa Group companies to be in contempt and imposed a daily fine of $100,000 until the contempt was purged. The fine was to increase to $300,000 per day after thirty days, and to $400,000 per day thirty days after that. Within hours, a Russian bailiff rescued Telenor's shares in Vimpelcom by serving an order on a Moscow share registry. Telenor said the dispute involved 'illegal acts, supported by the Russian courts'. A1 knew how to play the game in Russia.

Woodhouse asked the board of IBRC to approve a joint venture between IBRC and A1. The Department of Finance was contacted, and the Russian embassy and the Department of Foreign Affairs were asked to check out the company's bona fides. All reports came back positive. An international investment bank was brought on board to advise on the potential joint venture. Woodhouse then worked out the finer points of the deal.

The bank would provide A1 with power of attorney to represent its interests in Russia and Ukraine. A new joint venture company, NewCo, would be established, and IBRC's claim in the assets transferred to it. The bank would own 75.1 per cent of NewCo and A1 would have 24.9 per cent. Recovery proceeds would be used first to offset the set-up costs of the new company. The next $31 million would go straight to A1, while the next $100 million would be split 80 per cent to IBRC and 20 per cent to A1. If they reclaimed another $100 million, A1 would be entitled to 30 per cent of the recovery with the bank getting 70 per cent. After that, it was 50/50, split evenly right down the line. A1 would bear all the costs of the recovery process. It would also continue to use the bank's foreign lawyers and stick by its legal strategy.

For the bank and Woodhouse, it was a massive roll of the dice. The bank had admitted it had failed in its efforts to recover the Quinn assets and was prepared to pay a high price for specialist help. Woodhouse felt he had little choice. The stand-off had gone on for far too long, he thought. Having finally acknowledged moving the assets, the Quinn family were claiming they no longer controlled them. Whoever was controlling the assets – and Woodhouse firmly believed it was the Quinns – they now had a bigger problem on their hands than a nationalized Irish bank. The oligarchs had taken a seat at the table.

13

Prisoner 82809

On 1 November 2012, Sean Quinn, sixty-six years old and bankrupt, made the 140-kilometre road trip from his home outside Ballyconnell to the Four Courts on Dublin's north quays. He was accompanied by Sean Junior, recently released from his three months in the Mountjoy Prison Training Unit. His wife, Patricia, and his four daughters did not make the trip. They feared what might happen that day and they did not want to be there to see it.

It was a bitterly cold day. The newspapers and radio bulletins carried reports that Concerned Irish Citizens, the pro-Quinn lobby group, was warning there would be 'civil unrest' if Sean Quinn was jailed. Whatever fears there might be about civil unrest, the jailing of Sean Quinn was a likely prospect.

In her judgment in June, finding Quinn guilty of contempt of court on three counts, Ms Justice Elizabeth Dunne had described him as an 'evasive and uncooperative' witness whose evidence was 'not credible'. Sean Junior and Petey had been handed prison sentences that day, and Sean Senior had only escaped with his liberty because IBRC thought he might make progress in recovering the properties in Russia, Ukraine and India while his son was jailed. If he did so, he could help the bank get what it wanted and purge his own contempt of court. But it had not happened. Today, he would have to explain to the High Court why it had not.

Father and son were in the courtroom by 10.20 a.m., ten minutes before the case was due to begin before Ms Justice Elizabeth Dunne. There was a media scrum on the way in; RTÉ and BBC broadcast vans were parked across from the front door of the Four Courts and every major newspaper and broadcaster was represented.

The stage was Court 6, a long rectangular room on the ground floor of the Four Courts complex. Unlike many courtrooms, Court 6 has a pleasant view, with three large windows looking out across a small courtyard to the quays and the River Liffey. By the time the Quinns opened the door, the room was already packed. Dozens of journalists were in situ. Barristers, some gowned and wigged, were preparing their lines for routine applications in other cases. There were supporters, onlookers, besuited businessmen who had looked in from other cases.

This was a commercial court, not a criminal one, so there was no dock, no prescribed area in which Quinn had to sit. He was free to sit or stand wherever he wanted. He chose the back row, furthest from the door and as far from Justice Dunne's bench as he could possibly be.

'Is there any room there for a fella to sit?' Quinn had inquired of the border countrymen who had ventured to Dublin in support.

'Sure, I can always make myself smaller,' came the reply from one of them.

The veteran journalist Vincent Browne, who had interviewed Quinn in August for his television programme, stood at the back of the courtroom alongside Quinn. The interview had been confrontational at times, but now Browne exchanged words with the businessman. Three rows in front sat Mike Aynsley and Richard Woodhouse. Sean Junior opted to stand by the window, declining offers of a seat.

For the next five minutes, there was no talk of banks, assets, contempt or jail. Quinn and his border companion discussed the weather, chatted about shared friends and chewed the fat about the local GAA scene. It was, despite the situation and the setting, just a gentle exchange between old associates. It ended only when Eugene Grant, the lawyer who would represent Quinn, called him aside for a quiet word.

This was unfamiliar territory for Grant. He was a Queen's Counsel who practised in Belfast. He specialized in criminal practice; he was a founder of the Criminal Bar Association (NI) and was a member of the Criminal Justice Review which had drawn up the blueprint for reform of Northern Ireland's legal system back in 1999. He was not a complete stranger to the Four Courts – for a short period, Grant had acted as lead barrister for John Gilligan, the alleged ringleader in the plot to murder the *Sunday Independent* journalist Veronica Guerin, in 1996. He had withdrawn from that case.

On this occasion, Grant was assisted by his daughter, Maddie, a practising barrister in Dublin. Through his career, Grant had developed a reputation for rhetorical flourishes, for delivering heartfelt pleas on behalf of his clients. He knew he would have to deliver one today.

After Justice Dunne took her seat at 10.34 a.m., Niall McPartland, the husband of Ciara Quinn, stood to inform the judge he would speak on behalf of the other family members, if necessary. It was noted that Peter Darragh Quinn, described as the ninth-named respondent, was 'not present or represented'. The judge began by outlining the legal ramifications of the Supreme Court's decision in the appeal by Sean Quinn Junior against his imprisonment. As Dunne talked about the 'coercive' and 'punitive' elements of her earlier judgment, Sean Quinn Senior sat forward on his seat, clasped his hands, yawned and looked out at the November sunshine.

Then the lawyers for IBRC were on their feet. In the offices of McCann FitzGerald that morning, Richard Woodhouse had sworn another damning affidavit – sixty-three paragraphs, twenty-one pages in total, outlining IBRC's latest position on the asset-stripping case. As the bank's barrister began to read it into the court record, Woodhouse's words described a situation of mounting urgency, bordering on desperation. The 25 October meeting between IBRC's senior management and lawyers, and Sean Quinn and his family, had been 'wholly unproductive and unsatisfactory from the perspective of IBRC', he said. It was now necessary, the banker said in his affidavit, to take 'further steps' if there was to be any reasonable prospect of recovering the €500 million worth of Quinn overseas property assets.

It was at this point the bank revealed its decision to hire Russian asset managers to deal with their particular Russian problem. With the Quinns continuing to maintain they had no control over the properties and could do nothing further to help the bank, it would be 'the only viable means' of recovering the properties. Woodhouse did not mince his words, describing 'a conspiracy' by the Quinns to put the assets beyond the reach of the bank. Significantly, he referred for the first time to 'fraudulent activity', raising the prospect of future criminal, rather than just civil, litigation.

As the IBRC lawyer read details of the bank's loss of control once more of the Kutuzoff Tower, Father Gerry Comiskey, the Quinns' family friend and parish priest, squeezed into the crowded court-room. When parties involved in other cases that were due to be heard at 11 a.m. also packed in, Justice Dunne took a moment to ask them to come back 'not before 12'. The reading of Woodhouse's affidavit continued, describing the precarious position of each of the properties.

The Kutuzoff could be sold from under the bank at a knock-down price and the bank feared other assets could suffer a similar fate. In the bluntest terms, the bank was admitting its approach to recovering the assets had failed. Despite nearly eighteen months of litigation in ten jurisdictions, including Russia, Ukraine, India, Belize and Panama, it had failed to gain control of a single one of the assets in the Quinn International Property Group.

Woodhouse reiterated IBRC's view that Sean Quinn Senior had done little to purge his contempt other than sign and dispatch vague letters to all and sundry. Quinn had asked the recipients to forget previous orders from him and his family, and instead take future direction from the bank. The batch of letters made no reference to previous asset-stripping; they just asked the recipients to give IBRC their cooperation. Though Quinn denied it, the bank was steadfast in its belief that the businessman and his family continued to control the overseas properties and were profiting from them.

'There has been no meaningful attempt to restore any of the assets, and in particular it has not been possible for IBRC to regain and retain control of any of the assets,' Woodhouse's affidavit said. 'On the contrary, the defendants have largely ignored the findings of contempt. IBRC has come to the view that the defendants have no intention of abiding by the [court] orders or reversing the steps taken to put the assets beyond the reach of IBRC.'

As the reading of the affidavit continued, a middle-aged man joined the crowd in Court 6. He stood out in the crowd because he had brought his family – two small girls, no more than five years old, and a boy aged about ten. They looked on bewildered as the last of Woodhouse's affidavit was read into the record, culminating in financial details of the planned asset recovery link-up with A1. There were eleven assets to be recovered in Russia and Ukraine. Under the profit-sharing agreement with IBRC, A1 stood to make up to $123 million if it could recover them all. As the details were read out, Sean Quinn Junior shook his head.

When the bank's lawyers retook their seats, Eugene Grant rose. He started slowly. 'At the outset, we would submit respectfully that you should not consider imprisoning Sean Quinn today,' he said, addressing Dunne directly. With rising passion, he said that his client had once 'stood tall as a leading light of the Celtic Tiger' but was now 'a man bereft of all financial and economic dignity'. He spoke, too, of extensive medical problems afflicting Quinn, which had not previously been in the public domain. A medical report, signed by a Dr Geoffrey Bourke, based in Ballyconnell, described Quinn's poor health, including a severe heart condition.

Quinn was suffering from hypercholesterolemia, the presence of dangerously high levels of cholesterol in the blood. He had had heart surgery to install stents in 2003 and 2005, a fact not widely known up to that point. Then there was an inflammation of the gullet which, if left untreated, could lead to serious disease. Quinn also had recurring tabular adenomas, a benign tumour in the large intestine which required regular screening 'as a result of its malignant potential'. He also had a slow-growing skin cancer, basal-cell carcinoma, which had been removed from his upper back in August. And there was also reason for concern over prostate cancer, with a recent test coming back 'borderline' – a further test would be required in a few months.

Quinn had admitted that he sanctioned the asset-stripping scheme in 2011 to frustrate the bank's efforts to seize the valuable overseas properties, said Grant. He didn't dispute that, but he argued it was 'a lawful protection of those assets'. And he denied having any part in implementing the plan after 14 April 2011, when the bank appointed Kieran Wallace as share receiver to the Quinn Group. Yes, Quinn had moved assets. Since then, however, the 'unfortunate unravelling and spin-out of the original decision is that, as far as he knows, many of those assets may well be beyond reach'.

As the time approached noon, a uniformed Garda took up position outside the door of the courtroom, a reminder of the seriousness of the proceedings. 'Sean Quinn has totally cooperated as best he can to purge his contempt,' continued Grant. During the three months his son was in prison, he had signed every document the bank had asked him to sign and told his family and in-laws to do the same. Quinn had even asked a member of the Ukrainian Parliament for help securing a document from the National Bank of Ukraine, said Grant. By 12.20 p.m., Mike Aynsley had removed his glasses and was pinching the bridge of his nose like a man struggling to stay awake. Beside him, Richard Woodhouse shifted awkwardly on the wooden bench.

Quinn, Grant said, had signed the various Quinn Group companies over to his family in 2002, more than a decade earlier. He had never held any ownership or authority over the Russian assets. He had not been to Russia since 2007 and had no contact with Russian persons. Even IBRC had made no allegation to suggest this, said Grant, and none of the information the bank had gleaned from the repaired server in the Kutuzoff Tower referred to Quinn Senior. The lawyer went further: when all 26,000 emails on the server were disclosed, they would 'categorically refute' that the Quinn family was still involved in the properties.

'He has always made the case that he was only involved in sanctioning the asset-stripping,' said Grant. 'He is not in a position in any remotely detailed fashion to deal with the nuts and bolts. If he could, he would have done that prior to the incarceration of his only son.' As he spoke, Quinn's supporters dotted around the courtroom, many dressed in fleeces, jumpers and anoraks, nodded in agreement. Quinn remained silent at the back of the court, twisting a navy handkerchief in his hands. Summing up, Grant made a final plea. Quinn was 'absolutely committed' to purging his contempt, he said. The asset-stripping and the court case had 'negatively consumed' his life and had 'a devastating effect' on his family life. If he could reverse the asset transfers, he would. 'He is not the Svengali behind it.'

As Grant continued, a man by the name of Ken Drumm walked into the back of the courtroom. A businessman, he was having his own legal difficulties in relation to his former construction firm, Okohaus Superstructures. Okohaus had been involved in building schools for the Department of Education but went into receivership at the end of 2008. There was an irony to Drumm's presence – his brother was David Drumm, the former Anglo Irish Bank chief executive whose career had become so intertwined with that of Sean Quinn and his family.

Grant concluded by appealing for Quinn to remain free, allowing him to work with IBRC to recover the property assets and thus purge his contempt. Instead of jailing him, it would be more productive to consider ending 'the shocking bitterness and breakdown of trust' between the bank and Quinn and get them to work together. Jailing him would give some advantage to IBRC – 'a bank which effectively ruined the Irish economy for our children and children's children' – in other actions against the Quinns, said Grant. If Dunne decided not to jail Quinn, 'any objection from IBRC would be overzealous if not vindictive', given his age, health and history.

'I urge you not to jail this man,' said Grant, coming full circle, back to the start of his statement. By the time he finished, the clock was touching 1 p.m. The whole courtroom seemed exhausted.

It was a perfectly pitched appeal, based as much on emotion as evidence. It was designed to highlight the best of Quinn and downplay the worst. It remained to be seen, though, if Grant had done enough to keep Sean Quinn out of prison.

When the Northern barrister was finished, Shane Murphy, the lawyer for IBRC, rose to his feet. Any decision to jail Quinn was, of course, for the court alone, he said, though he highlighted once again the difficulties the bank had encountered in getting information from the businessman. The bank, however, was willing to show leniency, or at least forbearance. If Justice Dunne imposed a custodial sentence, Murphy said IBRC would not object to a stay being put on the sentence pending the outcome of any appeal to the Supreme Court – a concession that had not been offered in the case of Sean Junior just over three months earlier.

Elizabeth Dunne, however, was not about to make a quick decision. She quickly announced that she would give her verdict the next day, 2 November. Journalists rushed to get the day's events into news bulletins and on to internet reports. Aynsley and Woodhouse left the courtroom quietly.

Sean Quinn's supporters crowded around him, shaking his hand and saying words of support. He could breathe freely – until the following morning, at least.

As he took up a position at the back of the courtroom just before 11 a.m. on 2 November, Sean Quinn Junior chatted with supporters about the bank's proposal to join forces with A1.

'It's absolutely unbelievable,' Sean Junior said, shaking his head. Again he stood, declining an offer of a seat. 'Honest to God, I'm a lot younger than you are,' he said to one man who offered his place.

His father, dressed in a sombre suit, striped blue shirt and navy and gold striped tie, sat in the second-last row, surrounded by supporters. Mike Aynsley sat directly in front of the businessman. As on the previous day, Quinn's wife and daughters were not present in the courtroom.

Justice Dunne was in a businesslike mood. There was another case on the court list ahead of the Quinns, a petition from a liquidator to restrict two directors of a collapsed building company, Blueprint Construction. 'I'll deal with it shortly,' she said. Then she turned her attention to Sean Quinn Senior and Eugene Grant.

Her judgment on 26 June had found Quinn guilty of contempt in a number of respects. He had admitted to taking steps to put assets beyond the reach of IBRC. The only issue before her was 'the imposition of punishment', she said. The judge had read and considered Richard Woodhouse's detailed affidavit from the day before, as well as new affidavits from Sean Quinn and other Quinn family members.

She had considered the Supreme Court decision in Sean Quinn Junior's case and other relevant judgments. They said that imprisonment for contempt of court was primarily a 'coercive' tool and that a prison sentence was 'a last resort'. Dunne said she had 'no difficulty agreeing' with those judgments. To the media, the lawyers, the bankers, the Quinn supporters, the Quinns themselves, it was impossible to gauge how she would rule.

Dunne acknowledged Grant's 'impassioned plea' that Sean Quinn should not be jailed. She acknowledged, too, that Quinn had cooperated with IBRC in signing various documents, while his age, previous good character, close links with the GAA and charities were also noted. His health was 'a mitigating factor', the judge said. As she continued, Quinn sat with his head up, listening. With one shaky hand, he wiped at his mouth with a handkerchief.

The facts of the June judgment had not changed, however, said Dunne. Sean Quinn was guilty of contempt of court because he had signed documents transferring the overseas properties despite being injuncted from doing so. Giving evidence in the trial, he had been 'evasive and uncooperative' and taken every opportunity to embark on lengthy criticisms of Anglo. The judge said it was impossible to accept Quinn's evidence that he had 'no hand, act or part' in the property transfers after April 2011. 'His evidence is not credible; I am satisfied he was au fait with the arrangements.'

The judge said she acknowledged the 'serious dispute between the parties' but that did not change the fact that Quinn's contempt was 'nothing short of outrageous'. Noting Grant's comment from the previous day that the case had 'negatively consumed' Quinn's life, Dunne remarked, 'In my view, he only has himself to blame.' Taking into account the events of the foregoing days, weeks and months, the judge said she could not come to any conclusion other than that Quinn's actions constituted 'serious misconduct'. It was so serious, she said, it 'mandates that a term of imprisonment be imposed'.

Sean Quinn was going to jail.

The businessman barely flinched, though many heads turned to see his reaction.

The judge continued: taking into account Quinn's previous good character, his age, his charitable donations and his health, she was imposing a nine-week sentence. It was shorter than the three months served by Sean Junior, but long enough to keep him in prison over Christmas and into 2013. It was important, Dunne added, 'that the integrity of the court system is not set at naught by an egregious breach of a court order'.

As the judge spoke, Sean Junior's fingers hovered over the screen of his iPhone. 'He got nine weeks,' he typed into a text message to several family members. Standing at the back of the courtroom among journalists and family supporters, he had glanced over at his father when the sentence was delivered but given no visible reaction. The judge was still talking, however, and he waited to hear more before sending his text message.

Justice Dunne was now offering the possibility of a reprieve that would spare Quinn from immediate jail time, and perhaps give him the option of not spending Christmas in Mountjoy. If the business-man wanted to appeal to the Supreme Court and got an early hearing, a stay could be put on the sentence. IBRC's lawyers said the bank had no objection to a stay on the sentence, which would keep Quinn out of prison.

The court prepared to break up, but Grant was not finished. Sit-ting in the heart of the court, Richard Woodhouse and Mike Aynsley, the two IBRC bankers, were visibly shocked by what Grant said next: his client was considering not seeking a stay, and going straight to jail. Grant asked for time to take advice from Quinn on whether he wanted to start his prison sentence immediately.

The judge gave him until 12.50 p.m., about ninety minutes, to decide.

Sean Quinn got to his feet and made his way slowly to the door, delayed by a cluster of supporters and well-wishers. In the corridor he gathered in a huddle with his lawyers, his son and Niall McPart-land, his son-in-law, while journalists looked on. Beside the Quinn group, the young child of a barrister tried on his father's courtroom wig, laughing, oblivious to the drama unfolding beside him.

In truth, the decision had already been made. Sean Quinn was single-minded, a trait that had defined his life in business. The threat of jail had been hanging over his head for months, like a creaking guillotine that could fall at any moment. Enough was enough; Quinn wanted it over. He told Grant not to seek any more adjournments, not to engage in delaying tactics, not to look for a stay. He had been sentenced to jail and he would go to jail, today.

With his freedom ticking away, Quinn decamped to the bar in the bowels of the Four Courts, known as the Pit, with his son and son-in-law. The former billionaire sat down to a final meal of chicken curry with rice and chips, washed down with a pint of lager. On the other side of the bar were Mike Aynsley and Richard Woodhouse, the IBRC bankers, who had also dropped in for their lunch.

Back in the courtroom before lunchtime, Grant told the judge, 'In the light of your punitive sentence, Mr Quinn wishes to begin serving his prison sentence today. I am instructed he has chosen not to avail of the facility to apply for a stay and therefore remain at liberty today. He has made that choice himself.'

'So be it,' said the judge.

'The martyr tactic,' commented one courtroom observer.

The nine-week sentence meant Quinn would not be due for release until 4 January 2013. Would it be possible, Grant asked, to seek temporary release for his client for 22 December? His granddaughter Orna, born in August to Ciara Quinn and Niall McPartland, was due to be christened that day. The christening had already been postponed once because Sean Junior, the newborn's uncle, was in prison. Now it looked as though the baby's grandfather would be behind bars for the rescheduled ceremony. Justice Dunne said it was a matter for the prison authorities, not the courts, to decide.

Then it was all over. As a Garda moved in, a tearful Quinn, long known for his dislike of public speaking, held an impromptu press conference in the courtroom.

'The whole thing is a charade,' he declared. 'Anglo took all of my money, they took my companies, they took my reputation and they put me in jail. Yet they have proved nothing, they haven't proved that this money is owed, they haven't proved they had a right to put in a receiver [to the Quinn Group], they haven't proved that they loaned any money to the assets in Russia and the Ukraine.'

Asked how he felt about being in jail for Christmas, he said, 'You don't have to ask that, do you? If you have a wife and five children, grandchildren, you don't have to be asked about that. They put me into jail and my son in jail for dissipating assets. They [IBRC] have tried to drag us through the mill.' He continued, 'Did I apologize to the Irish public? Yes, I do. Is it small fry compared to the overall assault that has been launched on us, on our companies, and destroyed me? It is an absolute disaster.'

Clearly emotional, Quinn added, 'For sixty-four of my sixty-six years I made very little mistakes. I run my business very well. Did I make mistakes in the last two years? Did my family make mistakes in the last two years? Yes, I did, and I apologize to the Irish public for that, yes, I do. Are you saying to me, did we dissipate assets, did we make mistakes, did we do stupid things? Yes, we did. Was I stupid to believe the Anglo story? Was I stupid to believe all the brokers of all the institutions in Ireland that the Celtic Tiger was going to last forever? Was I stupid to believe that? Yes, I was.

'I'm wondering why you people [the media] can't say, Sean Quinn's an eejit and Sean Quinn done stupid things. I accept that. But did he run a great company for thirty-five years, one of the best ever, did he employ eight thousand people? Yes, he did. Did he ever owe anybody a penny, did he have rows with anybody else, did he pay his way? Do the people in the area respect what I done? Yes, they do.'

A final question was thrown in. 'Mr Quinn, there were suggestions of civil unrest, what appeal would you make to your supporters?'

He never got a chance to answer. The Garda interrupted Quinn and led him away. His last words were reported to have been, 'Get my pack of cards.'

At 1.55 p.m., after formalities and paperwork, a Garda van backed up to the door of the courts, ready to collect prisoner number 82809. After a final glance backwards, Quinn took a surprisingly sprightly jump into the cage in the back of the Garda van and was driven away, siren blaring and lights flashing. The former titan of business was on his way to jail.

Everyone present felt they had witnessed something momentous.

A businessman in a pinstriped suit, a former Quinn employee, stood weeping. 'When I was fund-raising for youth development for Fermanagh GAA, he gave me €100,000 and said "spend it well",' he told the *Irish Times*. 'That's only seven years ago. I felt I owed it to him to take two days here to support him.'

No sooner had the Garda van containing his father left for the Mountjoy Training Unit than Sean Quinn Junior was back in a courtroom. This time it was before Judge Peter Kelly in Court 1, where IBRC was seeking direction in a separate case. The bank wanted the go-ahead to cross-examine the five Quinn children and three of their spouses – including Sean Junior's wife, Karen Woods – about their personal finances. It did not believe they had fully complied with Judge Kelly's previous court orders to disclose all assets and bank accounts, and it didn't believe they had passed on all documents in relation to the asset-stripping. Getting them into the witness box would be a way to get to the bottom of things.

The bank started proceedings by notifying Judge Kelly of its joint venture with A1, the Russian company, revealed in Court 6 just over twenty-four hours earlier. Niall McPartland, acting for the family, queried the A1 arrangement and claimed that IBRC held no valid charge over Quinn assets in Russia and Ukraine. An offer from Sean Junior to help IBRC's efforts to recover the assets had been rebuffed, he said.

IBRC's lawyers said it was simply too late; the deal with A1 had to be done with 'urgency' to prevent the bank losing control of the assets forever. The lawyers reiterated the bank's fear that moves were afoot to take $8 million in cash from an account relating to the Kutuzoff Tower, divert its lucrative rent roll, and orchestrate a situation where the $188 million tower would be sold at a steep discount to a connected party.

Judge Kelly said he would not comment on the merits of the Quinn and IBRC counterclaims, because it would 'add to an already tense situation'. He dismissed a motion by the Quinns to have Declan Taite of RSM Farrell Grant Sparks removed as receiver to their personal assets over the alleged conflict of interest. The judge also set a date of 29 November to hear the bank's application to cross-examine the family members. Then Sean Junior was free to go home to his family, without his father.

After a cigarette in the grounds of the Four Courts, Sean Quinn Junior faced the media outside. At that stage, he had been so busy in the courts, he didn't know which prison his father was in. Questioned about his own three-month stint in the Mountjoy unit, he said he was 'well rested'. After consulting McPartland, Sean Junior read a statement from a handwritten scrawl on the ripped-out page of a diary.

'It's a very sad day to see Dad jailed at the behest of Anglo Irish Bank, the very bank who ruined this country,' he said. 'He is a father, grandfather and husband and he will be missed dearly during this time. I would like to thank all those who supported us in these extremely difficult times.'

Before climbing into a car driven by his sister Aoife, he was asked whether he believed his father had done wrong and was in contempt of court.

'No,' he replied.

With that, the car drove off.

The weekend newspapers were full of reports of Sean Quinn's jailing, how it had unfolded, how he had looked, how he reacted. The *Sunday Independent* said IBRC management had met the Garda Fraud Squad to discuss suspicions about alleged criminal actions taken by members of the Quinn family. There was more detail, too, about IBRC's joint venture with A1. The *Sunday Times* reported that Alfa Group, A1's parent, was the biggest financial and investment group in Russia with a sometimes murky way of doing business. Its three founders occupied the sixth, fifteenth and seventeenth spots on the list of Russia's richest people. One founder, German Khan, was reported to have told executives in BP, the oil group, that he considered *The Godfather* film 'a manual for life'.

The following morning, Monday 5 November, some Quinn supporters took matters into their own hands. About fifty workers at factories previously owned by Quinn – now controlled by the Quinn

Group lenders and IBRC – staged a walk-out. Together with former Quinn employees and other Quinn supporters, they used tractors, trailers and farm machinery to block the roads to the factories in Ballyconnell and Derrylin. The protest was peaceful, though there were reports of people being deliberately delayed and dismissed by the protestors. 'Licence plates were removed from all machinery and everyone denied ownership and refused to move them,' one witness told the *Irish Times*.

In a statement, the protestors said they were 'angered and dismayed at the ongoing senseless and damaging dispute' between IBRC and the Quinn family. 'We have no interest in covering old ground and we make no pronouncements on the rights and wrongs of either party in this pointless dispute. We demand, however, a resolution that will save our jobs, our communities and our future livelihoods.'

The Quinn supporters called for immediate mediation between IBRC and the Quinn family and wanted Quinn released while the mediation talks were taking place. They also called for the disposal of any former Quinn assets in Ireland or overseas to be halted until the conclusion of some independent inquiry. The final demand was for a 'return of the businesses to local management control and an acceptance by all stakeholders that local interests can only be properly represented in the future through the exercise of that local control'.

Paul O'Brien, the Quinn Group chief executive, was furious. From his point of view, the protestors were doing more to put jobs at risk than any bank or receiver ever could. Nobody would want to do business with a group that was under siege. IBRC was a 25 per cent shareholder in the manufacturing group but had no input into its day-to-day operations. The protests baffled O'Brien; he could not see how any Quinn supporter, no matter how fervent, could believe that Sean Quinn would ever regain control of the group.

The Gardaí and Police Service of Northern Ireland (PSNI) moved in to restore order and disperse the protestors. O'Brien appealed directly to the staff. The people attacking the company had chosen to 'stay in the shadows', he said. 'They have little or no interest in your welfare, in the preservation of jobs in this community or in the continuation of the very substantial contribution these businesses make both directly and indirectly to the economic health of these localities.' Jobs were on the line, he said. 'Your continued loyalty and dedication is very important to our businesses, to our customers and to each other.'

That afternoon, the manufacturing group issued a strongly worded public statement.

> Protest actions have this morning disrupted the operations of our manufacturing plants in Derrylin and Ballyconnell and are currently being dealt with by the PSNI and the Gardaí. These protests are linked to an ongoing legal dispute between the Quinn family and IBRC and are nothing to do with Quinn Manufacturing Group – which has no influence on these matters. Quinn Manufacturing Group employs over 1,000 people in the Cavan/Fermanagh area and we call on the people behind these protests to desist as they will only serve to have a negative effect on our businesses and damage employment prospects in the area.

The appeal fell on deaf ears. Before the week was out, an electrical substation at a wind farm close to the Quinn Group headquarters was set on fire. The wind farm had been owned by the Quinn family, but was now ring-fenced as an asset of Liberty Insurance. Two fire engines from Lisnaskea were called out to deal with the blaze, on the northern side of the border. No one was injured but there was substantial damage to the installation. The PSNI said openly they believed the fire had been started deliberately, though no one was apprehended for the crime.

Life in the Mountjoy Training Unit moved slowly for Sean Quinn. His age meant he could not work in the kitchen as his son had done, so the days were long. He had regular visitors, including Sean Junior and a visit from his daughter Ciara, who brought her three-month-old daughter to see her grandfather.

Father Gerry Comiskey visited, too, and told media afterwards that Quinn had found the jailing 'very traumatic'. The priest said, 'The whole drama of being brought across the city in a Garda van with lights and sirens blaring left him quite emotional. I assured his family he was okay but he was still traumatized by the events of the day. He was emotional but has great inner strength and I think he'll be able to call on that strength in the days ahead and I think will bear up reasonably well.'

Comiskey said there was 'palpable anger' in the Cavan/Fermanagh region and called for calm. 'I would like to add my voice to the others who have been calling on people to control their anger and not to do anything that would jeopardize the jobs or livelihoods of the hundreds of people dependent on income from the Quinn Group,' he said.

In a children's rights referendum, held on 10 November, there were reports of spoiled votes in Cavan, Monaghan, Sligo and Leitrim – on their voting slips, some voters had written 'Free Sean Quinn'.

On 15 November, just under a fortnight after Quinn's jailing, Liberty Insurance announced it would lay off 285 of its 1,400 staff at the former Quinn Insurance offices in Dublin, Cavan and Enniskillen. Eighteen months earlier, as Liberty was pushing ahead with the deal to acquire Quinn Insurance, Ted Kelly, the Liberty chairman, had said there would be 'no massive lay-offs or anything like that'. Quinn supporters had been sceptical at the time; now their fears were being realized. Though Liberty had decided to re-enter the insurance market in Northern Ireland and Britain, the volume of business there had 'declined sharply' and it needed fewer staff than it was carrying, the company said.

The round of lay-offs would reduce job numbers at the insurer to just over 1,100, less than half the number it employed when it went into administration in March 2010. Patrick O'Brien, the chief executive of Liberty, said it was 'fully committed to the Irish business' and would continue to invest. 'We have decided to make the right decision to position us for sustainable profitability and to protect in excess of 1,100 jobs remaining,' he said.

In a statement, the Quinn family condemned the lay-offs. 'We have repeatedly called for a public inquiry into the administration of Quinn Insurance,' they said. 'Following today's developments, we feel more than ever that a public inquiry is required.'

Concerned Irish Citizens called a public meeting for 2 December in the Community Centre in Ballyconnell to discuss what it called the 'crisis' at the former Quinn companies. 'The very survival of our communities is at stake,' the pressure group said. There was talk of lay-offs at Quinn manufacturing companies, though a group spokesman insisted they were unfounded.

The Ballyconnell Community Centre is a solid, unremarkable building, a single large hall used for local gatherings, like countless others in small towns around the country. A plaque on the wall declares it opened in 1990 and carries the Irish language saying 'Ni neart go cur le cheile' – there is no strength without unity. People started to gather in the early evening of 2 December. By the time the meeting began at 6 p.m., more than 250 people were in the building. Standing against a wall down the back was Sean Quinn Junior, flanked by Liam McCaffrey and Kevin Lunney. David Mackey, the close friend of Sean Quinn Senior and ex-director of Quinn Group, also attended.

The mood was agitated. A panel of local politicians from Fine Gael, Fianna Fáil and Sinn Féin was regularly heckled and criticized for not doing enough for the border region. Joe O'Reilly, a Fine Gael TD for Cavan/Monaghan, rejected the criticism. 'We formed an all-party group in 2010 and that group worked day after day and night after night,' he said. 'We went to every imaginable organization. We did our best to dam the river and stop the flow and we have not stopped yet.'

The meeting heard from Martin Maguire, chief executive of the Fermanagh Economic Development Organization, a group chaired by Peter Quinn. 'The future of the Quinn Group is concerning for all of us, whether you know Sean Quinn or not,' Maguire said. He suggested Quinn Group could face serious financial problems by May 2013.

Maguire's statement was flatly denied by the group afterwards. 'He is obviously looking at a cash-flow forecast that I don't have, because we are not going to run out of money,' Paul O'Brien, the Quinn chief executive, responded. 'We had a superb year for cash. It's all crap.'

A letter was read out from Denis Doogan, who had worked for

Quinn Group for twenty-six years and was chief executive of its radiator unit when he resigned in July 2011, three months after the share receiver was appointed. He was highly critical of the way the group was being run and alleged that dozens of senior staff had left the group but were bound by gagging clauses. 'Collectively, 450 years of industry and manufacturing experience has been obliterated,' Doogan's letter said. He claimed the group was losing business with customers who did not want any dealing with 'an Anglo-based enterprise' and alleged the group was spending an 'obscene' amount of money on consultants. The letter continued:

> When the decision was taken to remove Quinn Insurance and Quinn Group from the control of Sean Quinn, the dawn of one of the greatest cover-ups in the history of the Irish Republic had arrived. This cover-up has seen the persecution of Sean Quinn and his family over the last 2–3 years in an attempt to deflect the focus away from a failed banking system and a failed regulatory system. However, the vendetta against Sean Quinn has now become a vendetta against the people of this region, and is gradually impacting upon us all.

The reading of his letter was met with a sustained round of applause.

David Mackey addressed the meeting, saying he fully agreed with Doogan. 'What Denis Doogan said was fair and balanced,' he said, urging the politicians to read Doogan's letter. The meeting ended by asking Mackey to head a taskforce with politicians and others to monitor the situation and try to safeguard jobs. Mackey agreed he would go into talks about it. Sean Quinn Junior did not speak at the meeting, though a letter from the Quinn family was read out, thanking the organizers and local people for their support.

Ten days earlier, Sean Junior had appeared on *The Late Late Show*, the most watched television programme in Ireland. There was an irony in Quinn's *Late Late* appearance – the Quinn Group had previously sponsored the show and Liberty Insurance had taken over the sponsorship, worth more than €1 million a season, just months earlier.

Ryan Tubridy, the host, quizzed Quinn about his time in Mount-joy.

Quinn said it had been 'surreal', 'frightening' and 'humbling'. He recalled being brought away in the 'dog box' in the back of the Garda van and being able to hear the crowd in Croke Park, the GAA stadium near Mountjoy, on match days and wishing he was there. His father, three weeks into his prison sentence, had 'settled in reasonably well' in Mountjoy, Sean Junior said. 'He's doing very little, he's spending a lot of time in his cell, he's doing a bit of reading and, as he'd say, he's dodging about. There's not much to do in prison, I'll tell you that.'

The interview was pre-recorded for legal reasons, with Sean Junior's wife, Karen Woods, looking on. Sean Junior revealed that on honeymoon in Australia six months earlier, he had told his wife there was 'not a hope' of him going to prison. 'It never crossed my mind,' he told Tubridy. 'It was just not going to happen.'

The prison term had been hard on his wife, he said, who was photographed on every visit to Mountjoy. Media reports had detailed how Woods, a receptionist in a car dealership, had been paid more than €320,000 by a Russian company in the Quinn Group. 'We made a lot of mistakes – there's no question,' Quinn said. 'It was my bright idea to get Karen over to Russia and give her a salary. Karen now has court orders over her, her bank accounts are frozen . . . she has to go begging to receivers [for living expenses] and it's a hundred per cent my fault.'

Ill at ease, at first, Quinn grew in confidence as the interview progressed. He repeated the family position that they no longer had any involvement in the overseas property assets. 'I think the fact that we moved assets – and we accept that we moved assets in March and April [2011] – certainly had a negative impact. There is stuff going on in the Ukraine and Russia that we are just not involved in. We are not in control of those assets.'

Pressed by Tubridy on the fact the High Court and Supreme Court did not believe him, Quinn said the court judgments were 'not nice to hear'. But he added, 'There's two sides to every story.'

Of his father, he said, 'There is no doubt that he made mistakes.

He's on the record that he made mistakes with Quinn Insurance and taking money out of the company . . . And he certainly made a mistake getting so deeply involved in buying shares in Anglo Irish Bank. I've no doubt that a day doesn't go by that he doesn't think, "Why the hell did I get involved with that Anglo Irish Bank?"'

Asked if he thought his father had learned from his mistakes, Sean Junior said, 'I suppose he's not going to be given an opportunity . . . he's going to be bankrupt for eight, ten, twelve years and it's going to be difficult to see if he gets the opportunity to see if he has learned from his mistakes.'

Were they motivated by greed? Tubridy asked.

'I suppose, possibly,' he said. He also pledged to 'do everything in my power' to purge his contempt.

Within weeks, Sean Junior would offer to sell the home in Castle-knock in Dublin that he shared with Karen Woods and give his share of the proceeds to IBRC in an effort to purge his contempt of court. The bank accepted the offer. It was agreed Sean Junior would also travel to Moscow to get bank statements for various accounts held by family members there.

In early December, as Sean Quinn was almost halfway through his nine-week sentence in the Mountjoy Training Unit, three letters landed on the desk of Ned Whelan, the prison governor. All three concerned Prisoner 82809 and all had a similar request – for temporary release on compassionate grounds.

The letters were from Quinn's firm of solicitors in Belfast, from Father Gerry Comiskey, and from Ciara Quinn. 'My daughter, Orna, was born on August 12th this year; she was a much longed-for baby and her safe arrival has been a blessing on my entire family,' Ciara wrote. 'Indeed, the 12th August has been the only good day in my life over the past nineteen months.'

She was a practising Catholic and wanted the baby baptized as soon as possible after her birth. Initial plans had to be postponed because 'unfortunately my brother was incarcerated at that time'. The ceremony had been set for 22 December because the child's god-father was flying home from China and did not know when he would next be in Ireland. 'Without my father there, it will leave a large void in the ceremony and a dark cloud over the entire day.' She added, 'My father is a devoted family man, and to miss his granddaughter's christening would negatively affect him. His life revolves around his family and it is for these reasons I request temporary release for my dad from the 22 December to the 27 December.' She signed off, pointedly, 'Wishing you and your family a happy and healthy Christmas.'

Whelan, the prison governor, considered the matter, with input from the Attorney General, Máire Whelan, and Alan Shatter, the Fine Gael Justice Minister. It was a delicate situation. A prisoner convicted of contempt is not entitled to remission, unlike an inmate with a criminal conviction, so they would be making an exception for Quinn. They did not consent to releasing Quinn for the five days requested, but ruled that he could be released on Monday 24 December, Christmas Eve, and return to the Training Unit at Mountjoy on Thursday 27 December.

At 6 a.m. on 24 December, Sean Quinn Junior picked up his father from the Mountjoy unit and drove him home to Cavan for Christmas. The christening was rescheduled to 26 December. An *Irish Times* report said Quinn was 'in jovial form' at the event. Father Gerry Comiskey said Quinn was 'not a bit worried' about going back to Mountjoy. Quinn was receiving hundreds of letters of support from all over the country, Comiskey said, and they had 'strengthened his resolve'.

At 7.40 p.m. on 27 December, Sean Quinn Junior dropped his father back to prison. The *Anglo-Celt*, the local newspaper in Cavan, published its weekly issue that day. The lead report said the family would pursue 'a very large compensation claim' against the state. Their legal action against IBRC and the share receiver, Kieran Wallace, had been scheduled to begin in April 2013, but the Director of Public Prosecutions had asked for the case to be delayed because of criminal proceedings against former directors of the bank which dealt with overlapping issues, including the Maple Ten transaction in 2008.

Now the family was considering widening their case to include the Central Bank and the Department of Finance as defendants, according to Colette Quinn. She told the *Anglo-Celt*:

> Realistically the family see ourselves before the courts for at least the next three years. If we are successful in our cases, and I believe we will be, that will leave it open for us to take a very large compensation claim, not just against the bank, but also the Regulator and the Department of Finance. It's the taxpayer who will lose out. It's very important to establish, this was never our preferred option. What has happened and where this has all come to, this was the bank and the Regulator who brought it to this stage.

Adding the Central Bank and Department of Finance to the case, Mr Justice Peter Kelly said later, would 'change the whole landscape' of the case.

The reunited Quinns would have had other matters to discuss over Christmas. On 20 December, the same day Quinn got confirmation of his temporary release, Quinn Group management announced they were in talks to merge the Quinn building-products business with Lagan Cement. Quinn and Lagan were lifelong rivals – Sean Quinn had secretly funded objectors to a Lagan factory in 2000 – and a merger of their businesses would never have been considered during Quinn's reign. To Quinn supporters, it was further proof that the group was being dismantled before the Quinn family had had their court case heard on the legitimacy of the receivership.

That was irrelevant, Paul O'Brien, the Quinn chief executive told the *Impartial Reporter*. There was no 'going back'; the Quinns would never be back in control of Quinn Group. 'Even if they won the case, they don't get their companies back. It is only a claim for damages. That is a big misunderstanding,' O'Brien said.

Just before 9 a.m. on 3 January 2013, Sean Quinn was released from Mountjoy. His son was there to pick him up again and drive him home. In Virginia, the first Co. Cavan town they passed through on their way up the N3, someone had parked a large JCB forklift beside the town's massive Christmas tree. Hoisted on the forklift was a 10-foot white sign, professionally printed with black lettering and proclaiming, 'Welcome Home Sean Quinn'. He was back in Quinn country.

In an interview with BBC Northern Ireland that day, Quinn was filmed holding his granddaughter Orna. His tone was understated but defiant. 'The Quinns are not killed off. The Quinns are still there,' he said. The prison experience had been tough but the family had not been defeated. 'I could fit into most environments, and I fitted in. Of course, when you find a door slamming at nine o'clock at night, it's not nice. It's not something I was used to and it's not something I felt I deserved.'

He had received a 'very positive' response from other inmates in Mountjoy, he said. 'I think one hundred per cent of them felt I shouldn't be there. I certainly felt I shouldn't be there, after creating seven thousand jobs, after never in my life owing anybody a penny. Never in my life did I steal a penny or take a penny that didn't belong to me. I felt it was just wrong.' Prison had been 'a learning experience', he said. It had made him 'feel happy that I have a good wife and a good family, that I can come to a warm environment and a warm community. From that point of view, I felt lucky in some respects.'

Quinn acknowledged he might not have seen the last of Mountjoy. 'Can we go back to jail? Yes we can,' he said. 'They can continue this charade as long as they want, and as long as the public opinion and as long as the media backs them in doing that, they're very keen to do that. I have genuinely no idea what their next move is going to be.'

Epilogue

The civil servant lay in wait for Alan Dukes, the rangy chairman of IBRC. It was 6 February 2013, a Wednesday, and Dukes was attending meetings in the five-star Merrion Hotel opposite Government Buildings in Dublin city centre. As he made his way out the door of the hotel just after 5 p.m., the official, attached to the Department of Finance, pounced.

Dukes had been scheduled to meet Ann Nolan, the top banking official in the department and one of the three most senior officials in the entire Department of Finance. The meeting was due to begin at 8 p.m., but Dukes was told it had to be moved forward. There was pressing business that could not wait; his presence was required immediately.

'Do you have me under surveillance?' Dukes quipped to the civil servant as he was escorted across the road to the finance department's offices.

Mike Aynsley, the IBRC chief executive, was still en route from London for the 8 p.m. meeting with Nolan. With the meeting brought forward, Dukes would have to handle whatever was coming on his own. Beside Nolan at the table was John Moran, a former banker who had been appointed secretary-general of the Department of Finance exactly one year before. There was no small talk. Dukes was handed a letter dismissing the entire board of IBRC with immediate effect and informing him of the imminent liquidation of the bank.

The bank chairman was then introduced to Padraig Monaghan, a partner with KPMG, the accountancy firm. The legislation used to nationalize Anglo in January 2009 had granted the Minister for Finance the authority to appoint an officer to take control of the board of the bank. The Finance Minister, Michael Noonan, who had sat around the cabinet table with Alan Dukes in the 1980s, was now nominating Monaghan as that person. It was effectively a death sentence for the bank formerly known as Anglo Irish Bank.

Monaghan's appointment was temporary. The Dáil, Dukes was told, was convening late that evening to approve new legislation that would formally liquidate the bank. The President, Michael D. Higgins, was in Rome, but two officials had been dispatched to Italy to brief him on unfolding events. He would return to Dublin on the government jet to sign the legislation into law. Liquidators would be appointed to IBRC and it would be closed within months.

The mandarins thanked Dukes for his efforts. The meeting ended. Moran and Nolan were needed elsewhere. The liquidation of the bank was part of a much larger choreography, one they knew would stun the political establishment and surprise the financial markets. The government was attempting a radical restructuring of €30.7 billion in so-called 'promissory notes' used to bail out Anglo Irish Bank and Irish Nationwide, the two components of IBRC.

The promissory notes were a financial manoeuvre to bail out the institutions, as part of the government's guarantee of bank assets and liabilities in September 2008. Repayable with interest over ten years, they had fast become politically toxic. A debt repayment of €3.1 billion relating to the notes was due to be paid at the end of March. Pat Rabbitte, the Minister for Communications and a senior government member, had already said the government would not be paying the money. For months, the government had been working on a plan to replace the notes with bonds from NAMA. The liquidation of IBRC was central to the strategy.

Liquidating IBRC would resolve other headaches for the government. Relations between IBRC senior executives and the Department of Finance had been sour for some time. Neil Ryan, a senior department official, had been dispatched to Connaught House, the IBRC headquarters, on secondment in September 2012 to monitor events and report back to Noonan. Ryan had a frosty relationship with Mike Aynsley, and the two men had clashed on a number of issues. Noonan was unhappy with the bank's relationship with a number of its larger borrowers, particularly when embarrassing revelations emerged in a London court case about IBRC's support for Paddy McKillen, a property investor (and member of the Maple Ten) who owed the bank €900 million.

Noonan was unhappy, too, with the salaries and perks enjoyed by IBRC's top executives. Six executives at the bank, including Aynsley, Woodhouse and Tom Hunersen, were being paid more than €500,000 each a year. More than 200 IBRC staff were on salaries of more than €100,000 each. Some months before, Noonan had commissioned consultancy group Mercer to assess the remuneration of all banks covered by the government guarantee. It had yet to be published, but Noonan knew what was in it. The average remuneration for staff at AIB and Bank of Ireland was €57,900 and €60,500 respectively. The figure for Permanent TSB was €57,400. At IBRC, the average remuneration was €80,800.

Meanwhile, Brendan McDonagh, the chief executive of NAMA, a far larger organization, had taken a voluntary pay cut reducing his salary to €365,000 for 2012. Both NAMA and IBRC were effectively workout vehicles, charged with putting themselves out of business by winding down their loan books. Noonan decided he could kill two birds with one stone: facilitate a deal on the promissory notes, and finally bury the corpse of Anglo Irish Bank.

In the two weeks preceding the liquidation of IBRC, Sean Quinn's five children returned to the High Court. IBRC had won the right to cross-examine the family members about their personal financial affairs. The bank felt the Quinns had not disclosed everything about their finances, and the family had been unsuccessful in efforts to resist the bank's application for cross-examination. The High Court ruled in the bank's favour; Mr Justice Peter Kelly dismissed family claims that the bank was on a 'fishing expedition' for information that would disadvantage them in their main court case against IBRC. The Supreme Court subsequently refused an order deferring the case, following an appeal by the family.

During the cross-examination, the bank concentrated on the salaries paid to the family members by Russian companies in the International Property Group. Aoife Quinn was first up. 'I am not great at maths, especially in my head and under pressure,' she said.

She revealed that almost €370,000 had been paid by a Russian company into her bank account. Most of the money had been spent on legal fees, she said, but she had no receipts. She said that Ocean Bank in Moscow, where the family held accounts, did not issue statements, but she got a text message whenever there was a transaction on her account. She had withdrawn almost all of the money lodged to her Moscow account using a Visa card in Ireland. Aoife said she had also opened a bank account in Dubai, but had never lodged any money to it.

Questioned by Paul Gallagher, the lawyer for IBRC, about trips to Switzerland in late 2011 and early 2012, and whether they had any connection with any Quinn family trust, she said they did not. Stephen Kelly, Aoife Quinn's husband, told the court he earned €260,536 from the Russian property group companies between July 2011 and May 2012. Again, Kelly had made large withdrawals from his Moscow account through Irish ATMs. Most of the money had been spent. Under questioning, Kelly said that Eversheds, the Irish law firm that previously represented the family, was paid through Senat Legal in Dubai.

Sean Junior gave evidence on his own behalf and on behalf of his wife, Karen Woods. He said he was paid €399,308 from his Russian employment and his wife got €320,297. Asked how Senat got the money it used to pay Eversheds, Sean Junior said he did not believe that issue was covered by the discovery order granted to IBRC. 'I have been found guilty of contempt. I have served three months in jail. I have agreed to sell my family home with my wife, Karen. I am in a very precarious position,' he said.

Ciara Quinn had been paid €339,921 by Russian companies between July 2011 and May 2012. She told the court she had spent the money in Ireland, on legal fees. Like the other family members, she had no receipts. Asked by the judge how she got the money from her account, she said she withdrew it in cash and then gave the money to family members. Ciara Quinn's husband, Niall McPartland, a solicitor, said he received €281,048 from Russian companies between 2011 and 2012. McPartland's declared bank accounts included a UBS account in Switzerland.

Colette Quinn told the court she'd received €339,921 between July 2011 and May 2012. The money was paid into her Ocean Bank account and was withdrawn from ATMs in Ireland using a Visa card. On a single day, 14 July 2012, the court heard, she withdrew nearly €16,000 from ATMs in Cavan town and Belturbet in twenty transactions in the space of two hours. Judge Kelly later described the Quinns' evidence as 'substandard' and said it was 'simply incredible' that they could not produce documentation to justify their lucrative salaries. He ordered them to make a full and proper disclosure of their salaries and ownership of several Quinn companies.

Kieran Wallace woke early on Thursday 7 February 2013. The KPMG partner and share receiver to the Quinn Group had not watched the live news feed from the Dáil as the politicians debated the Irish Bank Resolution Corporation Bill 2013 through the night. Instead, he turned on the radio at 7 a.m. to check that everything had gone smoothly.

It had.

The legislation liquidating IBRC had passed both the Dáil and the Senate, despite sometimes raucous proceedings, and had been signed into law by the President. Wallace had just been installed as the state-appointed special liquidator of Irish Bank Resolution Corporation. He would take the lead on the litigation with a KPMG colleague, Eamonn Richardson.

Wallace had been involved for some time in Project Red, the Department of Finance's code name for the plan to resolve the promissory note situation. Within the department, Anglo and later IBRC had become known as 'Red' simply because they were so deep in debt. KPMG had produced a plan for the winding-down or liquidation of Anglo in 2010 for the previous Finance Minister, Brian Lenihan. The blueprint had languished in a drawer until the final months of 2012 when the KPMG accountants received a call from the Department of Finance. They were asked if the plans could be updated.

On Wednesday 6 February, Wallace had received a call from the Department of Finance, with the message: It's on. He headed to bed early that evening, knowing the biggest liquidation of his career would begin the following morning.

His first task on 7 February was difficult. With the bank in liquidation, there was little need for its top tier of highly paid executives. The Department of Finance had been clear on that one. Wallace decided to do the deed in person, walking from his city-centre home to Connaught House early in the morning.

The first person he met was Richard Woodhouse, the British banker who had spearheaded the Quinn case. Woodhouse and Wallace knew each other well; it was Woodhouse who had appointed Wallace as share receiver to the Quinn Group, and the two men had worked closely on the project. Wallace informed Woodhouse that his contract was terminated with immediate effect. Given his expertise, Woodhouse was asked whether he would be available on a 'consultancy basis' to run the Quinn cases. The banker declined; he had no desire to stay on at a bank that was in liquidation.

For almost the entirety of his time in Ireland, since the start of 2010, Woodhouse's working life had been consumed with Sean Quinn and the Quinn family. He had battled them in courts in Ireland and abroad. Woodhouse had been the bank's chief strategist on all the bank's actions and had sworn the affidavits in the various Quinn cases. Now, it was over. The quick conversation with Kieran Wallace ended Woodhouse's time at IBRC. The irony that Wallace was the share receiver to the Quinn Group was not lost on either man. Woodhouse packed his personal belongings into boxes and thanked all of the staff members who had worked with him. He left the building within hours. His Irish adventure was finished.

Wallace had a similar conversation with Mike Aynsley. The Australian banker knew what was coming. 'Go ahead, Kieran, I know what you have to do,' he told Wallace when the KPMG accountant made his way down the corridor to the chief executive's office.

Aynsley knew that his salary had become a thorny political issue. But he felt that he, along with his top team, was worth it. 'There are certain types of individuals that are critical for us in the tapestry of this workforce that we cannot get for less than this sort of money,' Aynsley had told the *Irish Independent* just months before. 'You can't lose qualified people who manage complex accounts and just transfer an IT specialist or a human-resource specialist to that position.'

Now the government was turfing out the IBRC management en masse.

Aynsley had heard the whispers that Noonan was planning something, but did not imagine the bank would be shut overnight. But like Woodhouse, he packed up his office and left immediately. There was no sentiment, just an acknowledgement that the game had changed. He had been the public face of Anglo Irish Bank after Sean FitzPatrick and David Drumm. He had stood on St Stephen's Green when the old Anglo signs were removed and taken away as museum pieces. Now that phase was over, too. He was part of history.

The purge continued. Wallace terminated the contracts of Tom Hunersen and Mark Layther, who dealt with the bank's recovery of smaller individual loans. Of the six IBRC staff who earned more than €500,000 a year, five were let go. Only Jim Bradley, the chief financial officer, survived.

There was shock news, too, for IBRC's 1,000 staff. Wallace confirmed they would be made redundant on statutory terms as the bank was liquidated. That meant they would get two weeks' pay, or a maximum of €1,200, for each year of service. There would be no exceptions; IBRC was in liquidation. The majority of staff were rehired on three-month rolling contracts to deal with the liquidation process.

The liquidation of IBRC received broad public welcome. Eamon Gilmore, the Tánaiste and Labour Party leader, captured the general mood: 'I'm delighted we now have torn up the promissory note and we have wiped Anglo Irish Bank off the business map.'

It was announced that the bank's assets, including its shareholdings in Quinn Group and Liberty Insurance, would be sold within six months if buyers were willing to meet independent valuations, though the time frame was later extended. The pursuit of the Quinn family for the international properties and repayment of loans would continue unabated, said Brian Hayes, the Department of Finance junior minister who had previously made diplomatic efforts to recover assets in Ukraine.

The legislation liquidating the bank gave Wallace and Richardson, the liquidators, the right to continue any litigation taken by IBRC or launch new cases, but it put a stay on all outstanding actions against the bank. That suggested the Quinn family's case against the bank over their billions of euro in borrowings was effectively at an end.

The family immediately went to the High Court to question this provision, stating they would challenge the constitutionality of the Act if required. Some weeks later, the stay was lifted. However, the liquidation of the bank would have massive consequences for the family's litigation against the old Anglo Irish Bank. They were now suing a bust bank; even if they won, they could not get any compensation or damages.

Eleven days after the IBRC liquidation, Kieran Wallace and Eamonn Richardson gave an interview to the *Sunday Business Post* to explain the liquidation and its consequences. The effect on the Quinn saga featured prominently. 'A lot of historical claims against the bank will rank as unsecured creditors. They fall behind preferential and secured creditors. Under current projections, there will not be any dividend for unsecured creditors,' Wallace said.

The liquidator said there would be 'no let-up' in legal actions taken by IBRC, including proceedings against the Quinns. 'We will be maintaining all the litigation around the world in relation to the conspiracy case, which relates to the €500 million property portfolio,' said Wallace. 'As liquidator, we have to recover money for the creditors. This involves pursuing this case. We will be continuing with the litigation.'

Richard Woodhouse's departure would not affect the conduct of the litigation, according to Wallace. 'We have a legal team in place who are fully briefed, and there are a lot of people within the bank who worked with Richard on it. We are confident it will continue on without any problems arising.'

During the interview, the liquidators confirmed that the Quinn loans were for sale. It would be open to a third party to buy the loans and pursue the Quinns for the money owed. If the loans were acquired during the six-month window, all of the bank's litigation would go with them. There was speculation that Russian groups, including A1, the joint venture partner selected by IBRC, would bid for the loans and take sole charge of reclaiming the valuable foreign properties.

The bank and the courts had de-Quinned the Quinn Group; now, liquidation was effectively de-Quinning the bank. Yet the property assets remained in a vortex of muddled claims, counterclaims and confusion. The liquidation of IBRC had changed everything, and nothing. Kieran Wallace quickly found himself in the role once filled by Richard Woodhouse, working with Karyn Harty in McCann FitzGerald to recover the assets, even as the IBRC liquidation unfolded.

Just weeks into the job, Kieran Wallace signed his first affidavit in relation to the Quinn litigation. The affidavit, lodged with the High Court in early March 2013, supported a bank application to have Senat Legal, the Dubai law firm that managed the Quinn family's international legal battle, added to the Irish conspiracy case. In it, Wallace outlined how the bank uncovered new evidence which, it claimed, linked the Quinn family to corporations in Switzerland, secretive bank accounts in Singapore and investment firms in Hong Kong.

The evidence had been obtained by the bank over several months. It outlined new claims that the Quinn family sought to strip millions of euro in cash from its international property portfolio. The affidavit stated that emails obtained by the bank showed how Aoife Quinn had attempted to move either $5 million or $3 million from a Russian company through a Hong Kong corporation called Orient Guide Investment and into a bank account in Singapore.

The attempted transaction happened in September 2011, IBRC said, months after the bank secured its injunction preventing the family from interfering with the property assets. Petey Quinn was also involved in the deal, the bank claimed. When Wallace signed the document, Petey remained in the North, with the warrant for his arrest still in place in the Republic.

New evidence was also produced showing that the family moved shares in the Q-City property in India, now valued at $80 million because of increased occupancy, to a company incorporated in Unterkulm, a small town in Switzerland. The bank discovered this

Swiss company, Logvis AG, for the first time in January 2013. Wallace said, in the affidavit, that it could link Logvis to Senat Legal through a Dubai-based firm called Logvis Middle East. Separately, a Slieve Russell Hotel company now controlled by IBRC launched legal proceedings against Ciara Quinn, seeking repayment of money it claims it is owed, including the cost of Quinn's lavish 2007 wedding.

On 6 March 2013, attention turned fleetingly to the old Anglo Irish Bank. Sean FitzPatrick, Willie McAteer and Pat Whelan, the three former Anglo executives, appeared in the Dublin Circuit Criminal Court where a case against them was up for mention. The three men face allegations that they permitted the bank to give unlawful financial assistance, prohibited under company law, to sixteen individuals – Patricia Quinn, the five Quinn children, and the Maple Ten customers of the bank – to buy Anglo shares as Sean Quinn's CFD stake was being unwound.

The trial is expected to begin in January 2014 and last between three and six months. Judge Mary Ellen Ring noted a larger-than-normal panel of potential jurors would need to be available, given the likely duration of the trial. If any jurors became unavailable, the trial could collapse. 'If the jury collapses due to the unavailability of jurors, an immediate retrial will be a problem,' the judge said. A second case against FitzPatrick, over the transfer of his personal loans out of Anglo each year to conceal from shareholders, is listed for hearing in October 2014.

The Quinn family case against the bank and Kieran Wallace, the Quinn Group receiver, will not even get under way until the trial of FitzPatrick, McAteer and Whelan is complete. That is likely to be 2015, a decade after Sean Quinn started his CFD investments and seven years after his disastrous investment was unwound.

On 9 April 2013, Matthew Elderfield made the surprise announcement that he would step down from his role as Financial Regulator and Deputy Governor of the Central Bank and return to the UK. Elderfield, seen as an effective Regulator during a tumultuous period that saw not only the Quinn Insurance administration, but also the nationalizing of five of the six Irish banking institutions, gave six months' notice and waived his €100,000 bonus entitlement. Elderfield later confirmed he would join Lloyds Banking Group, which racked up £12.1 billion of loan losses in Ireland during the credit boom, as its director for conduct and compliance.

The dispersal of the assets once owned by Sean Quinn continues apace. The Crowne Plaza Hotel in Cambridge was sold for €45.5 million in 2012, the Ibis Hotel in Prague fetched €12 million, and an industrial unit in Britain and two apartments in Manchester were also sold. The Hilton Hotel in Sofia and the Sheraton in Krakow were put on the market in February 2013. Quinn's main wind farm, on the slopes of Slieve Rushen, is for sale. Other assets, including the Prestige Mall shopping centre in Istanbul and the Leonardo office block in Kiev, are expected to follow.

Quinn Group faces the prospect of further losses if and when the Leonardo property is sold. The building is 45 per cent owned by employees, friends and family of Sean Quinn, who were given a personal letter by Quinn in 2007 guaranteeing the value of their investment. The building is likely to sell for a significantly lower price than Quinn paid and the manufacturing group is expected to make up any shortfall faced by the Quinn investors.

The former Quinn Insurance office on O'Connell Street in Dublin, opened with fanfare by Sean Quinn in 1996, has been shuttered and put on the market. The insurer's office block in Navan, Co. Meath, has been sold as the new headquarters of Meath County Council. In March 2013, Liberty Insurance announced it would lay off 425 of its 1,450 staff, after a larger-than-expected response to the redundancy programme announced in late 2012.

'Liberty Insurance remains fully committed to the Irish market, its customers and its staff in Cavan, Dublin and Enniskillen,' the company said. Liberty had sales of around €180 million in 2012, compared with more than €1 billion sales recorded by Quinn Insurance during Sean Quinn's reign. It made a €20 million underwriting loss for 2012, though its bottom line was saved by a €35 million gain on investments – driven, ironically, by the strong performance of Irish government bonds.

Liberty has moved away from insuring young drivers in favour of more business with female customers and drivers over forty. It is back in business in Britain, selling through price-comparison sites and aggregators. Patrick O'Brien, the Liberty chief executive, said Liberty Mutual, the US parent, wants to buy the 49 per cent stake held by IBRC in the Irish operation, 'sooner rather than later'.

Quinn Healthcare, a separate company, rebranded itself as Laya Healthcare in 2012 under the leadership of Donal Clancy and announced 100 new jobs, bringing its workforce to about 450 people. The business has 475,000 customers.

Joint venture talks between Quinn Cement and Lagan Cement ended without a deal in early 2013, though market observers believe Lagan may return to the table in the future. Paul O'Brien, chief executive of Quinn Group, said businesses or assets would be sold if the right price was on offer.

In May 2013, Quinn Group formally pulled the plug on the half-built chemical plant at Leuna in Germany, which swallowed almost €200 million during Sean Quinn's time at the helm of the group. The mothballed plant would have cost another €200 million to complete, but the group said 'a thorough and exhaustive global tender process' failed to identify a suitable partner to fund and finish the project.

The Quinn family name has been excised from the holding company for the Quinn manufacturing group. It has been renamed Gortmullan Holdings after a townland outside Derrylin. A letter sent in late 2012 to the group's lenders, whose approval was needed for the name change, said 'the selection of the new name respects the heritage of the business'.

The restructured Quinn Group had revenues of €639 million in 2011 and made an operating profit of €25.8 million after the financial restructuring. It lost €199 million after accounting for impairments and exceptional items, including 'staff reorganization' costs. The financial overhaul that dragged on through 2010 and 2011 cost the group €87 million in professional fees paid to advisers, accountants and lawyers, according to group accounts.

Talbot Hughes McKillop, the British restructuring firm that advised on the Quinn Group overhaul, reported profits of £21.6 million for the two years it worked on the Quinn project. Its partners, including Murdoch McKillop, shared nearly £19 million in remuneration.

By the end of 2012, Grant Thornton in Ireland and Britain had been paid €14.2 million for its work as administrator to Quinn Insurance. Quinn Insurance's legacy business remains in administration, under the management of Aidan Cassells, a former head of Axa in Ireland and chief executive of the Irish Insurance Federation, who was hired by Grant Thornton to wind down the remaining business in Britain. In July 2013, the President of the High Court gave the Quinn Insurance administrators the go-ahead to serve a summons on PricewaterhouseCoopers, the former auditors to the insurer.

IBRC and A1 formally announced their joint venture to recover the former Quinn properties in Russia and Ukraine at a press conference in Moscow in April 2013. It was attended by senior IBRC and A1 executives, as well as Philip McDonagh, the Irish ambassador to the Russian Federation. 'The lawful return of these assets to the Irish people is an extremely important issue for the Government of Ireland,' McDonagh said.

A1 is investing $18 million in the joint venture, less than the $30 million originally expected, after renegotiating terms when IBRC was put into liquidation. The Russian group will keep 30 per cent of the proceeds from the sale of Quinn properties. It expects the process to take one year. 'If we say we're going to return the assets, then there is no doubt that we will get them,' said Dmitry Vozianov, acting director of A1.

The recovery effort yielded its first results at the Ukraina shopping centre in Kiev, where the bank succeeded in installing a new director in early 2013. An audit of Univermag, the company behind the centre, however, indicated that up to $15 million may have been transferred out of the company's accounts between 2011 and 2012. The money was transferred to Lyndhurst, the British Virgin Islands company, and two Ukrainian companies.

On 27 May 2013, in an affidavit filed with the High Court on behalf of the family, Aoife Quinn cited a previously unreleased report prepared by Arthur Cox, the solicitors, for the government at the time of the Anglo nationalization. The family also got access to another report, prepared in 2009 for Donal O'Connor, the then Anglo chairman, by Pat Whelan, then managing director of Anglo in Ireland.

The Quinns claim both reports show the Financial Regulator was notified about Quinn's CFD stake in Anglo in September 2007, just after Sean Quinn shocked David Drumm and Sean FitzPatrick with the news that he held CFDs relating to 24 per cent of the bank's shares. In her affidavit, Aoife Quinn quoted the O'Connor report: 'After this meeting [in the Ardboyne Hotel], the board was informed of SQ's CFD positions, and it was decided that the regulator be informed immediately. David [Drumm] met and advised Pat Neary [the then Regulator] immediately.' The Arthur Cox report says: 'There followed a series of bilateral discussions between the bank and the regulator, and, as the bank understands it, Quinn and the regulator.'

The Quinn affidavit also claimed the Domestic Standing Group, a low-profile group comprising senior officials from the Department of Finance, Central Bank and the Financial Regulator, knew about Quinn's CFDs. The family allege that department officials, including Ann Nolan, the most senior banking official in the Department of Finance, were involved in a 'cover-up' of the extent of the department's knowledge. 'The department, knowing what went on in Anglo, has actively engaged in seeking to cover up the true state of affairs,' said Aoife Quinn in her affidavit. The department denied any wrongdoing.

Emails and transcripts of phone calls, granted to the Quinns in discovery and quoted by Aoife Quinn, showed the panicked mood within Anglo as management tried to find a way to unwind Quinn's CFD stake in 2008. In a call with David Drumm, then Anglo chief executive, on 22 April that year, John Bowe, the bank's head of treasury, said: 'When the share price falls we should think the share price is just falling. Instead of that, we think, "F★★★, we have to write cheques now [to meet Quinn's margin calls]. You know we get into this spiral, and we're in this spiral, and I just want the spiral to go away."'

In another call with Drumm on 30 June 2008, Bowe noted the Anglo share price was falling.

'Pat Whelan was writing cheques to Quinn again, I assume?' said Drumm.

'Yeah, I'd say so,' said Bowe.

Drumm replied, 'Stop, stop the calamitous event.'

A fortnight later, the bank finally unwound Quinn's CFD stake by assembling the Maple Ten group of investors. In an email quoted by Aoife Quinn, Drumm told an Anglo colleague the Regulator had been 'squared' in relation to the transaction.

In late June 2013, Bowe was catapulted to national prominence as the central figure in the 'Anglo Tapes' – audio and print extracts of phone conversations among senior Anglo executives in 2008, published over several weeks by the *Irish Independent* and *Sunday Independent*.

In the recording from early 2008, before the bank assembled the Maple Ten, Bowe discussed Sean Quinn with Matt Moran, the bank's chief financial officer.

'I was just thinking of your man, em, north of, south of the Border . . . he's down just over a bill [€1 billion],' said Bowe. 'It is frightening. The thing is that, Matt, it is not like a guy who can sell and realize cash. There is no cash to be raised here.'

Moran replied, 'The market is bigger than any man. It is the great leveller . . . He really put us at risk . . . So keep praying.'

On 18 July 2013, the Quinn family, having sought to have both the Department of Finance and the Central Bank added to their main case against Anglo, changed tack and said they would sue the department and the Central Bank separately. The move means the actions of the regulators and the department in relation to Anglo – and specifically the question of what they knew about the bank's funding of Sean Quinn's CFD position and the Maple Ten transactions – will be subject to scrutiny by the Irish courts.

On the same day, the Central Bank announced it had reached a settlement with Quinn Insurance over further breaches committed by the firm while it was under Quinn ownership, although it agreed to waive a €5 million fine, the largest possible financial censure, 'in the public interest', as the company was in administration. The breaches included a lack of adequate procedures or controls to manage assets representing its technical reserves, and a failure to maintain adequate solvency margins.

Peter Darragh Quinn has not returned to the Republic of Ireland since he was found guilty of contempt of court and sentenced to three months in jail in July 2012. The warrant for his arrest remains in place. He has not entered any defence to the contempt case but has lodged an application for a hearing at the European Court of Human Rights. On 14 May 2013, IBRC secured a judgment for $188 million – the value of the Kutuzoff Tower in Moscow – against Petey. Judge Peter Kelly said Quinn played a 'pivotal' role in stripping assets from the Quinn International Property Group and remained in flagrant contempt of court. Sources say that Petey is considering leaving Northern Ireland for Britain or Australia.

Sean Quinn Junior agreed in June 2013 to sell the penthouse apartment in Dublin he owns with Karen Woods and give his half of the proceeds to help purge his contempt of court. The penthouse was described in court as the 'last remaining owned asset' of Sean Junior, once the heir to a fortune. In the High Court, Judge Elizabeth Dunne told Sean Junior, 'in the nicest possible way', that she would be 'delighted to see the back of him'.

Several mornings a week, Sean Quinn can still be seen walking the grounds of the Slieve Russell Hotel, the 'baby of our own conception' he built more than twenty years ago. His walk takes him near the Cranaghan Suite, where he made his triumphant speech in March 2007. He passes the Giant's Grave, the tomb relocated from Slieve Rushen by a single-minded man who wanted to dig a quarry. Some say that disturbing the giant was the beginning of Sean Quinn's downfall.

In a different time, Quinn placed a bronze sculpture of Emer, wife of Cúchulainn, in the lobby of the hotel. Outside Connaught House in Dublin, the headquarters of Irish Bank Resolution Corporation, there is another bronze sculpture. The figure stands naked and defiant, holding a spear in one hand and the severed head of Ulster's prized bull in the other. It is Queen Maeve of Connacht, whose supporters slayed Cúchulainn, the champion of Ulster.

Acknowledgements

The *Citizen Quinn* project started in the summer of 2012, at the height of the contempt of court case against Sean Quinn, Sean Quinn Junior and Peter Darragh Quinn. Although the Quinn story was in the headlines daily, we felt there was still confusion about how Sean Quinn and his family, once the wealthiest in Ireland, had come to this point. From the outset, our aim was to tell the story of Sean Quinn's remarkable rise and fall as comprehensively and accurately as possible. We hope we have succeeded in some measure.

There are countless sources who made this book possible; people who provided important insight and clarity to a thoroughly complex story. Their input was invaluable. Most chose to speak on the condition they would remain anonymous or would not be quoted directly. They know who they are. We know who they are. Heartfelt thanks to all of them.

Special thanks to Tony O'Shea and Mark Condren, who contributed their remarkable photographs of the Quinns, separated by twenty-five years and very different circumstances. Bryan Walshe, the long-standing picture editor at the *Sunday Business Post*, and Eileen Martin, Jason O'Neill and Thomas Kelly of the *Sunday Times* gave generously of their time and allowed us to dip into the photo archives of those publications.

The book would not have existed without Michael McLoughlin, managing director of Penguin Ireland, who took a chance on two first-time authors. Writing a book is very different from writing a newspaper article, but he never doubted us (in public, at least). Brendan Barrington was an enthusiastic and no-nonsense editor and the book is the better for it.

Ian Kehoe writes:
I would like to sincerely thank my co-author, Gavin Daly, for helping

to turn a fledgling idea into a fully formed book. Gavin brought integrity, energy, knowledge and a monumental work ethic to the project. He is a former colleague and a long-time friend, and I could not have wished for a better person with whom to write this book.

I would also like to thank my wife, Miriam, for her unquestioned love and support during the entire process. Writing a book is a selfish business, and it eats away at evenings, weekends and holidays. Despite being routinely left on her own minding a rampaging one-year-old (while also pregnant), Miriam never once complained. I would also like to thank the kids, Ellie and Sam, for being perhaps the only people in the world not to talk to me about Sean Quinn.

Sincere thanks too to the small army of family and friends who provided essential back-up during the process, especially my parents, Carmel and Peadar, my sister, Andrea, and my mother-in-law, Helen. I would also like to acknowledge my many friends for their guidance and support along the way – Ciaran, Derek, Michael, Ian, Ronan, Brendan, Oliver, James and all the rest.

My work on *Citizen Quinn* spanned two employers, and the support of both was essential. I would like to thank all my former colleagues in RTÉ's *Prime Time* for a tremendous opportunity and learning experience, and my current colleagues at the *Sunday Business Post*, led by editor Cliff Taylor. I would also like to acknowledge the work of other journalists in covering the Quinn story in recent years, particularly Tom Lyons and Simon Carswell.

Gavin Daly writes:
My wife, Catherine, gave her unwavering love and support throughout the gestation and writing of *Citizen Quinn*. It would not have been possible without her constant encouragement and considerable personal sacrifices. I love you to the moon and back. Juliet, you will be pleased to know that 'Daddy's book' is finished and life can go back to normal at last.

My parents, John and Marie, gave us a love of books from an early age and I'm very proud to have my name on one. Thanks to them and to my sisters, Fidelma and Orla, and my brother, David, for their support in the past year and always. This undertaking would not have been possible either without the unswerving support of the Weadick clan.

My boss, Brian Carey, the 'big brain' business editor of the *Sunday Times*, provided inspiration, advice and encouragement. Thanks too to my other *Sunday Times* business colleagues, Niall Brady, Aine Coffey and Mark Paul (since departed to the *Irish Times*), and to Frank Fitzgibbon, the energetic editor of the *Sunday Times* in Ireland. I have learned a lot from you all. Cliff Taylor and all my former colleagues during twelve great years at the *Sunday Business Post* helped to shape me as a journalist, for which I am grateful.

Ian Kehoe, my co-author, friend and former colleague, was the one who believed that a book about Sean Quinn could – and should – be written. I would like to thank Ian for getting me involved and for making this joint project a surprisingly smooth experience. I hope it is as enjoyable to read as it was to write.

July 2013

Index